I0759580

VERONA CAMPIONE

VERONA CAMPIONE

The Miracle of 85

Richard Hough

First published by Pitch Publishing, 2025
1

Pitch Publishing
9 Donnington Park,
85 Birdham Road,
Chichester, West Sussex,
PO20 7AJ

www.pitchpublishing.co.uk
info@pitchpublishing.co.uk

A CIP catalogue record is available for this book from the British Library.

ISBN 978 1 83680 121 4

Typesetting and origination by Pitch Publishing

Printed and bound on FSC® certified paper in line with our continuing commitment to ethical business practices, sustainability and the environment.

Printed and bound in India by Thomson Press

Contents

Introduction

12 MAY 2025 marks the 40th anniversary of one of the most remarkable sporting achievements of all time. For a so-called 'provincial' club like Hellas Verona to win Serie A, Italy's premier football league, is a remarkable achievement. To have done so in 1985, when Italian football was in its strutting pomp, boasting some of the greatest names ever to have played the game, elevates an outstanding footballing triumph into the realms of a genuine sporting miracle.

The early 1980s was a golden age for football in Verona. It was the era of Elkjær, Briegel and Bagnoli. The unmistakable voice of Roberto Puliero. And the bold simplicity of that iconic blue and yellow kit.

Drawing on interviews with players, fans and local journalists, as well as contemporary newspaper accounts and archive footage translated from Italian, *Verona Campione: The Miracle of 85* tells the remarkable true story of a football team that came from nowhere to shock the sporting world and win a unique *Scudetto*, revealing for the first time how a club like Hellas Verona was able to win the Italian championship and what it still means to the city 40 years later.

Author's note

I have used the terms 'Hellas Verona', 'Hellas' or simply 'Verona' when referring to the football club now officially known as Hellas Verona Football Club. The term '*Gialloblù*' is also occasionally used, a popular nickname for the team and its fans, in reference to the traditional colours of '*giallo*' (yellow) and '*blu*' (blue) associated with the club. Of course, in the period in which this book is set, the football team subsequently known as Chievo Verona didn't exist and only one team could claim to truly represent the city – Hellas Verona.

1a Giornata

16 September 1984

'WHO'S GOING to mark Maradona?'

Deep in the bowels of the Bentegodi, a pungent blend of sweat, camphor oil and adrenaline fills the home changing room. From the terracing above, the rhythmic chanting of 41,000 expectant fans is reaching a crescendo. They have packed into Verona's cavernous stadium on the third Sunday of September for Diego Armando Maradona's competitive debut in Italy. The stifling heat of August has faded, giving way to the pleasant warmth of a late Indian summer. Back in the changing room, the towering figure of Hans-Peter Briegel stands up. 'I'll take care of it,' he says.

At a shade over 5ft 5in and weighing in at just over 11st, the mercurial Argentine is so stocky he is almost squat. With such a low centre of gravity, he is exceptionally powerful and mesmerisingly elusive with the ball at his feet. He can do things with that sphere of leather, rubber and inflated air that few others in the history of the game ever have, and, at 23 years of age, is now approaching his prime. After an explosive spell at Barcelona, culminating in the notorious Copa del Rey Final against Athletic Bilbao at the Santiago Bernabéu stadium, Maradona was in desperate need of a change of scenery.

Andoni Goikoetxea, 'the Butcher of Bilbao', had broken the Argentine's ankle the previous September and Maradona was intent on revenge. At the end of a frustrating encounter in which Barcelona couldn't find an equaliser to cancel out a 13th-minute Endika Guarrotxena Arzubiagam opener, Maradona exploded. Lashing out in a series of kung-fu style kicks and wild lunges, his first victim was Miguel Ángel Sola, an unused substitute who was knocked to the floor, then kneed in the face by an incandescent Maradona, leaving the prone Spaniard unconscious on the Bernabéu turf. If it's any defence, Maradona had been relentlessly fouled throughout the match before his frustrations finally boiled over and he toggled to streetfighter mode. This was no Ronaldo-style spit-the-dummy tantrum. This was raw, out-of-control violence.

As the situation escalated, Spanish riot police were deployed to restore order on the pitch. In the recriminations that followed, Maradona was handed a three-month ban. It was not, however, a sanction that would ever be enforced, as the volatile Argentine fled to Napoli for a world record fee of 14bn lire (£6.9m). On 5 July 1984, an estimated 70,000 fans, each paying 1,000 lire, turned out at Napoli's San Paolo Stadium to welcome their new signing. The Argentine would go on to lift two historic *Scudetti* but glory in Italy would be hard-earned, even for a troubled genius like Maradona.

By the time the Maradona circus came to Verona on 16 September 1984 for the opening game of the 1984/85 campaign, Hellas had already launched their season with an impressive cup run, albeit against lesser opposition. Back then, the Coppa Italia, the pre-eminent Italian cup competition, was split into three distinct phases: a summer group stage conducted before the start of the league season; a first knockout round played in February; and a final knockout phase played in June, after the league fixtures had concluded. With eight groups of six teams in the opening phase, the top two teams from each group progressed to the winter knockout phase. Hellas eased through with their new foreign signings, Danish striker Preben Elkjær Larsen and German defender Hans-Peter Briegel, contributing five goals between them.

So, who was this German 'panzer' who volunteered for the task of marking the volatile Argentine – the greatest player on the planet – and how did he end up at Verona, a lowly provincial team that just a couple of seasons earlier were struggling in Serie B?

Hans-Peter Briegel was born on 11 October 1955 in Rodenbach, in the Kaiserslautern district in what was then West Germany. The son of a well-to-do family of farmers, Briegel was an impressive athlete, winning eight German athletics titles: three in the long jump, three in the triple jump and two in the pentathlon. But football was where his true passion lay. At 19, he signed his first semi-professional football contract with Kaiserslautern and in the 1974/75 season, played in midfield for the youth team. He made his first-team debut on 10 April 1976 at the Olympiastadion in Munich against a Bayern team that included Franz Beckenbauer, Gerd Müller and Karl-Heinz Rummenigge but it was Kaiserslautern who prevailed, winning 4-3 against their highly rated opponents.

He was a formidable physical presence and a powerful man-marker who was also capable of devastating counter-attacks but it was the arrival of Karl-Heinz Feldkamp at Kaiserslautern in 1978 that marked the turning point in Briegel's career. After seeing the young midfielder in action, Feldkamp was convinced that, despite his searing pace and power, Briegel was a natural defender, capable of suppressing even the most talented opposition striker, while, in possession, he was given the freedom to break free and attack. It was a tactical switch that paid dividends. As a defender, Briegel scored seven goals in 40 appearances in the 1979/80 campaign and eight goals in 43 appearances the following season.

In the 1981/82 season, Briegel's form for Kaiserslautern was even more impressive, with 13 goals in 32 appearances in the Bundesliga and four goals from ten appearances in the UEFA Cup. Indeed, it was in a quarter-final of that tournament against Real Madrid that Briegel enjoyed one of the greatest nights of his career. Real prevailed 3-1 in the first leg at the Bernabéu but in the return leg at the Fritz-Walter-Stadion on 17 March 1982, something quite remarkable happened. With Feldkamp once again relying on Briegel to break up the Spanish attacks, the Germans were inspired to an incredible 5-0 victory. It remains Real Madrid's heaviest ever defeat in European football. In the subsequent semi-final, Kaiserslautern lost to a second-leg extra-time penalty against Swedish champions IFK Göteborg but Briegel would remember that victory against Real Madrid as the high point of his career to date.

Meanwhile, he was a regular presence in the West Germany side that progressed to the final of the 1982 World Cup, only to lose 3-1 against Italy, with iconic goals from Rossi, Tardelli and Altobelli.

Fast forward to the summer of 1984 and Briegel was with the German camp at the Intercontinental Hotel in Frankfurt preparing for the European Championship. His team-mates in that squad included the likes of Harald Schumacher, Karl-Heinz Rummenigge, Andreas Brehme and Rudi Völler. Briegel had agreed to meet with Emiliano 'Ciccio' Mascetti, Hellas Verona's sporting director, who, speaking through an interpreter, outlined a basic offer that the ambitious Italian club were prepared to make to secure the signature of the German left-back. It fell short of what he was looking for and the two sides parted company without reaching any agreement.

Mascetti was a club legend who set the club record for appearances in Serie A and who, for over three decades, was Verona's record scorer in the top division, surpassed only in 2015 by a certain Luca Toni. A popular and respected figure, Mascetti took over as the club's sporting director following his retirement in 1980 and was at the heart of an ambitious project to secure and consolidate Hellas Verona's status in Serie A.

In an increasingly unscrupulous world, Mascetti was an honest broker, simply incapable of being rude or impolite. Above all, he was highly competent, assembling a formidable group of rejects and cast-offs from bigger clubs. It was then up to coach Osvaldo Bagnoli to get the best out of them and create a team capable of consolidating their position in Serie A. The two men enjoyed an extremely close relationship built on personal friendship and professional respect. In all the years they worked together, they only ever disagreed once on the evaluation of one player and when that happened, it came as quite a shock to both men.

In the summer of 1981, Mascetti brought 22-year-old playmaker Antonio Di Gennaro from Perugia and goalkeeper Claudio Garella from Sampdoria. They were the second and third components of the team that would begin the 1984/85 campaign, joining young *libero* Roberto Tricella, who had been in Verona since being released by Inter in 1979. In 1982, those three were joined by the Brazilian legend, Dirceu José Guimarães, from Atlético Madrid (the following year he would move to Napoli), Władysław Żmuda from Widzew Łódź, Luciano Marangon from Roma, Pierino Fanna from Juventus, Luigi Sacchetti from Fiorentina and Domenico Volpati from Brescia. With a handful of new additions each summer, Bagnoli's team was slowly taking shape.

In 1983, three strikers arrived Giuseppe Galderisi from Juventus, Maurizio Iorio from Roma and Joe Jordan from Milan. Defender Silvano Fontolan was brought in from Como and goalkeeper Sergio Spuri from Anconitana, as well as defender Mauro Ferroni from Sampdoria and midfielder Luciano Bruni from Fiorentina. Verona also came close to signing the Argentinian midfielder Ossie Ardiles. 'We can get him,' Mascetti informed Osvaldo Bagnoli. Ardiles was the right fit, exactly what they were looking for. Good feet, outstanding technique but also a good goalscoring record, important because 'a midfielder who doesn't score goals is not complete', as Bagnoli always said. 'We always looked at players to acquire with the Panini almanac in hand,' Mascetti admitted. 'If a midfielder could score goals, then we started to think about it.' In the end, the deal fell through.

In the summer of 1984, striker Maurizio Iorio would return to Rome and Scottish striker Joe Jordan was heading back to England after three seasons in Italy. On the pitch, Jordan's impact had been limited (just one league goal in 12 appearances in the 1983/84 season) but he was a popular figure in the dressing room, a big brother to the younger squad members like Giuseppe Galderisi and Maurizio Iorio. Ferdinando Chiampan, the club's majority shareholder, even thought that he would make an excellent sporting director –

but, of course, Verona already had Mascetti in that role. The injury-plagued Polish defender Władysław Żmuda was also on his way out and left-back Luciano Marangon had put in a transfer request, so Mascetti still had plenty of work to do before the summer was over.

Scots Gordon Strachan and Steve Archibald were both considered. Bagnoli even made a trip to see Strachan in the flesh and a £500,000 bid was proposed but the Aberdeen midfielder ended up at Manchester United. Bagnoli and Mascetti had also been following a talented young German midfielder who could do everything – attack, defend, run, tackle, assist, score. When they finally decided to make an offer, the confident young German informed them that he'd just signed a deal with Bayern Munich. That young midfielder was Lothar Matthäus and he'd go on to win the Bundesliga seven times, Serie A once (with Inter), the UEFA Cup twice and the World Cup with West Germany in 1990, winning the Ballon d'Or in the same year. By the early summer of 1984, efforts were focussing on another German to replace the free-spirited Luciano Marangon.

Now in France preparing for the first game of the Euros, Briegel's telephone rang. It was Mascetti asking for another meeting. This time, Briegel was prepared. He had asked his international team-mate, Karl-Heinz Rummenigge, who had just signed for Inter, for his opinion. The feedback was good and a second meeting took place at the Hotel Saint-Germain in Paris. Accompanying Mascetti was the club's accountant, Liliano Rangogni, determined to seal a deal. On the opposite side of the table sat Briegel, the player's brother and a German lawyer. The negotiations were so protracted that Briegel left to do two training sessions that day and each time returned to find the discussions ongoing!

News of the German's imminent signing first appeared in *L'Arena*, Verona's local newspaper, on 12 June 1984, just as the European Championship was kicking off in France. Under the headline 'Briegel belongs to Verona', the sub-heading exclaimed: 'The yellow and blue club has pulled off a sensational surprise move.' It was certainly a massive coup for a lowly but ambitious provincial side but it wouldn't be the last transfer bombshell of the summer. Just a few weeks later, Maradona would be introduced to a euphoric San Paolo. Against the backdrop of the knockout stages, the negotiations continued. The Veronese delegation eventually met all of Briegel's demands and a two-year contract was finally agreed. Verona had got their *mann*.

Not only did Briegel effectively nullify the threat posed by Diego Maradona in the opening game of the season but the German also broke the deadlock with a 26th-minute leaping header from a pinpoint Pierino Fanna corner. In those days, the Bentegodi didn't have a roof, which is just as well, as it would have been blown clean off by the noise that erupted around the stadium as the German scored. Striker Giuseppe Galderisi doubled the home side's lead barely five minutes later, concluding a well-worked Verona attack that had left Napoli spectating.

In the second half, it was an Argentine making his Serie A debut for Napoli who pulled one back for the away side – but the player in question was winger Daniel Bertoni, not Maradona. Flashes of Maradona's brilliance threatened but Briegel was relentless, using a flailing arm to deflect the ball when Maradona's genius sent him sprawling on his backside. From the resulting free kick, the Argentine came close but it just wasn't Maradona's day. Deep in the second half, Hellas playmaker Antonio Di Gennaro got his head on the end of another exquisite delivery from Pierino Fanna to crown a famous opening-day victory at the Bentegodi.

With tempers rising on and off the pitch, Napoli captain Giuseppe Bruscolotti was sent off, the culmination of a running battle with Elkjær that had been simmering away throughout the afternoon. As the final whistle sounded, skirmishes broke out on the terraces between opposing fans, heralding a bitter rivalry that would endure for decades.

Post-match, it was Di Gennaro who captured the mood, speaking to Radiotelevisione italiana (RAI TV) in the tunnel afterwards: 'On paper, it was a match like any other but a bit special because there was the effect of this ace who could give something extra to the team [...] but Verona has shown itself to be a great team because we played with our brains and that is very important for the championship.'

Maradona, too, was generous in his praise for the victors. '[A] good team, without doubt,' he observed. 'Bagnoli's men mark very well. It was really difficult to touch the ball [...] they're not afraid of anyone.' When asked specifically about Briegel, the Argentine complimented his 'impeccable' performance but concluded his remarks on a sour note. 'They wound me up,' he complained. 'I can't stand it. These Veronese continued to taunt me throughout the game. Maradona [referring to himself in the third person] doesn't like being mocked.' It was a theme that would blight the Argentine's time in Italy but his day would come.

Elsewhere, Inter, Juventus and AC Milan could only manage draws (against Atalanta, Como and Udinese respectively), while Torino, Sampdoria and Fiorentina took maximum points. With three goals and two points on the board already, it was Hellas Verona who emerged as unexpected leaders of Serie A on day one.

1A GIORNATA

Atalanta 1-1 Inter
Avellino 0-0 Roma
Como 0-0 Juventus
Lazio 0-1 Fiorentina
Milan 2-2 Udinese
Sampdoria 1-0 Cremonese
Torino 1-0 Ascoli
Verona 3-1 Napoli

CLASSIFICA

Verona	**2**
Fiorentina	2
Sampdoria	2
Torino	2
Milan	1
Udinese	1
Atalanta	1
Inter	1
Avellino	1
Como	1
Juventus	1
Roma	1
Ascoli	0
Cremonese	0
Lazio	0
Napoli	0

2a Giornata

23 September 1984

ASCOLI ONCE boasted 200 towers. A bold statement of the town's prosperity and status. Its other claim to fame is an association with a delicious antipasto made using local green olives and ground beef or pork. Known as olive all'ascolana, a by-product that emerged in the 19th century from the kitchens of the town's aristocratic palaces, they are perfect with a dry white wine like Verdicchio or Pecorino. Ascoli is also known for hosting La Giostra della Quintana, an annual medieval festival of pageantry and armed jousting that takes place on the first Sunday of August. Today, the competition should be a little less fierce, but Verona can expect a tough battle against a proud and disciplined adversary, currently enjoying their longest-ever spell in Serie A.

In common with many smaller Italian football clubs, Ascoli Calcio 1898 FC have a chequered history of rebrandings, mergers and bankruptcies. Costantino Rozzi, a local construction engineer, took over the club in 1968 and only planned to remain in post for a few months, just long enough to restore equilibrium to the club's precarious balance sheet. Instead, the charismatic businessman would cling on to the office of president for 26 years, until his death in 1994, leading the club from Serie C to a best-ever fourth-place finish in Serie A in 1980. Blunt but likeable, Rozzi had that common touch familiar to many presidents of the era – Romeo Anconetani (Pisa), Angelo Massimino (Catania), Antonio Sibilia (Avellino) and Verona's very own Celestino Guidotti.

Coach Carlo Mazzone, a former Ascoli player, is also a highly popular local figure. He led the team for 12 years (his first spell from 1968 to 1975, his second term beginning in 1980).[1] In 1982, Ascoli secured a sixth-place finish, the highlight of which came when 35,000 filled the Stadio Cino e Lillo Del Duca to see the home side beat Turin giants Juventus 2-0. A remarkable turnout when you consider that the population of the town is only 50,000!

In the 1983/84 season, Ascoli slumped to tenth place, though still finished ahead of bigger clubs like Napoli and Lazio. So, even for an in-form Hellas bristling with talent and confidence, a trip to Ascoli for the second game of the season is no *passeggiata*. Ascoli are well resourced, well organised and highly motivated, with one of the best coaches in the business. Plus, they have a touch of Brazilian flair.

After short spells at Verona and Napoli, nomadic Brazilian midfielder Dirceu José Guimarães, better known simply as Dirceu, has just arrived at Ascoli. With a permanent smile and an instantly recognisable mop of thick curly hair, the attacking midfielder has played alongside the great Brazilian players of his generation, including the likes of Zico, Sócrates, Falcão and Léo Júnior. Extraordinarily talented, he brings a touch of class and colour to an otherwise decent but unspectacular Ascoli team.

Despite a morale-boosting victory against Napoli in the opening fixture, the objective for Hellas this season remains unchanged: to avoid relegation. The club have endured too many nerve-shredding campaigns that go down to the wire, with a point, or sometimes even two, required to stay up on the very last day of the season. By securing salvation at the earliest

---

1 Within just a few weeks, Rozzi would sack Mazzone after a poor start to the season with just two points from seven games. Mazzone would go on to have a long and distinguished coaching career at Bologna, Roma, Napoli and Perugia, to name but a few. In 2000, he took charge of Serie A newcomers Brescia, where he coached the likes of Roberto Baggio, Andrea Pirlo, Luca Toni, Igli Tare and Pep Guardiola. He is credited with being the first coach to deploy Pirlo in a deeper, more creative midfield role.

possible opportunity, the club hope to put their affairs, both on and off the pitch, on a more secure footing and begin planning for a more ambitious future. This, after all, is a golden age for Italian football and Hellas want to be part of it.

The decade began with an underwhelming European Championship on home soil in 1980 and culminated in the spine-tingling spectacle of Italia 90, one of the most dramatic World Cups in the history of the game. In between, it was punctuated by the national team's unforgettable triumph at the 1982 World Cup and Maradona's historic double *Scudetto* with Napoli in 1987 and 1990. It was also a decade that saw the ever-increasing commercialisation of sport, with lucrative sponsorship deals, spiralling transfer fees and fierce competition for kit endorsements.[2]

In the summer of 1981, Adidas became Verona's official kit supplier, while electronics giant Canon was unveiled as the club's first-ever official sponsor, with Ferdinando Chiampan, the Italian distributor of the Japanese brand, joining the Hellas Verona board of directors as a major shareholder.[3] The financial capital provided by the deal was transformative. The signings of Briegel and Elkjær would simply not have been possible without the financial muscle provided by the Canon investment, worth a reported 10bn lire. The objective was to establish Hellas Verona as a permanent presence in Serie A and avoid the last-day promotion/relegation lottery of the past. As Bagnoli was fond of saying, get points on the board as early as possible and then enjoy the rest of the season without having to worry about relegation. Needless to say, a possible championship run isn't even on the radar at this point. In fact, it is so far off the radar that even mentioning it at this stage in the season seems ludicrous.

---

2 On 26 October 1984, Michael Jordan signed his first contract with Nike, a five-year deal worth $2.5 million.

3 The sponsorship deal with Hellas wasn't the Japanese electronics giant's first foray into the world of football. In 1983, the English Football League was renamed the Canon League in a deal worth £3.3 million over three years.

Though Verona's form in recent seasons has improved under Bagnoli, few predicted the previous weekend's victory at home against Maradona's Napoli in the opening game of the season. An outstanding team performance, two points on the board and three goals to boot. The new international arrivals, Briegel and Elkjær, both demonstrated their quality and impact. Equally important, the foreigners have adapted quickly to life in Italy, integrating well in a close-knit but welcoming dressing room despite the obvious language barriers. That's not always the case with foreign imports to the *Bel Paese*.[4]

In his team selection against Napoli, Bagnoli took a tactical decision that was in equal parts pragmatic and inspired. When Luciano Marangon withdrew his transfer request, Bagnoli found himself with two left-backs. Briegel had expressed his willingness to play in midfield and Bagnoli was quick to recognise the German's potential, deploying him in that more advanced role against Napoli, leaving Marangon to occupy his favoured left-back berth. Not only did Briegel win his duel with Maradona, he also scored a decisive goal on his Serie A debut. A tactical masterstroke or just a lucky break? Time would tell.

The arrival of players like Briegel and Elkjær to Verona came just as Italian football was emerging from a self-imposed 15-year ban on signing foreign players.[5] By the mid-1980s, Italian clubs were busy making up for lost time, hoovering up the biggest names and most talented football players on the planet. Although it was a decade of defensive resilience and tactical innovation in which only the most accomplished midfielders survived, it was also an era that boasted the most creative and technically gifted attacking players in the history of the game.

---

4 Football historian John Foot has devoted an entire chapter of his book, *Calcio, A History of Italian Football*, to the plight of foreigners in the Italian game, many of whom fall into that unenviable category of '*bidone*' (rubbish).

5 Foreign players were banned from the Italian league between 1964 and 1980, with the objective of reviving the fortunes of the national team. The strategy was clearly effective, as Italy won the 1982 World Cup thanks to a generation of outstanding Italian talent.

With each club limited to just two foreign signings, those that arrived in Italy were the cream of the global footballing crop. In fact, in the summer of 1984, as the world's greatest athletes were converging on Los Angeles, the most prolific footballing talent in the world was flocking to the Italian peninsula. From Germany, Argentina and Brazil, as well as England, Scotland and the Republic of Ireland, Serie A was attracting the best international talent and some of the biggest names in the game. Brady, Platini, Maradona, Rummenigge, Sócrates, Júnior, Zico, Laudrup and Souness were among the jaw-dropping array of international talent to have converged on the peninsula, making Serie A the most prestigious league in the world. As the Italian triumph at the 1982 World Cup demonstrated, Italy was also producing some outstanding homegrown talent of its own, including the likes of Paolo Rossi, the controversial striker whose famous hat-trick against Brazil earned him the title of footballer of the year in 1983, Franco Baresi, the masterful central defender who spent his entire 20-year playing career at AC Milan, and Giuseppe Bergomi, another one-club legend who would spend his entire playing career at Inter.

It was Liam Brady, a player who would spend seven seasons in Italy, who described Serie A as 'the powerhouse of European football'. He was far from alone in reaching that conclusion. According to American magazine *Sports Illustrated*, Serie A in the early 1980s was 'the most undeniably competitive league the world has ever seen'. In fact, it was a decade in which no fewer than six different teams would be crowned champions of Italy.

On 23 September 1984, neither of the sides playing at Ascoli's Stadio Cino e Lillo Del Duca have any expectations of joining that list. Teams like Hellas Verona and Ascoli simply don't win Italian championships. Their primary objective at this point in the season is little more than survival.

Today, Silvano Fontolan returns to the Hellas defence after missing out against Napoli, liberating Domenico Volpati to push up into midfield alongside Briegel, forming a tactically astute and physically powerful double pivot that gives greater freedom of movement to the more creative outlets of Antonio Di Gennaro and free-roaming winger Pierino Fanna. In what will become Bagnoli's preferred starting XI this season, he deploys a 4-2-1-3 formation that combines defensive solidity with a potent offensive dynamism. Offensive full-backs provide width, overlapping runs and crosses into the box; two defensive midfielders, who shield the back four, disrupt opposition play and distribute the ball; while Antonio Di Gennaro in the role of central attacking midfielder is the creative engine room of the team, linking the defensive and offensive units, orchestrating play and providing key passes to unlock opposition defences. With Giuseppe Galderisi and Elkjær occupying the central striking positions, Pierino Fanna is given freedom to switch from one wing to the other.

In their opening game of the season, Ascoli lost narrowly to Torino, one of the strongest teams in the league. At home against Verona, they are determined to bounce back. The first half is a war of attrition, as the two opposing factions battle for every square inch of the field. It's an impressive display of manpower but both sides lack the precision to make a decisive breakthrough. In the first half, the only real incident of note occurs on the 27th minute, when Hellas captain Roberto Tricella challenges the ex-Milan championship winner Walter Novellino on the edge of the area. The home side demand a penalty but referee Pierluigi Magni is unimpressed and waves play on. Outraged, the stadium erupts. The controversy doesn't end there, as the encounter becomes increasingly ill-tempered and acrimonious.

Barely ten minutes into the second half, Hellas win an indirect free kick for a foul on Fanna on the edge of the box. Di Gennaro curls one into the top corner. Goal! The Ascoli players swarm the referee. Indirect free kick! How can it be a goal? The referee signals that the goalkeeper touched the ball before it crossed the line. And maybe he's got a point. A fingertip? Yes! The goal stands.

Just a few minutes later, following a foul on an Ascoli player, riled club president Rozzi leaps from the Ascoli bench and launches such a violent protest that he is sent off. A seething sense of injustice surges around the stadium. Sometimes, it's moments like this that ignite a game. A shared sense of outrage can galvanise the fans and provoke a reaction from the players. Can Ascoli profit from the injustice and turn things around?

Four minutes later, Volpati releases Tricella out wide. The Hellas captain has time and space to pick out Briegel inside the six-yard box. The big German, his socks rolled low around his ankles, easily holds off his marker for a simple tap-in on the volley. Ascoli 0 Verona 2!

Twenty-six minutes into the second half, Verona score a third. This time it's Elkjær who picks up a deep ball from Briegel and surges towards the area, turning the hapless Ascoli defender inside out before beating goalkeeper Roberto Corti with a precise diagonal shot for what is the Dane's first goal in the Italian championship.

Just four minutes later, Ascoli pull one back through Argentine midfielder Patricio Hernandez, who catches Claudio Garella off guard with a spectacular long-range effort. Bagnoli responds immediately by introducing midfielder Luciano Bruni for a fading Giuseppe Galderisi. In the closing minutes, Fanna makes way for Franco Turchetta, as Bagnoli seeks to run down the clock. The closing minutes pass without further incident and Hellas emerge more or less unscathed from a battlefield that was fraught with danger.

Two points on the road and three more goals – an impressive result against a tough opponent who will feel hard done by. Once again, Verona's summer signings have shown themselves to be genuine match-winners. Elsewhere, Zico's Udinese destroy Lazio 5-0, while Juventus thrash Atalanta 5-1. Inter narrowly beat Avellino 2-1, with a Giancarlo Pasinato winner just eight minutes from time. Both Napoli and Roma fail to win at home, while Torino lose in Cremona.

With just two games played, it would be unwise to read too much into this opening sequence of results. But, with four points from two games and six goals from four different players, Hellas are the only team in the league with maximum points. Though there will, of course, be sterner challenges along the way, it is a promising start and an early indication that even the giants of Turin, Milan and Rome might struggle for consistency this season. In fact, it's the first time in Verona's 14 Serie A campaigns that they find themselves with maximum points after two games. As Bagnoli's men leave this proud hill town in Le Marche, fewer than 50 of Ascoli's towers remain but the view from the top of the table is still one to savour.

2A GIORNATA

Ascoli 1-3 Verona
Cremonese 2-1 Torino
Fiorentina 0-0 Milan
Inter 2-1 Avellino
Juventus 5-1 Atalanta
Napoli 1-1 Sampdoria
Roma 1-1 Como
Udinese 5-0 Lazio

CLASSIFICA

Verona	**4**
Udinese	3
Juventus	3
Inter	3
Sampdoria	3
Fiorentina	3
Cremonese	2
Milan	2
Como	2
Roma	2
Torino	2
Avellino	1
Napoli	1
Atalanta	1
Ascoli	0
Lazio	0

3a Giornata

30 September 1984

THE AERO Trasporti Italiani DC-9 touched down at 13:52 on 15 June 1983. As he disembarked, Arthur Antunes Coimbra was met by 5,000 screaming fans who had shown up at the small Trieste airport to greet him. Transferring, along with his wife, several journalists and a few club officials, to the four-star Hotel Là di Moret in a specially commissioned coach, thousands more fans were waiting for him at the hotel.

In the 1982/83 season, Udinese Calcio had finished in sixth place, narrowly missing out on a coveted European place. The following season, they aspired to go one better and the ambitious but unfancied club had just pulled off the transfer coup of the decade.

Two days after landing at Trieste airport, Coimbra made his debut on Italian soil in a friendly match against Flamengo, his former club, coming on as a 40th-minute substitute. He played for just five minutes but the mere sight of the Brazilian legend in an Udinese jersey was enough to satisfy the 40,000-strong Friuli crowd.

Zico, as the legendary Brazilian is better known, was an outstanding creative playmaker with an eye for goal.[6] He had scored 123 goals in 212 appearances for Flamengo during the most successful period in the Brazilian club's history. A genuinely two-footed player, he was deadly from set pieces.

---

6 Zico's nickname originated in his family from increasingly shortened versions of 'Arthurzinho' (Little Arthur) which then became Arthurzico, then Tuzico and, finally, Zico, a version created by his cousin Ermelinda 'Linda' Rolim.

For many commentators and fans, he was, quite simply, the best football player in the world.

Udinese, like Sampdoria, Napoli and Verona, are an ambitious but underachieving football club that seem to be operating outside the normal financial constraints. It is, after all, the 1980s, a period of ostentatious displays of wealth and profligate spending. And there is nothing more ostentatious than the statement signing of a bona fide South American legend.

Aside from the cavalier approach to spending by those lucky enough to have money or credit, the 1980s is a difficult decade to define. The story of those years, as the popular historian Dominic Sandbrook (2019) has testified, is bitterly contested: '[T]here is no consensus about the 1980s, and there never will be.' On the face of it, it was a time of political conservatism, of Reaganomics (industrial deregulation, reductions in government spending and tax cuts for individuals and corporations) and Thatcherism (a belief in free markets and a smaller state). It was also an era that promised great social change. In the summer of 1984, Walter Mondale, the Democratic candidate for president of the United States, chose Geraldine Ferraro, the first female vice-presidential nominee, as his running mate. Forty years later, we still haven't had a female 'leader of the free world'. Following the turbulence of the 60s and 70s, the dawning of a new decade heralded a fresh era of peace and prosperity that gave rise to a surging tide of individualism, materialism and consumerism, personified in the form of the 'yuppie', whose conspicuous spending and behaviour caricatured the mindset of a generation. Northern Italy was booming. After the devastating *anni di piombo*, a decades-long wave of domestic political terrorism, a period of peaceful calm had returned to the streets and piazzas of the peninsula. With oil prices low, people even spoke of a 'new economic miracle'.

Of course, not everyone was cashing in. In Italy, the early 1980s are also remembered for double-digit inflation, as prices rose by as much as 20 per cent from one year to the next.

In the UK, it was also a time of double-digit inflation that peaked at 22 per cent, while unemployment surged towards two million. As the British manufacturing industry lurched towards oblivion, street violence, football hooliganism and terrorist bombings dominated the headlines.

The 1980s also saw the emergence of a garish new popular culture in which neon colours, bold patterns and flashy accessories defined the look. New forms of mass media, most notably the launch of CNN in 1980 and MTV in 1981, revolutionised the way the world consumed news, music, dance and fashion. Mullets and moustaches were in, as punks and New Romantics pushed the boundaries of decency and taste. You only have to browse a Panini sticker album from that era to get a sense of the look. Blockbuster franchises like *Indiana Jones*, *Back to the Future* and *Star Wars* captivated a generation of cinema-goers while, at the other end of the cultural spectrum, *Il nome della rosa*, a 500-page debut novel by an Italian professor of semiotics, was published in 1980. It sold more than 50 million copies, becoming one of the best-selling books ever published.

What does any of this have to do with Hellas Verona's fixture against Udinese on 30 September 1984? Very little, if the truth be told. But without a little historical context, we are only getting a small piece of a bigger picture. Context gives us a sense of time and place and triggers memories that might otherwise have been lost, particularly in a decade so rich, colourful and evocative as the 1980s. And few things capture that rich colour like the name Zico.

Despite competing offers from Roma and Milan, in 1983 the Brazilian icon accepted a 6bn lire offer to join Udinese. His impact was immediate and not just on the pitch. With 26,611 season tickets sold, the 1983/84 campaign started with a bang for Udinese, with a convincing 5-0 victory on the road at Genoa in which Zico contributed two goals. The following weekend, Udinese beat newly promoted Catania 3-1, with the Brazilian once again making a significant contribution. Speaking after the game, Zico expressed surprise that his marker hadn't followed him into the changing room after the final whistle, such was the diligent Italian defender's commitment to his task. The defender in question was named Claudio Ranieri and he couldn't, despite his best efforts, stop Zico from scoring twice that day.

In Zico's first season in Italy, a string of impressive results propelled Udinese to the upper echelons of the league table but, in March, the Brazilian suffered a strain which forced him to miss five games on the trot as Udinese slumped from third to ninth place in the league. Despite his injury, the Brazilian scored an impressive 19 goals in 24 Serie A appearances in the 1983/84 season (just one less than Platini at Juventus), plus five more in the Coppa Italia, as Udinese finished in a respectable but ultimately disappointing ninth place.

At the beginning of the 1984/85 season, Brazilian coach Luís Vinício was appointed to take charge at Udinese. Though the immensely experienced Franco 'The Baron' Causio (304 appearances for Juventus and a 1982 World Cup winner) had moved on to Inter and Pier Paolo Virdis to AC Milan, Udinese still had the look of a team that meant business. The Brazilian central defender Edino Nazareth Filho, better known as Edinho and a veteran of the 1978 and 1982 World Cups, had joined Udinese in 1982, scoring seven goals in his first season in Italy.[7] A dead-ball specialist, Verona fans remember him for a remarkable free kick that hit both posts but somehow didn't go in.

So, the Udinese who arrive at the Bentegodi in September 1984 will certainly be no pushovers. Already, in the opening two games of the season, they have drawn 2-2 with AC Milan at the San Siro and destroyed Michael Laudrup's Lazio 5-0 at the Stadio Friuli. To the disappointment of most, even Verona fans hoping to catch a rare glimpse of footballing royalty, Zico will be watching from the stand, once again the victim of a lingering injury. Even without the Brazilian legend, Udinese are a quality team that pose a serious threat to Verona's unbeaten start to the season.

---

7 As captain of the national team, Edinho would go on to play in all five of Brazil's matches at the 1986 World Cup.

It's a match that Bagnoli is determined to win, and, in a sign of a more offensive approach, he drops defensive midfielder Domenico Volpati in favour of the more attack-minded Luciano Bruni. For Udinese, 23-year-old striker Andrea Carnevale is playing his second season in Serie A, having arrived at Udinese from Catania. The youngster emerged from a deeply traumatic childhood to become one of the Italy's most potent and intelligent strikers.[8] It seems unlikely that Maradona would have been watching this game but Carnevale provides an early prototype for the 'Hand of God' that would forever tarnish the Argentine's reputation (at least as far as the English are concerned). Thankfully for Verona, experienced referee Luigi Agnolin spots the infringement and Carnevale's 'goal' is disallowed. In the build-up to the handball, Verona keeper Claudio Garella demonstrates what would become one of his trademark saves – improvising to block the ball with his feet.

Verona create numerous chances in the opening exchanges but it requires a somewhat theatrical second-half dive by Elkjær inside the box, with referee Agnolin pointing to the spot, to provide the breakthrough. The penalty kick is coolly dispatched on the 59th minute by Giuseppe Galderisi, giving Verona a slender lead going into the final third of the game. At just 5ft 6in (1.68m) tall – placing him somewhere between Maradona and Messi – Galderisi, who has now scored two goals in three games this season, is known by players, fans and friends alike as 'Nanu'.[9] The diminutive striker makes up for what he lacks in stature with speed, agility and determination (what the Italians call *grinta*). He began his playing career

8 In 1975, Andrea Carnevale's father murdered his mother with an axe when he was just 13 years old. In 1983, his father committed suicide while in prison. At the end of the 1985/86 season, Carnevale signed for Napoli for a reported 4bn lire. Playing alongside Maradona, he scored 13 goals in his first season and won the historic 1987 championship. His form with Napoli would earn him a starting place at the 1990 World Cup alongside Gianluca Vialli, although he was substituted for the largely unknown Salvatore Schillaci, who would go on to become the leading scorer and best player of the tournament.

9 'Nano' in Italian means dwarf.

in Turin, making his Serie A debut in 1980 for Juventus when he was just 17 years old. The following season, with the prolific Roberto Bettega sidelined through injury, Nanu made 15 appearances for Trapattoni's side and scored six goals, including a memorable hat-trick against AC Milan. The following season, the youngster couldn't find space in a team bolstered by the arrivals of Paolo Rossi, Michel Platini and Zbigniew Boniek. Nanu roomed with Rossi and even helped him with the sacks of fan mail that arrived from every corner of the globe after Italy's 1982 World Cup triumph had propelled him to international stardom. But, in the 1982/83 season, Nanu managed just seven appearances for Juventus. Notwithstanding his tender years and limited contribution on the pitch, he picked up two championship medals and a Coppa Italia as the Turin giants enjoyed a period of domestic dominance in the early 1980s.

But the promising young striker craved more than just medals. He needed to play. So, in the summer of 1983, Galderisi joined Hellas Verona, where a rebuilding project had already begun under Bagnoli's quietly effective leadership. Not long after he arrived in Verona, on the second day of the summer training camp in Cavalese, Bagnoli wrote his starting XI on a blackboard. This was characteristic of Bagnoli's approach to management – clear, direct and uncompromising. Galderisi was unhappy. His name wasn't on the list. Outraged, he called Juventus president Giampiero Boniperti to tell him that he'd changed his mind and wanted out. Boniperti told him to stay put and get on with it. In the end, Nanu made 41 appearances in all competitions in the 1983/84 campaign and it was the veteran Scottish striker Joe Jordan who found himself on the fringes.

In that first season with Hellas, Galderisi formed a brilliant partnership with Maurizio Iorio, who had arrived in Verona having just won the championship with Roma. In fact, playing alongside Nanu, Iorio enjoyed the best season of his career, scoring 14 goals in 25 league appearances, with seven more in Verona's historic cup run that took them all the way to the 1984 Coppa Italia Final. Despite his impressive form and blossoming partnership with Nanu, Iorio returned to Rome at the end of the 1983/84 season in a deal worth more than 2.5bn lire. Galderisi scored seven goals that season and, more importantly, made 27 appearances in Serie A. Finally, he was getting the game time that he needed.

Now, with three games and two goals already under his belt this season, Nanu is emerging as one of the most promising Italian strikers in the league. Udinese, though, respond immediately to Galderisi's goal, forcing another superb stop by Garella from an Edinho free kick. Bagnoli is quick to react, replacing Fanna with Franco Turchetta and, with four minutes remaining, bringing on Domenico Volpati for Galderisi. Volpati is immediately involved, saving a certain goal on the line from a shot by Paolo Miano. Once again, Bagnoli's timely intervention and in-game management has proved decisive. Or have Verona just got lucky again?

Remarkably, at this early stage in the season, in his post-match interview with Gian Piero Galeazzi on RAI television, Hellas captain Roberto Tricella has to dismiss talk of a potential championship challenge, while Bagnoli insists that his objective remains the 25 points that will secure Verona's place in the top tier for at least another season.

Elsewhere, Lazio hold Inter to a 1-1 draw, AC Milan and Sampdoria take maximum points from Cremonese and Ascoli respectively, while Torino, producing the result of the weekend, hammer Napoli 3-0. So, after three matches, Hellas are a point clear of their closest rivals, Sampdoria, and two clear of a chasing pack that includes Juve, Inter, AC Milan and Torino.

Although some formidable individual talent has converged on the peninsula, including some of the world's greatest and most ambitious players, none of the major teams are without their flaws. While some are in transition, others lack that clear sense of identity that is common to the most successful teams. Others are too dependent on a single player or, in the case of Napoli, have yet to learn how to get the best out of the superstar at their disposal. This has left the door open for a club with a clear identity, a cohesive and well-organised team of players and a manager with the tactical awareness and in-game experience to bring it all together.

It's still early days and Hellas can once again consider themselves fortunate to have taken two points thanks to a generous penalty award. Can they maintain such form and expect such luck against the biggest teams and best players in the league? They now face a run of games that includes Inter, Juventus, Roma and Fiorentina. Despite a promising start, no one expects Verona to take much from these fixtures.

3A GIORNATA

Atalanta 0-0 Roma
Avellino 0-0 Juventus
Como 0-0 Fiorentina
Lazio 1-1 Inter
Milan 2-1 Cremonese
Sampdoria 2-0 Ascoli
Torino 3-0 Napoli
Verona 1-0 Udinese

CLASSIFICA

Verona	**6**
Sampdoria	5
Juventus	4
Torino	4
Inter	4
Milan	4
Fiorentina	4
Udinese	3
Como	3
Roma	3
Cremonese	2
Avellino	2
Atalanta	2
Napoli	1
Lazio	1
Ascoli	0

4a Giornata

7 October 1984

VERONA'S AWAY record in Milan is dire. In fact, since the stadium was inaugurated in 1926, Hellas Verona have never won at the San Siro, a record that stands to this day. The San Siro (or the Stadio Giuseppe Meazza as it was officially renamed in 1980) is located on the western outskirts of Milan, on the site of an ancient church (the San Siro alla Vepra) from which first the neighbourhood and then the stadium took its name. Milan, according to the 1984 *Let's Go* travel guide, is 'easily Italy's most industrious and vital city' and 'one of her most artistically important and enjoyable'. That latter characteristic does not, of course, apply if you are a Hellas Verona fan, where Milan is generally a place of defeat. What separates it from the art cities of Florence, Venice and Rome, according to our guide, is 'its contemporary attitudes, its energy and its sparkle'.

That's the one thing the vastly experienced squad of Football Club Internazionale Milano (known universally as Inter) is lacking this season – a bit of sparkle. While the Inter squad is bristling with homegrown talent like Walter Zenga, Giuseppe Bergomi, Giuseppe Baresi, Andrea Mandorlini and Alessandro Altobelli, as well as Irishman Liam Brady (recently arrived from Sampdoria) and the Bayern Munich legend Karl-Heinz Rummenigge, their form so far this season has been less than convincing, with low-scoring draws against Atalanta and Lazio and a narrow victory at home against Avellino. Might this finally be the moment for Hellas to cause an upset at the San Siro?

One man who is certainly capable of providing a bit of sparkle is Brady. When he left Arsenal in 1980, he was the first foreign player to sign for Juventus since the Italian borders reopened to foreign transfers in 1980. The talented 24-year-old was taking a calculated risk. He was arguably the most gifted player in English football at the time but success in the more demanding context of the Italian Serie A was by no means a given. In the 1960s, the first wave of English-based players to arrive in Italy, including the likes of Jimmy Greaves and Denis Law, struggled to adapt to life on the peninsula. But Brady, who led a second wave of incoming talent in the 1980s, was determined to succeed where others had failed.

The Irishman spent two seasons wearing the famous No.10 shirt of Juventus, where he picked up back-to-back championship medals in 1981 and 1982. But, with the imminent arrival of Michel Platini and Zbigniew 'Zibì' Boniek, Brady was informed just before the end of the 1981/82 season that, because of the strict two foreigner rule, there was no space for him the following season. At the time, Brady was Juve's regular penalty taker and he reacted to the news by telling manager Giovanni Trapattoni that he wouldn't be taking penalties for the remainder of the season. Then, in the closing stages of the decisive final game, with their designated penalty taker already substituted, Juve were awarded a spot kick! In desperation, Trapattoni turned to Brady. The Irishman didn't let him down.

Brady's goal secured an historic 20th *Scudetto* for the Turin giants, depriving Fiorentina of a spectacular upset at the last minute. For Brady, it was a bittersweet moment. He had just won the championship but he knew this would be his last appearance in the famous black and white stripes of Juventus. He spent the next two years at Sampdoria, before signing for Inter at the start of the 1984/85 season, where he was joined by powerful German striker Rummenigge.

Rummenigge broke into the legendary Bayern Munich side as a youngster in the 1975/76 season and made his international debut the same year. In 1979/80, his form exploded and 'Kalle', as he was known, was the league's top scorer with 26 goals as Bayern won the Bundesliga. At 25 years old, he was already the leader of a young, ambitious West German team full of big personalities and no shortage of talent and they were amongst the favourites to win the 1980 European Championship hosted in Italy.

Europa 80 was, if the truth be told, an underwhelming tournament that failed to capture the public's imagination. Across four host cities (Milan, Turin, Rome and Naples), attendance was low, except for those matches involving the host nation. Italy scored just two goals in four games, with a 1-0 victory against England and draws against Spain and Belgium, but progressed to the third-place play-off anyway, which they drew 1-1 with Czechoslovakia. In the subsequent penalty shoot-out, after 17 successful attempts, AC Milan defender Fulvio Collovati missed for the host nation, handing the bronze medal to the Czechs and consigning the Italians to an inglorious fourth-place finish on home soil. In a sign of the kind of problems that would tarnish the game for the next decade and more, a riot in the crowd during England's opening match against Belgium in Turin resulted in the use of tear gas that temporarily forced both teams off the pitch as half-time approached.

Rummenigge's West Germany emerged as the superior team, beating a strong Belgian side 2-1 in the final. 'Kalle' went on to win back-to-back Ballon d'Or (in 1980 and 1981) and, in 1982, he came within inches of winning the European Cup Final for Bayern with an outrageous overhead kick against Aston Villa. Just a few weeks later, at the World Cup in Spain, he scored five goals to take West Germany to the final against Italy. By 1984, he was one of the biggest names in world football and his transfer to Inter Milan for 8.5bn lire was one of the biggest transfer deals in football history.

This season, another new addition to the Inter squad is an elegant young defender named Andrea Mandorlini. He would go on to make 180 appearances for Inter but it was as a coach that Mandorlini would achieve the impossible. In 2010, Hellas Verona were languishing in second-to-last place in the Lega Pro Prima Divisione when Mandorlini was appointed. After an initial series of five consecutive draws, Hellas embarked on a run that would see them reach the play-offs. Eliminating Sorrento and then Salernitana, Verona returned to Serie B after a four-year absence. But better was to come.

In Serie B the following season, setting out with the aim of salvation, Mandorlini's newly promoted Verona came close to securing immediate promotion to Serie A, finishing the season in fourth place with 78 points but losing out in a play-off semi-final against Varese. In 2013, Mandorlini finally led Verona back to Serie A after an 11-year hiatus, achieving automatic promotion behind Sassuolo, the first coach in the club's history to achieve two promotions. In the 2013/14 season, which once again began with the simple objective of staying up, Mandorlini's Verona achieved a stunning tenth-place finish. That season, he equalled Verona's record of six consecutive home victories in Serie A and his team scored more goals (62) than they had ever scored in a single Serie A season before, as well as the highest number of victories (16). The following season, with salvation once again the objective, Mandorlini's Verona finished in 13th place, with veteran striker Luca Toni lifting Serie A's top scorer title alongside Inter's Mauro Icardi and the team recording some impressive results against Napoli, Milan, Inter and Juventus along the way. For his record in those years, Mandorlini is widely regarded as one of the outstanding coaches in Verona's history. That, however, is all in the future. Today, he is wearing the famous black and blue stripes of Football Club Internazionale Milano.

Alongside Mandorlini at the back for Inter, Baresi already has seven Serie A seasons under his belt, while the *libero* Bergomi is beginning his fifth Serie A campaign. Alessandro Altobelli, widely regarded as one of the finest Italian strikers of the post-war period, is another name that is intrinsically linked to the club. Between 1977 and 1988, 'Spillo', as he was known, made 466 appearances and scored 209 goals for Inter (second in the all-time list behind Giuseppe Meazza), winning a *Scudetto* (in 1979/80) and the Coppa Italia twice (in 1978 and 1982).

In Ilario Castagner, Verona's opponents today have the first coach in the history of Italian football to finish a Serie A championship undefeated. That he achieved this miraculous feat with lowly Perugia makes it even more remarkable. In that unbeaten 1978/79 season, Perugia finished in second place, the greatest result in the club's history. In 1980, however, the club was caught up in the *Totonero* match-fixing scandal and would start the following campaign with a five-point penalty. After spells at Lazio and AC Milan, Castagner arrived at city rivals Inter at the beginning of the 1984/85 season, succeeding outgoing coach Luigi Radice, who was on his way back to Torino.

With the arrival of Rummenigge, Brady and the legendary Juve winger Franco Causio, Castagner is expected to improve on last season's fourth-place finish. In fact, despite their lack of sparkle so far this season, the Milan giants are, with such a formidable squad, regarded as serious title contenders – something Hellas full back Luciano Marangon concedes in his pre-match interview with Gian Piero Galeazzi on RAI TV. With a West German international playing on each side, the national team coach, the legendary Franz Beckenbauer, is at the San Siro today to observe proceedings. From Verona, a few thousand have made the trip to Milan and are rewarded for their troubles with a thrilling encounter between two teams full of top quality players.

Nicknamed 'The Doberman' for his loyalty and aggression on the pitch, versatile Verona defender Mauro Ferroni is assigned the unenviable task of suppressing Rummenigge. Ferroni, a lifelong bachelor, loves to cook and is known to prepare delicious *Bucatini all'amatriciana* for his friends, washed down with a nice bottle of Frascati. Such elegance doesn't stop him from mauling Rummenigge. Meanwhile, Silvano Fontolan, nicknamed '*il corazziere*'[10] on account of his size and bulk, faces Alessandro Altobelli, while Luciano Marangon,

---

10 A '*corazziere*' was a heavily armed cavalry soldier from the 15th century. Today the term is used to describe a tall, robust person.

the Casanova of the team, faces off against the great Franco Causio. A formidable trio at the heart of Verona's defence, Ferroni, Fontolan and Marangon are the defensive bedrock of this Hellas Verona team. In neutralising Rummenigge, Ferroni will play one of the greatest games of his career.

Alessandro Fiorio, who was then a 17-year-old student, vividly recalls those glorious Sunday afternoons, even though Verona were playing away from home and he hadn't travelled. He'd meet his friends from the neighbourhood and they'd go to play football in a small square near his house in Veronetta. Back then, there weren't as many cars as there are now and it was quite safe to play football on the street. They'd put a small wireless radio near the goal so whoever was in goal could follow Roberto Puliero's commentary and alert the others if something important was happening. 'There were', Alessandro remembers, 'no live matches on TV, only *Tutto il calcio minuto per minuto* on the radio and Puliero's mesmerising commentary. We didn't need anything else.' Indeed, for many local fans, Puliero was the voice of the championship.

His is a name that few outside Italy will have heard of but Roberto Puliero is one of Verona's favourite sons. In the brash and often shallow world of football punditry, Puliero was a profoundly cultured commentator, a bedazzling blend of refined intellect and unrestrained passion. Urbane, eloquent and artistic, he was a genuine free spirit, a nonconformist whose unmistakable commentaries provided an instantly recognisable soundtrack for a generation of football fans. Puliero was, as the local news outlet *Verona Sera* explained, 'a man loved by all for his subtle humour, the refinement of his language and intelligence which embraced popular tradition'. Tim Parks, in his seminal work, *A Season with Verona*, offered the following evocative portrait of Puliero: 'A highly cultured man, warm, liberal and charismatic [...] his broad, wrinkled mobile face is the result of years of extravagant mimicry and clowning. He wears his fuzzy hair long and absolutely unkempt. His voice, strained with overuse, rich and nasal, with dialect intonations and generous with emotion, is absolutely distinctive, immediately seductive.'

In goal for Verona, Claudio Garella is at his unconventional, spectacular and courageous best, while Briegel's imposing presence in midfield snuffs out more than one Inter attack. But it is home goalkeeper Walter Zenga who pulls off the save of the match, a remarkable double block to deny Verona a first-half lead.

In the end, the two sides effectively cancel each other out and the match ends goalless. For Verona, it is a mature, if unspectacular, performance. Although it's the first time this season Hellas haven't scored, to return, for once, from the San Siro unscathed and with a valuable point is a powerful statement of intent, underlining that Hellas are a team not to be underestimated. There is, as Bagnoli himself observes in his post-match interview, 'still much water to pass under the bridge'. And, in case anyone is getting carried away with delusions of grandeur, Bagnoli brings them back down to earth by revealing that the city can't even provide his players with a hot shower at their training ground![11]

Elsewhere, Juventus and AC Milan draw 1-1, Torino win at Udine and Fiorentina, the only team in the championship not yet to have conceded a goal, crush Atalanta 5-0. Having survived the trip to Milan, next week brings another stiff challenge, as Juventus travel to Verona. The Turin giants are unquestionably the dominant Italian club side of the decade, winning four championship titles between 1980 and 1986. At the heart of Juve's success is a Frenchman known simply as '*Le Roi*'.

---

11 In the aftermath of the draw with Inter, Bagnoli complained to the press that on Saturday evening Briegel, Fanna, Galderisi and Volpati were sick because of the cold showers they took after training that week.

4A GIORNATA

Ascoli 0-0 Lazio
Cremonese 0-0 Avellino
Fiorentina 5-0 Atalanta
Inter 0-0 Verona
Juventus 1-1 Milan
Napoli 3-0 Como
Roma 1-1 Sampdoria
Udinese 0-1 Torino

CLASSIFICA

Verona	**7**
Fiorentina	6
Sampdoria	6
Torino	6
Inter	5
Milan	5
Juventus	5
Roma	4
Udinese	3
Como	3
Napoli	3
Cremonese	3
Avellino	3
Atalanta	2
Lazio	2
Ascoli	1

5a Giornata

14 October 1984

MICHEL PLATINI won the Ballon d'Or three seasons in a row and was the pre-eminent football player of his generation. In fact, between 1982 and 1985, a Juventus player won the Ballon d'Or in four consecutive seasons (first Paolo Rossi in 1982 then Platini in 1983, 1984 and 1985). At Euro 84, a Platini-inspired France were crowned champions of Europe, with the No.10 scoring nine of France's 14 goals in just five games, a record that stands to this day. In the final against Spain at Parc des Princes in Paris, Platini's second-half free kick broke the deadlock and helped secure France's first major tournament in world football. Just a couple of seasons previously, Platini had inherited Juventus's famous No.10 shirt from the outgoing Liam Brady, inspiring *La Vecchia Signora* (The Old Lady) to yet another Italian Serie A title. According to Pelé, who knew a thing or two about such things, Platini was the European footballer of the 1980s. Going into the 1984/85 season, the experienced Frenchman, known by his compatriots as '*Le Roi*' (French for 'The King'), had just turned 29.

Like Platini, the versatile Polish midfielder Zbigniew Boniek arrived at Juventus in 1982, after impressing with the Polish national team at the World Cup that summer. He lifted the Coppa Italia in his first season in Turin in which Juventus had to settle for a second-place finish in the league and also reached the European Cup Final. With Juventus, he would go on to win the Italian championship in 1984, the Coppa Italia, the European Cup, the European Cup Winners' Cup and the European Super Cup. With his blistering pace and a killer instinct, Maradona thought 'Zibì' was the best counter-attacking player in the world. He is certainly one of the greatest Polish players of all time, having inspired Poland to a third-place finish at the 1982 World Cup.

Legendary *libero* Gaetano Scirea was beginning his 11th consecutive season in Serie A with Juventus. By now, he'd already won just about everything in the game; six Serie A titles (he would go on to win one more), two Coppa Italia, a UEFA Cup, a Cup Winners' Cup, a Super Cup and a European Cup, as well as a World Cup in 1982. A symbolic figurehead and captain of the Trapattoni-era Juventus, Scirea had been part of one of the most formidable defensive units in the history of the Italian game, alongside the now retired Dino Zoff and Antonio Cabrini. World Cup winners Marco Tardelli and Paolo Rossi were amongst the offensive talent that the defending champions boasted as they travelled to Verona to face the league leaders on matchday five.

For ten years (from 1 July 1976 to 30 June 1986), Giovanni Trapattoni was head coach of Juventus as they won every UEFA and international club competition going. He won the Serie A league title six times (in 1977, 1978, 1981, 1982, 1984 and 1986), the Coppa Italia twice (in 1979 and 1983), the European Cup and the Intercontinental Cup in 1985, the UEFA Cup Winners' Cup and the European Super Cup in 1984 and the UEFA Cup in 1977. One of the greatest managers in the history of the game, he was renowned for his expert man-management and unrivalled tactical awareness.

As early as the late 1960s, the style of football known as *catenaccio* was in decline. With the advent of 'Total Football' and zonal marking, such a defensive approach was gradually losing favour. But, as the concept of 'first, don't concede' continued to dominate, the true tactical successor to *catenaccio* was born: *la zona mista*. Under this system, a player who moves out of position is immediately replaced by another from his team, thus retaining the team's overall shape. Each player is required to fill a variety of different roles, making it more versatile, fluid and offensive than the more rigid style commonly used in Italy at the time. Trapattoni and Gigi Radice, at Juventus and Torino respectively, began to apply the concepts of 'Total Football' (such as pressing and player fluidity) to the tried and tested principles of *catenaccio*. The Italian national team also adopted the so-called 'mixed zone', winning the World Cup in 1982 under the guidance of Enzo Bearzot while relying on the Juventus rearguard, whose players were so accustomed to playing it. Under this system, each outfield player – except the *trequartista* – occupied a particular zone on the pitch, giving the playmaker, a player capable of creating something from nothing, the freedom to roam the field to find pockets of space to exploit and break down the opposition's defence. The success of the system relied on the quality of the *trequartista* – the No.10. Juventus were fortunate in this regard. First, they had Brady, now Platini.

The only possible glimmer of hope for their rivals is that Juventus are an ageing squad whose period of dominance at the top of the Italian game is now coming to an end. What's more, their primary focus this season is the European Cup. Might that give Verona a glimmer of hope as they host the reigning champions at the Bentegodi?

With barely ten minutes remaining and Hellas already one up thanks to a second-half Galderisi goal, Antonio Di Gennaro launches a long speculative clearance. With lightning speed and astonishing power, Elkjær seizes on the loose ball, shrugging off the young Juventus defender given the unenviable task of marking him. As he surges down the wing and into the box, the great Dane lopes past a flailing Gaetano Scirea, one of the most refined defenders in the history of the game, somehow losing his boot in the process. Without missing a beat, Elkjær fires off a shot into the far-right corner of the net, beyond the sprawling Stefano Tacconi, known somewhat disparagingly as 'the best back-up keeper in the world'.[12] With or without his boot, even Tacconi has no chance, as Elkjær

---

12 Despite being one of the greatest goalkeepers of his generation, Stefano Tacconi earned just seven caps for the Italian national team. He is the only goalkeeper to have won all international club competitions but at international level he spent much of his career in Walter Zenga's shadow.

scores one of the most memorable goals in the club's history to seal a rare victory against Trapattoni's all-conquering Juventus.

As the Bentegodi erupts in a thunderous cacophony of joy, Elkjær points playfully at his shoeless foot as he is engulfed by his incredulous team-mates. Fourteen-year-old Verona fan Emiliano Cipriani and his dad were amongst the Juventus fans in the *Curva Nord* that day (the *Curva Sud* was full). When Elkjær scored, they jumped for joy, forgetting for a moment where they were. In local dialect, Emiliano's dad said: '*Sta sentà che no ciapemo do sberle* (sit down before they slap us in the face!)' Somehow, father and son survived to tell the tale of a truly iconic moment that is remembered in Verona more than any other goal scored that season.

On the radio commentary, Roberto Puliero's jubilant exclamation will echo down the decades: '*Rete! Rete! Alé alé alé alé alé alé alé alé alé! Alé bum bum bum bum bum bum bum bum bum bum bum bum bum! Il Verona amici sportive Veronese è la migliore squadra di Italia!*'[13] Universally remembered for that goal, the rest of game seems inconsequential.

Splendid October sunshine floods the Bentegodi as a capacity crowd of 43,000 fills the stadium that Sunday afternoon. Verona start strongly, taking Juventus by surprise with the intensity of their play, with Di Gennaro dictating the flow and tempo of the game from midfield. With barely 11 minutes on the clock, Volpati forces an excellent save from Tacconi. Barely five minutes later, Tacconi is forced into an outstanding double save, first from a shot from Briegel and, immediately after, from a Fontolan header from the rebound. After 21 minutes, Verona have a good penalty claim denied as Elkjær goes down in the box. Pierino Fanna, not deemed good enough for Juventus by Trapattoni, is rampant against his

---

13 A translation can barely do justice to the euphoric commentary of Roberto Puliero as Elkjær scored that iconic shoeless goal against Juventus. '*Rete*' means 'net/goal', while '*alè*' is the Italian version of the French '*allez!*' meaning 'let's go!'. '*Bum*', of course, is the Italian version of the onomatopoeic 'boom'. He continues his exultation by exclaiming 'Verona, my Veronese sports friends, is the best team in Italy!'

former club and, even against a team as formidable as Juventus, it is one-way traffic. At half-time, remarkably, it is goalless.

Finally, in the 62nd minute, Verona take a well-deserved lead. From Volpati to Fanna, Tacconi tries to intercept, but Galderisi is lurking and scores with a header. Another Juve reject making the difference! Verona 1 Juventus 0! Trapattoni immediately responds by putting on attacking midfielder Beniamino Vignola in place of the dazed sweeper Nicola Caricola, moving Tardelli back into defence. As Juventus desperately seek an equaliser, Verona fall back. After 80 minutes, Garella blocks a shot from Tardelli and then the rebound from Platini at point-blank range. Moments later, it is a long clearance from a goal kick that releases Elkjær for his wonder goal. Juventus are stunned and Galderisi comes close to grabbing a third just five minutes later, hitting the crossbar on the counter-attack.

As Elkjær leaves the pitch at the end of game, he wipes tears from his eyes. It's only October but it's now obvious to him that something special is happening. So, where did this wild Dane who outshines even Platini come from and how did he end up in Verona?

With five minutes to go to the interval, Belgium were 2-0 up in a fractious encounter that had frequently threatened to boil over. A penalty in the dying minutes of the first half gave Group One rivals Denmark a lifeline. Fifteen minutes into the second half, Denmark grabbed an equaliser and then Preben Elkjær Larsen stole the show with a late winner. From the moment he picked up the ball deep in his own half, there was only one thing on his mind. It was classic Elkjær, combining searing pace, power and close control with a ridiculously impertinent finish as he dinked the ball over the on-rushing Belgian keeper. That evening in June 1984, as the Danish players celebrated with characteristic swagger in a Strasbourg hotel, Elkjær was weighing up his options. He had just lost his grandfather and, at 26 years old, his life was at a turning point.

Back in 1976, 18-year-old Elkjær had left Denmark for West Germany, signing for FC Köln, then one of the leading clubs in the Bundesliga. Expectations were high and the rigorous regime was tough for the young Dane taking his first steps in the world of professional football. He had gone from two training sessions a week to two sessions a day, struggling to fit in with the physical and mental demands of the tough German system. Despite the challenges, Elkjær made 13 appearances and scored three goals in his first season with Köln. The following year, still just 19, he scored twice on his full international debut as Denmark won 2-1 in Helsinki against Finland.

Thrown in at the deep end with FC Köln as a precociously talented but rebellious teenager, Elkjær clashed frequently with his disciplinarian coach, Hennes Weisweiler, who disapproved of the young Dane's flamboyant lifestyle. In one notorious episode that has shaped Elkjær's reputation ever since, Weisweiler asked him if it was true that he had spent the early morning hours at a nightclub in the company of a bottle of whisky and a lady. Elkjær assured him it was false. In fact, he explained to his exasperated coach, he'd been in the company of a bottle of *vodka* and *two* ladies!

At the end of the season, Elkjær was transferred to Lokeren in Belgium, where he found the environment and expectations more suited to his temperament and lifestyle. He spent a happy but trophyless six years in Belgium. It was the beginning of the 'Danish Dynamite' era and Elkjær, as usual, was in the thick of things. When Denmark's manager, Sepp Piontek, imposed 200 kroner fines for every five minutes late a player returned after curfew, Elkjær simply handed over a down payment at the start of each international break to cover his fines. Despite his off-field reputation, Elkjær had the quality to deliver when it mattered.

He was a notorious chain smoker and was even said to take a sneaky draw on a cigarette during the half-time interval (a habit that he has denied). Despite this, Elkjær was blessed with searing pace and a seemingly endless lung capacity – 'the human locomotive' as one Spanish newspaper described him. Clinical in front of goal, he had perfected a variation of the

Cruyff turn while watching children playing football on the beach in Barbados. Irrepressible, the life and soul of the party, he claimed not to drink but sometimes he drove his team-mates mad with his incessant storytelling and chat. He was also known to enjoy nights out before big games and met his future wife, Nicole, at a nightclub in Lokeren.

However, by the summer of 1984, Elkjær's hardest partying days were behind him. Outrageously talented and at 26 years of age, he was about to enter his prime. Yet, notwithstanding his impressive goalscoring record for club and country, he had little in the way of silverware to show for his undoubted talents.

At the hotel where he was staying with the Danish squad for Euro 84, Elkjær had fielded several phone calls from some of the top clubs in Europe, including the likes of Barcelona, Real Madrid, Tottenham and Hamburg. With an offer already on the table from Bologna, Hellas Verona had also expressed an interest in the in-form Danish striker. For advice, Elkjær turned to international team-mate Michael Laudrup, who was playing for Lazio at the time. The feedback was positive. A top-six club, a beautiful city and a nice place to live. What more could you ask for?

Hellas Verona sporting director Emiliano Mascetti had been at the De Meer Stadion, the home of Dutch giants Ajax, earlier that year when the Danes had been on the wrong end of a six-goal thumping against the Netherlands. This was the era of 'Total Football' and the talented Dutch side put on quite a show. As unlikely as it seems, given the result, this was the match that convinced Mascetti that Elkjær was the perfect fit for Verona; a powerful striker with formidable physical strength, a fierce competitive spirit and the kind of raw pace that strikes fear into any defender.

If Hellas Verona were to get their man, they had to move quickly. Mascetti and club accountant Liliano Rangogni favoured a personal touch and were in France to speak to the player face-to-face. Rangogni, an accountant by profession, was responsible for agreeing salaries and bonuses and for negotiating new signings. The three men talked all night, away from the prying eyes of team-mates and the press. From a footballing perspective, Italy was appealing. It was the best championship with the greatest players in the world and Elkjær wanted to be part of it. Rangogni made an offer of 2.5bn lire. Within the context of an annual turnover of just 15bn lire, it was a significant outlay for a single player. As Denmark were preparing for their semi-final encounter with Spain, negotiations continued and Volker Schmidt, the Swiss agent who also represented Briegel, was called in to mediate. But Elkjær had made up his mind.

Though Elkjær had set the Euros alight and his signing was a massive coup for Verona, *La Gazzetta dello Sport* somehow managed to confuse him with Jesper Olsen when they reported his signing on the day of the Euro semi-final. With Denmark eliminated on penalties, Elkjær arrived in Verona for pre-season training and immediately recognised Bagnoli as the kind of coach he could work with. Despite the language barrier, he understood immediately who Bagnoli was and what he wanted, explaining to *La Repubblica* many years later that Bagnoli was '[a] tough gentleman, an honest man who asked you to work. He [Bagnoli] spoke little … [but] we always understood each other by looking at each other.' His first impressions of his new team-mates, however, were less convincing. 'Briegel and I ended up living next to each other,' Elkjær explained in a recent interview with *Mundial* magazine. 'We had houses together at Lake Garda. Every day, we'd take one car to training. After the first training session, we went back to our houses and we spoke on the way back. We said "Wow, we can't win anything here!" They were so small. Technically, they were okay but they had no power. It was a big surprise for us. We also had to play against Juventus, Milan, Inter, Roma, Napoli and Torino. To even be number five or six in Italy, you had to have a really good team. We weren't very impressed at the start.'

Everyone you meet in Verona of a certain age claims to have been in the *Curva Sud* the day Elkjær scored that shoeless goal. One person who probably wishes he hadn't been there was the Juve defender left flailing in Elkjær's wake as he surged towards goal, an 18-year-old named Stefano Pioli. The baby-faced defender tried his best to bring Elkjær down but was no match for the Dane's blistering pace.[14]

Elsewhere that day, AC Milan beat Roma 2-1, Sampdoria won 2-0 against Fiorentina and Torino and Inter ground out a 1-1 draw. With four goals in five games, Milan's English striker Mark Hateley was off to a flyer, the league's top scorer in his first season in Italy. Hellas, meanwhile, had the best goalscoring record in the league, with nine goals scored and just two conceded, maintaining their one-point lead at the top of the table. Back at the Bentegodi, the celebrations continued long into the night, as Hellas fans began to eulogise about a miraculous goal scored by the Danish dynamite.

Michel qui?

---

14 Pioli would recover from the indignity of being humiliated by a shoeless Elkjær, and would, in fact, play alongside the Dane in Verona just two years later. Pioli won the Serie A championship as a coach with AC Milan in 2022, the second of his career, having won his first *Scudetto* as a young player with Juventus in 1986.

5A GIORNATA

Atalanta 1-0 Cremonese
Avellino 2-0 Ascoli
Como 2-0 Udinese
Lazio 1-1 Napoli
Milan 2-1 Roma
Sampdoria 2-0 Fiorentina
Torino 1-1 Inter
Verona 2-0 Juventus

CLASSIFICA

Verona	**9**
Sampdoria	8
Torino	7
Milan	7
Fiorentina	6
Inter	6
Juventus	5
Avellino	5
Como	5
Roma	4
Napoli	4
Atalanta	4
Udinese	3
Cremonese	3
Lazio	3
Ascoli	1

6a Giornata

21 October 1984

USING EVERY part of his body – feet, knees and torso – Claudio Garella reinvents goalkeeping and single-handedly ensures that Hellas come away from the Stadio Olimpico with a point. For 14-year-old Barbara Salazer, Garella's performance against Roma is one of the highlights of the entire season. In tomorrow's player ratings in *La Gazzetta dello Sport*, Garella will receive a nine (at least that's how Barbara remembers it) – which is practically unheard of for a goalkeeper, while the sports section of Verona's daily newspaper, *L'Arena*, leads with 'Garella stops Roma'. The legend of 'Garellik' is born.

It was *L'Arena* journalist Valentino Fioravanti who first coined the term 'Garellik' to describe Verona's unconventional superhero goalkeeper. Fioravanti took his inspiration from the classic Italian comic series *Diabolik* in which the comic's protagonist was a misunderstood anti-hero with incredible superpowers, in much the same way that Garella overcame adversity to become an unlikely hero for Verona.[15] Garella's transformation, from an error-prone figure of fun, nicknamed 'Paperone' (the Italian name for the Disney cartoon character Scrooge McDuck), to one of the most outstanding goalkeepers in the league can be traced back to this game in Rome. In fact, Garella had been a key player for Verona in recent seasons, as Hellas progressed from the depths of Serie B to the summit of Serie A.

---

15 The series, created by sisters Angela and Luciana Giussani, was incredibly popular in Italy in the 1980s and spawned the *fumetti neri* (black comic) sub-genre.

Garella made his Serie A debut in the 1972/73 season with Torino (his one and only appearance in Torino colours). He then spent a couple of seasons in the lower leagues before transferring to Lazio. Famously described by Giovanni Agnelli, the industrialist and leader of the Fiat motor company, as 'the best goalkeeper in the world', before adding mockingly, '[w] ithout hands, though', Garella was a formidable shot-stopper, though he carried with him a certain reputation for making mistakes – which somewhat unkindly became known as *Garellate*.

In the 1977/78 season, Garella conceded 36 goals in 29 appearances for Lazio, including a string of howlers. After poor performances against Lens in the European Cup and Vicenza in the championship, Lazio fans began calling him 'Paperella' (a *paparella* is a rubber duck in Italian) and his days in the Italian capital were numbered. He was sold to Sampdoria, then in Serie B, where he played for three seasons, amassing 113 appearances and conceding 97 goals. Though much improved, question marks remained about the unconventional keeper's aptitude as a top-level keeper. Tall with round shoulders and disproportionate limbs, Garella had never been elegant-looking in the mould of Dino Zoff, the outstanding Italian goalkeeper of his generation, and had an alarming tendency to use his fists rather than his hands … not to mention his legs, feet, torso or any other part of his body that might get in the way of the ball. Somehow, it seemed to work, though no one could really understand how. Although the schoolboy howlers were now in the past, the reputation for calamity, like a bad aftershave from the 1970s, lingered.

In the summer of 1981, Garella was amongst the first to join Bagnoli's quiet revolution in Verona, earning promotion to Serie A in his first season with the club. With a striking head of thick dark hair, that garish red jersey, often with a conspicuous goal medallion hanging round his neck, and a roguish smirk, the unlikely-looking keeper soon became a fans' favourite, an integral and instantly recognisable part of the project under way at Verona. Garella's performance in Rome in October

1984 marked the culmination of his personal journey from gaffe-prone figure of ridicule to a match-winning superhero.

Prior to facing Verona, Roma have had a decidedly underwhelming start to the season, despite boasting a squad which still contains the nucleus of the team that won the championship in 1983. So far, they have managed only four draws and been beaten 2-1 against AC Milan. Pre-match, Swedish coach Sven-Göran Eriksson – impressing with flawless Italian despite having only been in Italy for a couple of months – acknowledges that it will be a difficult encounter against an in-form Hellas. The son of a bus conductor, also called Sven, Eriksson made his debut for Swedish Division Four team Torsby IF at the tender age of 16. In 1975, he quit playing aged just 27, never having fulfilled his dream of playing professionally.

As a young coach, he achieved remarkable success at IFK Göteborg, winning the Swedish treble in his third season. In 1982, he won the UEFA Cup, the first time a Swedish club had ever done so. On the back of such success, Portuguese side Benfica took a gamble on him and he won the Primeira Divisão and the Taça de Portugal, as well as finishing as runner-up in the 1982/83 UEFA Cup, losing to Anderlecht in the final. Sven's sensational record at Benfica of 57 victories in 78 games (a win rate of 73 per cent) brought him to the attention of Europe's biggest clubs and, after winning a second consecutive league title in Portugal, he moved to Italy, becoming the 'technical director' of Roma on 1 July 1984, with the unenviable task of succeeding compatriot Nils Liedholm and restoring Roma's place as a major force in Italian football. The pragmatic Swede favoured results, tactical discipline and workrate over performance and flair. He played a rigid 4-4-2 system with zonal marking and aggressive pressing. In Italy, he embraced the so-called *zona mista* system, the tactical evolution of *catenaccio* pioneered by Radice and Trapattoni. In background, temperament and style, the elegant, intellectual and urbane Swede couldn't have been more different to his opposite number on the Verona bench.

Born in 1935, Osvaldo Bagnoli was from Bovisa, an industrial neighbourhood in northern Milan. His father was a metalworker and his mother worked in a local factory. With a prominent nose and a thick mop of dishevelled hair, he was known fondly by his family as 'Zaso' (a contraction of *zazzera*, which literally means 'mop of hair'). The young Osvaldo played football barefoot in the street with the neighbourhood kids and left school with few qualifications to find work in the local factories. He continued to play and, in 1955, was invited to join the AC Milan youth set-up. One day, he was called into the manager's office. 'Bagnoli, you're in the first team,' he was told. 'I can't,' the startled youngster replied, 'I've got a job at the factory.' 'How much do you earn at the factory?' they asked him. 'Twenty-eight thousand a month,' he replied. 'We'll give you 35,000 but tomorrow you quit.'

Bagnoli was soon making his Serie A debut with the *Rossoneri,* playing the last eight games of the 1955/56 season. In June 1956, the penultimate edition of the Latin Cup (an international club tournament involving sides from France, Italy, Spain and Portugal) was held in Milan and Bagnoli was amongst the scorers as Milan beat Athletic Bilbao in the final. In all, Bagnoli made ten appearances and scored three goals in that breakthrough season as Milan finished second behind Fiorentina. The following season, Milan went one better and won the league, with Bagnoli once again making ten appearances, scoring a single goal in the last game of the season. Amongst his team-mates in the Milan squad that season were Swedish midfielder Nils Liedholm and Italian defender Luigi Radice, both of whom would go on to become influential and successful coaches.

At the end of the 1956/57 season, 21-year-old Bagnoli found himself surplus to requirements at AC Milan (forced out by the arrival of a promising young midfielder named Giovanni Trapattoni) and on his way, of all places, to Verona. These were tough times for the *Gialloblù*, who struggled for consistency despite impressive home victories against

AC Milan, Sampdoria[16] and Napoli. Despite suffering a debilitating bout of pleurisy that kept him on the sidelines for a spell, Bagnoli made 23 appearances and scored three goals in the 1957/58 campaign. But his first season with Verona would end in disappointment as Hellas finished at the foot of the table and faced an inter-divisional play-off against southern rivals Bari, runners-up in Serie B. With both legs played at neutral venues, a touch of A-list glamour appeared in the stands in the shapely form of the iconic Italian actress Marisa Allasio, star of *Arrivederci Roma,* whose father was the Bari coach, Federico. Verona lost 3-0 on aggregate, condemning Bagnoli and Verona to Serie B football the following season.

While Verona languished in Serie B, Bagnoli thrived, making 38 appearances and scoring 15 goals in the 1958/59 season, making him the club's top scorer. Despite his impressive personal contribution, Verona finished in a disappointing sixth place. Bagnoli would repeat the feat the following season, with 36 appearances and 12 goals, but this time Verona finished in an even more disappointing eighth place. It was during this period that Bagnoli met a local girl named Rosanna. On their first date, he took her to the cinema to see *Love in the Afternoon,* a 1957 romantic comedy directed by Billy Wilder and starring Gary Cooper, Audrey Hepburn and Maurice Chevalier. Before long, the young couple were married and starting a family. Two daughters arrived, Francesca and Monica, and, though his career often took him elsewhere, Bagnoli's marriage to Rosanna tied him to Verona for the rest of his life.

In 1960, Bagnoli's impressive form in Serie B earned him a transfer to Udinese, where an ambitious rebuilding project was under way. Bagnoli managed just 14 appearances in all competitions, with a solitary goal against Wiener Neustädter SC in the Coppa Mitropa.[17] After just a single

---

16 On 9 February 1958, the Brazilian striker Emanuele Del Vecchio scored all five goals in an impressive 5-3 victory against Sampdoria.

17 The Mitropa Cup, officially called La Coupe de l'Europe Centrale or Central European Cup, was one of the first major international European football cups for club sides. It was discontinued in 1992.

season with Udinese, Bagnoli moved on in the summer of 1961 to Catanzaro, 'the city of the two seas' that overlooks the Tyrrhenian to the west and Ionian to the east. Unione Sportiva Catanzaro 1929, as the club were more formally known, were a team for whom survival in Serie B was the sole objective. That goal was only reached in the very last game of the 1961/62 season, with a point against Reggiana. Once again, Bagnoli made a valuable contribution, scoring six goals in 33 league appearances while playing in a more offensive attacking role. Bagnoli spent four solid years on the Tyrrhenian coast, his best season coming in 1963/64 in which his 11 goals earned him the title of the club's top scorer. But, by the summer of 1964, his southern adventure was over.

Società Polisportiva Ars et Labor, better known by the acronym SPAL, is the football club of the elegant renaissance city of Ferrara. Founded in 1907 as a religious-cultural centre, the football club went their own way in 1919 and achieved their best finish in the 1959/60 season, earning fifth place in Serie A. In 1962, the club reached the final of the Coppa Italia, losing to Napoli. In 1964, after 13 consecutive years in Serie A, SPAL returned to Serie B, at which point Bagnoli entered the scene, finding himself playing alongside a talented young midfielder named Fabio Capello.

Bagnoli scored on his debut and again in a 1-1 draw against one of his former clubs, Hellas Verona. With Capello emerging as an exciting young prospect, Bagnoli was an influential member of the team that earned immediate promotion back to the top flight, scoring five goals from midfield. The following season, with Bagnoli once again a reliable presence in midfield, SPAL finished in 15th place, a point above the drop zone. Bagnoli contributed six goals, including a vital 70th-minute equaliser against Brescia in the last game of the season.

The 1966/67 campaign was another tough one for Bagnoli and SPAL, who once again only secured salvation on the last day of the championship, this time by virtue of a frenetic 3-2 home victory against an already relegated Venezia. It was a bleak cycle that Bagnoli would learn to deplore. In 1967, at the age of 32, Bagnoli returned to Udinese, who had, in the meantime, slumped to the third tier. At the end of the season, he was involved in a car crash and considered retiring. Instead, he accepted an offer from Verbania, newly promoted to Serie C, where he suffered another injury. The following season, he assumed the role of player-manager, assisted by the more experienced Franco Pedroni. Bagnoli finally brought his playing career to an end in 1973 at the age of 38, having made 110 appearances in Serie A and 209 in Serie B.

Bagnoli's playing career was solid rather than spectacular. Aside from that brief spell with AC Milan, he never played with a 'big' team nor for the national side. Instead, he travelled the length and breadth of the peninsula and experienced more than his fair share of ups and downs with an array of provincial teams struggling in that perilous chasm between Serie A and Serie B. He learned about survival, about promotion and relegation, about communication and man-management. He wasn't a showman – his personality wouldn't allow that. But he knew football inside out and had gained a wealth of experience at every level of the game. At the end of his career, he had no pretensions about going into coaching but his good reputation and work ethic would be enough to get him on the first rung of the managerial ladder.

By October 1984, Bagnoli has nearly 15 years' managerial experience under his belt and, in today's clash against Eriksson's Roma, will need to draw on every ounce of it. Not least because Brazilian legend Falcão is back in the Roma side after a six-week lay-off following an injury to his left ankle sustained in a Coppa Italia clash against Lazio back in September. Paulo Roberto Falcão is now in his fifth season in the Italian capital. One of the most talented South American players of his generation, his salary is the highest in the Italian championship, at more than 1bn lire a year. At the 1982 World Cup, he played alongside the likes of Toninho Cerezo, Léo Júnior, Zico, Éder Aleixo de Assis and Sócrates, making five appearances and scoring three goals from midfield, including one in that epic 3-2 second-round group stage loss to Italy. In the 1982/83 season, Falcão won his first Italian championship with Roma, the second in the history of the club, making 27 appearances and scoring seven goals in the league, two in the UEFA Cup and one in the Coppa Italia. A leader on the pitch, he was a key presence the following season as Roma lifted the Coppa Italia, finished second in the league and reached the final of the European Cup in 1984, losing to Liverpool on penalties.

Alongside Falcão, Antônio Carlos Cerezo, more commonly known as Toninho, one of the greatest defensive midfielders of all time, is beginning his second season in Serie A. A veteran of the 1978 and 1982 World Cups, he has made 57 appearances for the star-studded Brazilian national team.

In goal for Roma, the vastly experienced Franco Tancredi, widely regarded as one of the best Italian goalkeepers of his generation. Winger Bruno Conti, a World Cup winner and, like Tancredi, a veteran of the Roma team that lifted the *Scudetto* in 1983, is a formidable talent. On the other wing, Franceso Graziani is another vastly experienced World Cup winner with a formidable goalscoring record; having won the *Scudetto* with Torino in 1976, he was the league's top scorer the following season. Finally, a defensive midfielder who made his Serie A debut with Roma back in 1979 and won his first trophy (the Coppa Italia) the same season. In October 1981, Carlo Ancelotti ruptured his right cruciate ligament in a seemingly innocuous clash with Fiorentina's Francesco Casagrande, an unmistakable figure on the pitch due to his long hair and conspicuous moustache. Following surgery and rehabilitation, Ancelotti managed 23 appearances and two goals in the 1982/83 season when Roma won the championship but suffered another catastrophic injury, this time to his left knee, and made only nine appearances the following season. With the appointment of Eriksson, Ancelotti is once again emerging as a natural leader in the heart of Roma's midfield. The Roma side also boasts two former Hellas players, Emidio Oddi and Maurizio Iorio, giving the encounter an added competitive edge. All round, it's a formidable-looking Roma team that takes to the pitch in front of an estimated 61,000 at the Stadio Olimpico.

As the players emerge from the tunnel, the air inside the stadium turns an acrid red and yellow. Bagnoli has set up with a familiar-looking formation, one that has been so effective against Inter and Juventus in recent weeks. Garella is soon called into action, making a string of impressive saves, prompting the RAI commentator to describe it as '*il Claudio Garella show*'. For Hellas, it's Briegel who comes closest to breaking the deadlock when his low diagonal strike veers just past the far post. At half-time, it's left to a rather shaken-looking Antonio Di Gennaro to capture the mood, conceding that a draw today would be a good result against a dominant Roma.

In the second half, Roma continue to dominate, playing outstanding attacking football and creating countless chances, while Verona venture out of their own half on just a handful of occasions. With 15 minutes to go, Garella pulls off a remarkable double save, first from Antonio Di Carlo and then from Iorio on the rebound. With Roma unable to beat Garella, it ends goalless at the Olimpico.

Post-match, the grinning goalkeeper rather unconvincingly suggests that it was a team effort rather than his own individual brilliance that earned Verona a point today. Of course, he is being modest. If there is a miracle this season, it is surely Garella's performance against Roma. His former team-mate, Iorio, agrees: 'Garella's not a goalkeeper, he's a monster!' Falcão, meanwhile, has a few choice words to say about Pierino Fanna, who has left a deep laceration on the Brazilian's shin. 'Fanna is a killer. I won't shake his hand' is the screaming headline the following day. Indeed, the Roma players feel that Fanna should have been sent off for his tackle on the Brazilian legend and slate the referee for his handling of the match.

Elsewhere, Inter beat Como 1-0 and Torino see off Lazio by the same margin, while Napoli and AC Milan battle out a goalless draw at the San Paolo, where torrential rain seems to curb Maradona's Argentine flair in what the media had been keen to bill as a battle between Argentina (Maradona and Bertoni) and England (Hateley and Wilkins), with memories of the Falklands War still fresh in the mind. While Torino move up to second, Sampdoria's defeat against Udinese sees them lose ground in the standings. There is a useful result also for Fiorentina, whose slender victory against Avellino nudges them up to third place.

For Hellas Verona, another formidable adversary has been thwarted, another global icon tamed and another unlikely hero has emerged in the rounded shape of Claudio Garella, who hasn't conceded a goal for 375 minutes. Today, Verona's unconventional keeper has displayed his full repertoire, making no fewer than nine decisive saves to deny Roma. Even his opposite number, the great Tancredi, is fulsome in his praise for the Verona keeper, telling the *Corriere della Sera*: 'My colleague was world class. Hands or feet, it doesn't matter – he was everywhere.' Only Bagnoli, the ultimate party pooper, offers a less charitable perspective: 'We were lucky that the ball always ended up where Garella was.'

6A GIORNATA

Ascoli 0-0 Atalanta
Cremonese 1-3 Juventus
Fiorentina 1-0 Avellino
Inter 1-0 Como
Napoli 0-0 Milan
Roma 0-0 Verona
Torino 1-0 Lazio
Udinese 1-0 Sampdoria

CLASSIFICA

Verona	**10**
Torino	9
Fiorentina	8
Sampdoria	8
Milan	8
Inter	8
Juventus	7
Udinese	5
Avellino	5
Roma	5
Napoli	5
Como	5
Atalanta	5
Cremonese	3
Lazio	3
Ascoli	2

7a Giornata

28 October 1984

FROM THE changing room of Sport Club Corinthians Paulista, Sócrates Brasileiro Sampaio de Souza Vieira de Oliveira led a small outpost of democracy in the heart of Brazil's military dictatorship. A qualified doctor, Sócrates, as the Brazilian midfielder is more commonly known, was also one of the greatest and most iconic football players of his generation. His playing career began at Botafogo-SP, a small club in the town of Ribeirao Preto about 300km north-west of São Paulo, before signing for Corinthians, the legendary Brazilian club based in the sprawling metropolis of São Paulo. It was here that Sócrates began to talk about the democratisation of football. The towering central midfielder led a revolution at the football club, developing and implementing a model of democratic self-management, while insisting that he be allowed to continue his medical studies in tandem with his playing career.

In the summer of 1984, the 30-year-old Brazilian icon signed for Fiorentina for 5.3bn lire. Captain of the Brazilian national team and the 1983 South American footballer of the year, his signing was a massive coup for the Tuscan club. Instantly recognisable with that trademark headband and dark beard, Sócrates stood an imposing 6ft 3in tall, a dominating figure in central midfield, having previously played in attack. A heavy smoker, he was also known to enjoy a beer or two, though neither habit seemed to impact his performances on the pitch.

Famously knocked out of the 1982 World Cup by a dour, defensive Italian side (who went on to win the tournament), he wasn't the only one to associate that defeat with the death of Brazilian football and the rebirth of the Italian game.[18] It certainly marked the beginning of the recovery of Italian football from the traumatic *Totonero* affair and, more specifically, the rehabilitation of Paolo Rossi, who emerged from the tournament as a national hero.

Italy won that remarkable second-round group game against Brazil thanks to a Rossi hat-trick, with Brazil falling short despite twice equalising through Sócrates and Falcão. It was Rossi again, this time with an unanswered double, who overcame Poland in the semi-final, setting up a final at Madrid's Bernabéu Stadium against a West German side that included the likes of Toni Schumacher, Karl-Heinz Rummenigge and a promising young midfielder named Lothar Matthäus, as well as an athletic full-back in Hans-Peter Briegel. Despite the Germans' potent blend of youth and experience, power and intelligence, it was the Italians who emerged triumphant. Who can forget Marco Tardelli's enraptured celebration as he gave the Italians a 2-0 lead after Rossi had once again scored to set up a famous 3-1 victory which gave the Italians their third World Cup title?

One of the most iconic images to emerge from that World Cup was the sight of Italian president Sandro Pertini on the flight home playing *scopone* with Enzo Bearzot, Franco Causio and Dino Zoff, with the gleaming World Cup sitting on the table between them. The following day, *La Gazzetta della Sport*, the most widely read daily newspaper in Italy, sold 1.5 million copies with the simple headline '*Campione del mondo*'. After years in the doldrums, Italian football was back on top of the world. Such was the impact of that victory, many of the biggest international stars of the tournament would soon be playing club football on Italian soil, while the names of the Italian World Cup heroes would continue to dominate Serie A for years to come.

---

18 For a comprehensive account of the context and implications of the 1982 World Cup semi-final between Brazil and Italy, see Trellini (2023).

By now, Italy was also emerging from the 'Years of Lead'. While the scars of domestic terrorism were still raw, the search for truth and justice would rumble on for decades to come. Economically, the country was on the verge of a decade of growth after a prolonged period of stagnation; a new era of political stability beckoned, following the turbulence and division of the 60s and 70s. At the heart of this new political dawn was Pertini himself, helping to restore the public's faith in the Italian government and its institutions and representing the country abroad with dignity and vigour. This would be a decade in which the fashion industry would replace the steel industry, Armani, Dolce & Gabbana and Versace coming to dominate the world's catwalks, and Italian football would take centre stage – both tactically and commercially, a legacy of that 1982 World Cup victory.

By the beginning of the 1984/85 season, only veteran keeper Dino Zoff from that World Cup-winning Italian team has hung up his boots. The other 12 Italian players who featured in the final that day are all still playing in Serie A, including Claudio Gentile and Gabriele Oriali at Fiorentina, and have been joined in Italy by Sócrates, Zico and Léo Júnior, Rummenigge and Briegel, Maradona and Passarella, to name but a few.

Inspired by the arrival of Sócrates, Fiorentina have enjoyed a strong start to the 1984/85 season, remaining unbeaten in the opening four games of the campaign (including an impressive 5-0 demolition of Atalanta), before dropping points to a rampant Graeme Souness-inspired Sampdoria. Meanwhile, Hellas have, against all expectations, emerged more or less unscathed from a month of fixtures involving Inter, Juventus and Roma. In recent days, pundits and commentators have suggested that Hellas have been lucky. Today, they face yet another stern test and Bagnoli is determined to prove his critics wrong and demonstrate that Verona's success is down to more than simply good luck.

But Verona has always been a happy hunting ground for Fiorentina. To date, the Tuscans have won seven of the 13

Serie A encounters between the two sides at the Bentegodi. Hellas, meanwhile, have triumphed just once, almost exactly a year ago, when Bagnoli's men won 3-1. Fiorentina won the return fixture 2-0 and went on to finish the 1983/84 season in third place behind Juventus and Roma. Were it not for a serious injury to influential playmaker Giancarlo Antognoni, Fiorentina might even have won a famous *Scudetto*.[19]

Under coach Giancarlo De Sisti, Fiorentina play a modern 3-5-2 formation and, with eight points on the board, are in the chasing pack that includes Inter, AC Milan and Sampdoria. They have conceded just two goals (both against Sampdoria) in six matches, one of which was an own goal. Such a strong defensive record is hardly surprising when you consider that they have the best *libero* in the world, the Argentine Daniel Passarella, playing alongside the ex-Juventus legend and World Cup winner Claudio Gentile. Passarella joined Fiorentina in the summer of 1982 after an impressive World Cup campaign. Now considered the greatest Viola defender of the last 50 years, he also has an impressive goalscoring record, netting seven times in 27 Serie A appearances the previous season.

Notwithstanding the array of homegrown and international talent at their disposal, the biggest name on the Fiorentina teamsheet is, of course, Sócrates. As it happens, the task of subduing the great Brazilian icon at the Bentegodi falls to another member of the medical fraternity, the versatile Hellas midfielder known to his team-mates as '*il Dottore*'.

Born in 1951, Domenico Volpati started out with his local team, Voluntas Novara. He made his senior debut in 1968 with Borgomanero, an amateur team from a small town about 110km north-east of Turin. He played just three games in that first season but managed 21 appearances (and two goals) in his second season. Between 1970 and 1975, while playing in Serie C with Solbiatese, he was also studying medicine. It was at Solbiatese that Volpati first encountered a

---

19 On 21 February 1984, in a match against Sampdoria, Antognoni suffered a compound fracture of the tibia and fibula of his right leg. He would be out of action for almost two years.

taciturn coach named Osvaldo Bagnoli: 'I played as a striker, he moved me back to midfield.' Following a disagreement with the club president, Bagnoli was sacked at the beginning of the second half of the 1973/74 season but the gruff coach and the urbane medical student hadn't seen the last of each other.

Volpati stepped up a level with Reggiana, then playing in Serie B, before being reunited with Bagnoli at Como, where the up-and-coming young coach had progressed from the youth team to the first team. At Como, Volpati joined a squad that also included Silvano Fontolan and Mario Guidetti, both of whom would subsequently be reunited with Bagnoli at Verona. Como finished in sixth place that season and it was only a series of poor results, taking just two points from the last six matches, that scuppered their hopes of promotion. Volpati's second season at the lakeside club didn't go so well. Bagnoli, with whom he had formed a close personal relationship, had moved on and Como struggled all season at the foot of the table. With Como consigned to Serie C, Volpati made the short move to Monza, where he caught his first glimpse of a striker named Domenico Penzo, a player who would go on to be a key figure for Hellas Verona in the early Bagnoli years.[20] In a single season with Monza, Volpati made another impressive contribution, making 34 appearances as they narrowly missed out on promotion to Serie A.

By now, Volpati's form had caught the attention of several bigger clubs and he made his breakthrough in Serie A with Torino in the 1979/80 season at 27 years of age. Torino finished third in the league and were also finalists in the Coppa Italia, with Volpati establishing himself as an integral member of the

---

20 In the 1981/82 season, Penzo scored 14 goals in 31 Serie B appearances for Hellas Verona. In the 1982/83 season, he scored 15 goals in 29 Serie A appearances and was the league's second top-scorer behind Platini. In 1983, he signed for Juventus as backup for Paolo Rossi in a part-exchange deal that involved Giuseppe Galderisi. Sold on to Napoli after a year, he played alongside Maradona until the arrival in 1986 of Bruno Giordano. After a season on the fringes of the squad, Penzo ended his career in Trento, in Serie C1.

team. The following season, he was once again a key player, making 45 appearances in all competitions (more than any other Torino player that season). *Il Toro* couldn't improve on the previous season's achievements, however, and finished in a disappointing ninth place. They were once again defeated finalists in the Coppa Italia and enjoyed a decent run in the UEFA Cup, losing a third-round penalty shoot-out to Grasshopper Zurich.

The following season, Volpati returned to Serie B, this time with newly relegated Brescia, where once again he was a consistent and reliable presence in midfield. It was, however, a disastrous season for the *Bresicani*, who suffered the ignominy of back-to-back relegations. It was the summer of 1982 and, disillusioned and ready to return to his medical studies, Volpati decided it was time to quit the game. It was at this point that Bagnoli re-entered his life.

It was 13 June 1982, the last day of the Serie B championship. Hellas (already promoted to Serie A) faced Brescia (on their way down to Serie C). Bagnoli's one objective that day was to convince Volpati to join him in Verona. Forty years later, Volpati does a convincing impression of Bagnoli's distinctive Milanese dialect, as he explains how the coach approached him after the game: 'Volpe, I need a player like you.' 'Thank you, Mister, but I'm 30,' came the polite reply, 'I'm retiring at the end of the season.' In fact, the match was suspended in the 75th minute when a violent storm rendered the pitch unplayable. Bagnoli suggested that he take a few days to think things over. A couple of days later, when the match was rescheduled, Volpati accepted Bagnoli's offer and, a few weeks later, signed for Hellas Verona for 160m lire, a fraction of the billions spent on Sócrates, Rummenigge and Maradona. It was the best deal Emiliano Mascetti ever did!

Volpati was intelligent, versatile and tactically astute. The kind of player that every coach wants in his team, capable of covering a variety of roles in midfield and defence. Wherever he played, Volpati applied himself with determination, concentration and intelligence. He played with ruthless pragmatism, nullifying the opponent he was marking and bringing out the best in Antonio Di Gennaro by always providing cover or offering a safe pass. Off the pitch, Volpati was an equally influential figure, central to the unity of the group, exemplifying the standards and expectations that were expected and placing the needs of the team above any personal goals or ambitions.

Today, he is up against Sócrates, a similarly altruistic figure.[21]

As kick-off approaches, it's a grinning and wise-cracking president Guidotti who fields the questions from RAI TV's Gian Piero Galeazzi. Less guarded than the more reserved utterances of Bagnoli, Guidotti boldly proclaims that it should be 'easy' for Verona to achieve salvation in Serie A this season. Claudio Gentile, meanwhile, concedes that Hellas have been the best side in the championship so far.

It's a mild mid-autumn afternoon and a carnival atmosphere prevails at the Bentegodi thanks to the *gemellaggio* (twinning) in place between the two opposing sets of fans. One theory behind the origins of the long-standing friendship involves a mythical leader of the Fiorentina *curva* known as '*Il Pompa*'. According to legend, during a game in the mid-1970s, '*Il Pompa*' infiltrated Verona's *curva* on a *motorino*! It was a brash and reckless gesture and one that won the instant approval of the home fans, who value outrageous gestures above all else. The twinning became official in the 1975/76 season and has continued ever since, meaning that rival fans can enjoy each other's company without the usual risks.

On the pitch, though, a fierce contest is in progress, with neither side expecting any favours. But then, a 25th-minute Fanna corner finds Fontolan, whose header deflects off the unfortunate Fiorentina defender Luca Moz, deceiving the visiting goalkeeper. A second consecutive own goal conceded

---

21 During the COVID-19 pandemic, Dr Domenico Volpati came out of retirement and volunteered at his local vaccination centre on Lake Tesero in the Italian Dolomites. It was a typically altruistic gesture from a man who has always been a great team player.

by Fiorentina and Verona are 1-0 up. Yet another stroke of good fortune for Hellas!

There's nothing lucky about the second goal, which arrives late in the first half. Briegel finds Volpati, who has momentarily abandoned his responsibilities marking Sócrates, surging down the left wing. Somehow, '*il Dottore*' beats Passarella to the ball and flicks a beautiful lob to the far post, where Galderisi is lying in wait. The diminutive striker makes no mistake and Verona lead 2-0 at the break. Volpati will observe later that it was the best move of the game.

With a post-mortem already under way, Fiorentina arrive five minutes late for the second half, although Sócrates still finds time to sign a few autographs on his way back to the pitch. It's a much-improved Fiorentina who get some luck of their own in the second half, with a goal direct from an Eraldo Pecci corner leaving Garella looking for once this season a bit goofy as he tries to comprehend how the ball has somehow found its way into his net. It's the first goal he's conceded in 431 minutes of play, the last coming against Ascoli on matchday two. Moments later, 'Garellik' is back at his imperious best when Sócrates fires a free kick over a flimsy looking Verona wall towards the left corner. Final score: Hellas Verona 2 Fiorentina 1.

Despite the victory, Bagnoli is far from happy, castigating his team for allowing their two-goal advantage to be halved, resulting in a tense final 30 minutes. Giancarlo De Sisti, meanwhile, laments the chances his side squandered in the final 20 but admits he can't really complain about the end result.

So, Verona have reached the end of their '*ottobre di ferro*' (iron October), during which they defeated Juventus and Fiorentina at home and drew away against Inter and Roma. It's an impressive run that may even silence the sceptics. Bagnoli, who has already had to fend off speculation linking him to several bigger clubs, remains humble: '[I]n a month we will no longer be at the top of the table but this terrible cycle [of games] will remind us of our potential.'

Meanwhile, in Milan, it's derby day and the English striker Mark Hateley has scored a powerful header to seal a famous victory for the *Rossoneri*. Elsewhere, Atalanta beat Napoli 1-0, Juventus and Roma tie 1-1 and Sampdoria and Torino share the points in Genoa following a four-goal thriller. For Hellas, it's another favourable set of results, with none of their closest rivals securing maximum points. Verona's lead at the top of the table is now extended to two points.

Next weekend is the international break and something quite extraordinary will happen. A Hellas player will be called up for the national team! It's just a friendly against Switzerland but Antonio Di Gennaro will receive his first cap. It won't be his last and, on current form, he won't be the only Hellas player this season to receive a call from Mr Bearzot.

For those not on international duty, the break provides a welcome opportunity to rest and reflect on what has been achieved so far. At this point in the campaign, Bagnoli has relied on just 12 key players – with substitute Luciano Bruni carving out a few minutes in most matches. Of the other squad members, only Franco Turchetta and Dario Donà have featured, just a few short minutes each. It has been an intense month, with demanding fixtures against some of the biggest clubs in the league and featuring individual battles against some of the greatest names in world football – none bigger than Sócrates. For the moment, at least, Hellas Verona remain unbeaten.

7A GIORNATA

Atalanta 1-0 Napoli
Avellino 4-1 Udinese
Como 1-0 Ascoli
Juventus 1-1 Roma
Lazio 2-1 Cremonese
Milan 2-1 Inter
Sampdoria 2-2 Torino
Verona 2-1 Fiorentina

CLASSIFICA

Verona	**12**
Torino	10
Milan	10
Sampdoria	9
Juventus	8
Fiorentina	8
Inter	8
Avellino	7
Como	7
Atalanta	7
Roma	6
Udinese	5
Napoli	5
Lazio	5
Cremonese	3
Ascoli	2

Politically, this period also coincided with the demise of Christian Democracy (which would claim 35 per cent of the national vote in the 1985 regional elections) as the major political force in country. In fact, Italian politics in the 1980s was dominated by a long-standing, though self-serving, alliance between the Christian Democrats and the Italian Socialist Party. The Christian Democrats represented 'small c' conservative efficiency, though the Italian economy remained mired in debt, corruption and inefficiency throughout the first half of the 1980s. The period featured eye-watering budget deficits, inflation that lingered at around 15 per cent (after reaching a high of 21.1 per cent in 1980), a pernicious black market and organised crime that was rampant in certain regions. By 1983, the Christian Democrats were in serious decline and in August that year, Bettino Craxi became the first socialist in the history of the Italian republic to be appointed prime minister. In fact, the Italian Communist Party was still a significant force in Italian politics, harnessing 30 per cent of the vote in the 1985 regional elections. Nicknamed *il Cinghialone* (the big boar) by his political detractors due to his physical size, Craxi's socialist-led coalition was Italy's 44th government in less than four decades. Craxi was a towering presence in Italian politics throughout the 1980s, leading the third-longest-serving Italian government of the post-war period. Meanwhile, in the UK, the towering presence in the political landscape was a grocer's daughter known in Italy as '*La Lady di ferro*' (The Iron Lady). A female head of government and a prime minister who held office for more than a few months – both concepts that seemed inconceivable to the stubbornly patriarchal and intrinsically chaotic political system of Italy in the 1980s.[23]

Notwithstanding its complex problems, Italy was, in the era before mass tourism and budget airlines, a popular destination for travellers and backpackers: 'The trains may not run on time, the economy may be ailing and doubtless

23 Silvio Berlusconi would subsequently serve as prime minister for nine years in total, but that was in three separate terms of office. Italy's first female prime minister, Giorgia Meloni, wouldn't take office until 2022.

the government will be in its usual turmoil but none of these need detract from a visit to Italy.' Verona itself had long been a popular destination for travellers. Set on a loop in the river amidst manicured vineyards and ceremonial cypress trees, it is a breathtaking patchwork of Roman ruins, renaissance piazzas and ornate palaces and sepulchres. Amid all this grandiosity sits one of the oldest high schools in Italy, Liceo Ginnasio di Stato Scipione Maffei or, more simply, Istituto Maffei. The school was officially founded in 1808, though it had been operational for some years previously, and specialised in the teaching of the classics, Latin and ancient Greek. In 1903, a group of students from the school founded a football team. Looking for inspiration for a name for their new team, they approached their Greek teacher, Professor Decio Corubolo. The professor suggested 'Hellas', the ancient Greek word for 'Greece', and the rest, as they say, is history.

One thing that isn't consigned to the past is the Italian custom of using the term 'Mister' when referring to the coach. The habit is traditionally attributed to the introduction of football to Italy by British sailors in the late 19th century. In fact, it was probably with the arrival of William Garbutt from Stockport that the custom really began. Garbutt played professionally for Reading, Woolwich Arsenal and Blackburn Rovers and, when injury forced him out of the game, he emigrated to Genoa. He soon began coaching at Genoa CFC, a club with obvious Anglo-Saxon origins (the CFC in the name, that remains to this day, denoting Cricket and Football Club). With an emphasis on fitness, tactics and technical ability, Garbutt's Genoa finished second in the Northern Championship in 1913. In deference to his status and professionalism, Garbutt's players always addressed him as 'Mister', a custom that continues across Italy to this day.

After an eventful playing career, Osvaldo Bagnoli got his foot on the first rung of the managerial ladder in 1973. From then on, he would always be known as 'Mister'. Bagnoli began his coaching career in Serie C with Solbiatese, the local team of Solbiate Arno, a small town in the province of Varese in

Lombardy, north-west of Milan on the road to Lago Maggiore. One day, the club president casually entered the changing room, smoking a cigarette as if he were in a bar. Bagnoli ordered him out (ironic given that he would subsequently tolerate Elkjær's habit) and was dismissed the very next day. It was an inauspicious start to Bagnoli's coaching career but demonstrated the principled approach that would become a hallmark of his management style.

Bagnoli didn't have to wait long for his next opportunity and was appointed assistant coach (and head of the youth team) of Serie A side Como in 1974. Midway through the 1975/76 season, he was promoted to first-team coach following the departure of Giuseppe Marchioro. Among the players on his roster were a troubled young striker named Paolo Rossi, who had been released by Juventus, and a young defender named Silvano Fontolan, who would subsequently be reunited with Bagnoli at Verona. Rossi managed just six appearances for Como that season (his career would take off the following season at Vicenza, where he would score 21 goals in 36 appearances). Bagnoli couldn't turn things around, as Como were relegated to the second tier. The following season, Como finished in sixth place, though it was only a run of poor results at the tail end of the season (just two points from the last six games), that denied the *Lariani* an immediate return to Serie A.

At the end of that season, Bagnoli moved on to rival Serie B side Rimini but, after a disappointing year, could only manage a 16th-place finish. His managerial career appeared to be on the slide before it had even taken off and he spent the next season in Serie C2 with Alma Juventus Fano 1906, who he successfully led to promotion. In 1979, Bagnoli was hired by Cesena, a perennial Serie B side from the central region of Emilia-Romagna. His impact was almost immediate. Between mid-December and the end of the season, they went on a remarkable run, losing just one game – against Verona, of all teams. In the end, Cesena managed a fourth-place finish, narrowly missing out on promotion, but it was a massive improvement on the 12th-place finish a season earlier. The following season, Bagnoli went one better, as Cesena finished joint second alongside Genoa, with AC Milan (relegated from Serie A for involvement in the notorious *Totonero* match-fixing scandal) winning the Serie B title. For Bagnoli, it was an impressive achievement in a highly competitive league that also included Lazio and Sampdoria.

Cesena's promotion that season was built on remarkable consistency (23 points by the midway point in the season and 25 more in the second half), as well as an exceptional defensive record (conceding just 26 goals in 38 matches, compared to Genoa and AC Milan, who each conceded 29). Bagnoli got the best out of his strikers, Antonio Bordon and Oliviero Garlini, both of whom reached double figures, and also nurtured young talent like Massimo Bonini, who would go on to make 192 appearances for Juventus.

While Bagnoli achieved an historic promotion with Cesena, Hellas Verona were languishing precariously at the foot of Serie B. In the 1980/81 season, Hellas finished in a humiliating 16th place. The average gate at the Bentegodi that season was just 11,720, with barely 3,000 season tickets sold. Nicola D'Ottavio and Enzo Scaini were joint-top scorers that season with just ten goals between them! Hellas only avoided relegation to the third tier on the last game of the campaign. From that season of abject failure, only defender Roberto Tricella would survive the quiet revolution that was about to take place.

In the summer of 1981, faced with the choice of leading Cesena, with whom he had just won promotion to the top tier, or accepting an offer to return to Verona, who were struggling at the foot of Serie B, Bagnoli chose Hellas. It was an idiosyncratic choice but not one that Bagnoli would ever regret. He began by guiding Hellas Verona to promotion in his first season with the club.

Now, in the 1984/85 season, Cremonese are playing in Serie A for the first time in 54 years but, with just three points on the board, they are living up to their pre-season billing as relegation favourites. Pre-match, club president Domenico Luzzara insists that his club are 'small but serious'. The local businessman has invested heavily in the club in recent years and is delighted that, as with the visit of Juventus two weeks ago, today's match is a complete sell-out.

The Cremonese squad is almost exclusively made up of the same group of players who won promotion from Serie B the previous season. The one notable exception is Jorge dos Santos Filho, the nomadic Brazilian striker better known as Juary. Another diminutive striker – just 5ft 5in (1.69m), Juary can't claim to be in the same league as Zico, Sócrates or Falcão but he nonetheless brings genuine quality and a touch of the exotic to an otherwise limited Cremonese team. He achieved a degree of fame with Avellino, where he spent two seasons, for his trademark corner flag dance and was snapped up by Inter, where he made 21 appearances and scored two goals. He moved to Ascoli in 1983, where he made 27 appearances and scored five goals, before being signed by Cremonese at the beginning of the current season. It has, however, been a frustrating start for the Brazilian, who has spent nearly four months on the sidelines. Finally, against Verona today, he is ready to wear the red and grey stripes of Cremonese.

After waiting more than 50 years to return to Serie A, Cremonese have taken just three points from seven games (a run of form that sees them three points adrift at the foot of the table alongside Aseoli) and Hellas approach today's match as clear favourites. Despite Cremonese's difficulties, the team have enthusiastic backing, with 5,371 season ticket holders determined to enjoy their status in Serie A for as long as it lasts. Notwithstanding their limitations on the pitch, Cremonese like to put on a show and play an entertaining brand of football. With little or nothing to show for their efforts at this point in the season, they are clearly missing the goals of the teenage striker they sold to Sampdoria in the summer – but Gianluca Vialli was simply destined for greater things.

Verona, playing in all yellow, remain unchanged as they seek to extend their unbeaten run to eight games. Thousands of Hellas fans have made the trip from Verona, inevitably resulting in a few minor scuffles along the way. In the morning, a police car rushing to the stadium to greet the first supporters' buses collides with a car and two officers end up in hospital. At midday, a group of Verona fans, after burning a Cremonese scarf, leave the north stand to attack the home fans in the south stand. Only the swift intervention of the police, who make a handful of arrests, prevents more serious clashes between the opposing sets of fans. Those who had left their seats looking for trouble then have difficulty getting back into the stadium, as their tickets have already been checked. In the ensuing crush at the gates, there are numerous injuries, including four fans (two from Verona and two from Cremona) who require hospital treatment. Despite the off-pitch issues, the game itself kicks off without delay.

Verona struggle to make an impact and, with the game still goalless, Bagnoli calls over captain Tricella to relay some instructions to Di Gennaro, who is being marked out of the game. For 70 minutes, Cremonese acquit themselves well against a team nine points above them in the league. Then, from yet another enticing Pierino Fanna free kick, the ball strikes Walter Viganò's raised arm for an indisputable handball inside the box. Galderisi coolly converts the resulting penalty for his fifth goal of the season, joining Mark Hateley as the league's top scorer. At this point, the Brazilian, Juary, is finally introduced and, with his first involvement in over four months, wins a penalty when he's brought down inside the box by Mauro Ferroni. Alviero Chiorri, one of Cremonese's best players on the day, steps up to take the spot kick but Garella pulls off yet another heroic save. Barely two minutes later, Briegel rampages up the right flank, slaloms gracefully past two defenders and slams home Verona's second from just inside the box. In the stand behind the goal, the travelling supporters erupt.

As the clock winds down, Garella is once again in outstanding form to deny Cremona a well-deserved consolation goal. As the final whistle blows, it's another disappointing result for Cremonese and a scoreline that, if the truth be told, flatters the visitors. Post-match, Bagnoli admits as much, conceding that it had been a difficult game that either side could have won. He is modest enough to admit that, to achieve certain results in football, you need the occasional dose of good luck. President Guidotti concurs: '[I]t could have ended 0-0 and no one would have been able to complain. If it had ended 1-1, it would have been fair and we would all have been happy.' Once again this season, Verona have been fortunate. But, at crucial moments in the game, the contributions of Galderisi, Briegel and, yet again, Garella prove decisive.

Meanwhile, in Milan, Inter stun Juventus with a 4-0 hammering (the first time in five years that Juventus have lost by four goals) as Rummenigge bags his first goal in Serie A, while Torino's 2-0 victory over AC Milan also keeps them in the chase. But, with 14 points on the board, Verona remain in pole position with a two-point cushion and as the only unbeaten team in the league.

8A GIORNATA

Cremonese 0-2 Verona
Fiorentina 1-1 Ascoli
Inter 4-0 Juventus
Napoli 0-0 Avellino
Roma 0-0 Lazio
Sampdoria 1-0 Como
Torino 2-0 Milan
Udinese 2-0 Atalanta

CLASSIFICA

Verona	**14**
Torino	12
Sampdoria	11
Inter	10
Milan	10
Fiorentina	9
Avellino	8
Juventus	8
Udinese	7
Como	7
Roma	7
Atalanta	7
Napoli	6
Lazio	6
Ascoli	3
Cremonese	3

9a Giornata

18 November 1984

UNIONE CALCIO Sampdoria is a football club on the cusp of a golden age. Founded in 1946 with the merger of Sampierdarenese and Andrea Doria, Sampdoria is now bankrolled by Paolo Mantovani, a businessman who made his fortune trading oil during the 1970s energy crisis.[24] With the appointment of sporting director Paolo Borea, they have assembled a potent blend of proven champions, seasoned international professionals and young talent capable of competing for silverware. These include Pietro Vierchowod, Graeme Souness, Trevor Francis and Roberto Mancini, as well as an exciting young striker recently arrived from Cremona – Gianluca Vialli.

Though Sampdoria fans enjoy an intense rivalry with city rivals Genoa,[25] the relationship with Hellas is warm, thanks to a *gemellaggio* that has existed since 1973, back when Emiliano Mascetti was Verona's leading scorer. It was the beginning of May, the third-to-last game of the season and, with Juventus and AC Milan fighting it out at the top, Sampdoria and Verona still required points to guarantee their survival in Serie A. Back in December, the two sets of fans had clashed in Genoa but, this time, the mood was different. The match finished 1-1 with a second-half Mascetti penalty cancelling out a first-half Sampdoria spot kick. The result, favourable to both

---

24 Paolo Mantovani was born in Rome but settled in Genoa in 1955 when he began working in the petroleum sector.

25 The intense city rivalry between Genoa and Sampdoria continues to this day. As recently as September 2024, violent clashes marred the 'Derby della Lanterna', resulting in 38 injuries.

teams, seemed to bring the fans together. Incidentally, in the last game of that season, just a couple of weeks later, Verona played AC Milan, for whom victory would have secured the championship. Hellas won 5-3 and the title went to Juventus. Verona stayed up and the legend of 'Fatal Verona' was born.[26] Verona were relegated the following season and Sampdoria also dropped to the second tier in 1977.

Now led by ambitious entrepreneur Paolo Mantovani, Sampdoria won promotion in 1982 (finishing in second place behind Bagnoli's resurgent Hellas) and finished seventh in both the 1982/83 and 1983/84 seasons in the top flight. The club made some shrewd investments in English-based players who adapted well to the Italian game and Sampdoria now boast some of the most exciting young talent in Italy. With the winning mentality of Souness, the guile of Trevor Francis and the raw hunger of Roberto Mancini and Gianluca Vialli, Sampdoria are now serious contenders for silverware.

Back in the early summer of 1984, while Liam Brady was finalising his move from Sampdoria (where he had made 58 appearances and scored five goals) to Inter, Scotland and Liverpool captain Graeme Souness landed in Genoa for a pre-season medical. According to the *Corriere della Sera*, the Scotsman was welcomed at Genoa's Christopher Columbus airport by more than 2,000 flag-waving Sampdoria fans. The midfielder returned to England barely 24 hours later, medical completed and a three-year contract signed in a deal worth a reported 2.5bn lire. Speaking to the Italian media once the contract negotiations had been finalised, Souness explained his decision to come to Italy: '[I]t was the most difficult choice of my career. It will be hard to leave England but I willingly accept the challenge of Italian football, today the true epicentre

26 In fact, Milan have lost two championships at the Bentegodi – the first in the 1972/73 season and the second in 1989/90, when Arrigo Sacchi's Milan lost out to Napoli. It was the penultimate game of the season and Bagnoli's Verona won 2-1. Despite the victory, it would be Bagnoli's last game in charge at the Bentegodi as Hellas were subsequently relegated to Serie B.

of the game. It will be a difficult challenge because this year I won everything – the League Cup, the championship and the European Cup. Altogether, I've won 12 trophies so far and, for my part, I certainly don't plan on stopping because as you get older, you get greedy.'

Two years previously, the arrival of English striker Trevor Francis, described by the *Corriere della Sera* as 'certainly the most famous British player after Kevin Keegan', attracted fewer headlines but was another important signing for the ambitious club. Mantovani had been looking for someone to 'nurse' his 18-year-old striker, Roberto Mancini, and the experienced Francis, alongside Juventus reject Liam Brady, seemed to fit the bill. To the alarm of Sampdoria's medical staff, Francis was reported to frequently enjoy a beer and barbecued steak at his seaside villa at Nervi, a picturesque fishing village on the Ligurian coast. Souness rented a neighbouring apartment as the two embraced the *dolce vita* of the Italian Riviera. Though he had already won so much with Liverpool, Souness was hungry for success and keen to lead the ambitious young squad at Sampdoria.

As well as the two foreigners, Sampdoria had Pietro Vierchowod, widely regarded as one of the greatest Italian centre-backs of all time. He was of Ukrainian descent and nicknamed *lo Zar* (the Tsar) on account of his pace, defensive ability, physicality and tenacious playing style. Roberto Mancini was playing in his third season for Sampdoria in Serie A alongside the frighteningly ambitious young talent from Cremona, Gianluca Vialli. Italian journalist Giovanni Brera would soon coin the nickname 'Stradivialli', making an analogy between the beauty of his goals and that of the violins made by Antonio Stradivari in his hometown of Cremona.

From the sublime to the malignant, the evolving 'ultra' scene of the 1980s represented an uglier aspect of the Italian game. While the culture of the ultras shouldn't necessarily be equated with hooliganism, violence and criminality were an intrinsic part of the scene. Trouble in and around the stadium, such as the incidents at Verona's game against Cremonese the previous week, was not uncommon. Though Verona itself projected a veneer of affluence and respectability, it wasn't immune from the social ills of the time.

It was, in fact, Verona's affluence and tranquillity that made the city such an appealing market for organised crime. Coupled with a police service and judicial system unaccustomed to dealing with such threats, it was fertile ground for criminals looking for new turf. By the early 1980s, a massive heroin epidemic was sweeping the globe and Verona, of all places, found itself at the epicentre. The city's marble-paved streets were haunted by junkies and pushers, the grand piazzas littered with discarded needles. The 1982 edition of the *Let's Go* travel guide included a pretty stark warning: '[T]he drug scene [in Verona] is fairly dangerous.' Indeed, for those growing up in Verona in the late 1970s and early 1980s, these weren't so much the 'Years of Lead' as the years of broken glass and discarded syringes. Piazza delle Erbe became a popular meeting place for drug addicts and dealers and it wasn't long before the habit found its way to the city's more affluent suburbs. At one point, the growing epidemic brought more than 20,000 people on to the streets to demonstrate against the so-called 'merchants of death'.

Barbara Salazer, a young Hellas fan, remembers having to call the emergency services when she was barely ten years old. From the public telephone at the neighbourhood bar, she would give the location of the bench or park where she had seen the tell-tale foaming mouth of another overdose victim and would then wait for the ambulance to arrive. She knew which families distributed wraps of heroin from their windows and which local kids were being used as couriers. In her neighbourhood, they even had a name for the addicts – *sbusoni* ('sbusar', in the Veneto dialect, means to pierce or shoot up). They were easily recognisable; many of them were friends of an older brother or children of a parents' friend. Her grandmother warned her to avoid certain places because of the drug addicts but, despite having met several, they never scared her. They were usually just slow but kind: '[W]e kids were obviously curious and imagined incredible things happening in those abandoned carriages on that disused section of the railway.'

Many of Barbara's middle school classmates wouldn't survive the epidemic that swept the city in the early 1980s, a time when Hellas were enjoying unprecedented success on the football pitch. Barbara considers herself one of the lucky ones. She studied and learned, travelled the world and found a decent job. These were, after all, the years of the economic boom; everyone was looking for qualified staff and, with an entire generation swallowed up by heroin, there was very little competition. The notorious *Brigate Gialloblù* experienced first-hand the impact of the heroin epidemic, spread by the so-called *Mala del Brenta*, a mafia organisation established in Veneto in the 1970s. Many of those young addicts who frequented the Bentegodi on Sunday afternoons didn't live long enough to see the end of the season.

Today, Sampdoria have arrived in Verona with a confidence bordering on the arrogant. Four thousand Samp fans have descended on the city, as well as club president Mantovani, with the clear expectation that they will return to Genoa with something to celebrate. Verona are wearing a slightly modified kit, with the stripes running horizontally, while Samp are in all white. Hellas are without their injured playmaker Antonio Di Gennaro, giving Luciano Bruni a rare start, and Elkjær has returned from Denmark with a slight thigh strain. After a serious injury, Luigi Sacchetti finally returns to the squad. A versatile and tireless midfielder, Sacchetti is a welcome reinforcement on a threadbare Verona bench. Sampdoria, meanwhile, are without the injured Mancini.

Sampdoria begin strongly, with Souness dominating the midfield and Verona creating few genuine chances. Sampdoria come closer to breaking the deadlock, with two efforts by Vialli thwarted, including an overhead kick deflected by Garella, and Ferroni heading one off the line when Garella charges out to meet the oncoming Trevor Francis. Verona come close to scoring just once, when Bruni's long-distance effort strikes the post. In the end, the two teams prove too similar and cancel each other out. For Sampdoria, it is a valuable point on the road. For Verona, the unbeaten run continues but it's the first time this season that they have failed to win at home. Once again, Garella is at his impervious best. Earlier in the week, Elkjær scored two in a World Cup qualifier for Denmark against the Republic of Ireland but today he is practically anonymous. Defender Mauro Ferroni suffers an injury that will rule him out of the biggest game of the season so far, next week's trip to Torino, who beat Juventus 2-1 in the Turin derby to set up a mouth-watering top-of-the-table clash.

For Juventus, on just eight points, it's their worst start in 15 years.

Post-match, journalists swarm around the narrow corridors outside the changing rooms, waiting for players to emerge for a few unguarded comments. The post-match exchange with Bagnoli goes something like this:

How do you rate Sampdoria?

A good team. They can win the championship.

And Verona?

Fourth or fifth … (he laughs and then leaves).

The headline tomorrow will read: 'Verona Slip But Stay On Their Feet'. As the home fans trudge away from the stadium, they grumble about a point dropped. How quickly they have become accustomed to winning at the Bentegodi! The referee, who seemed to favour a draw, didn't do Verona any favours and nor did the absence of Di Gennaro and the muted performance of a fatigued-looking Elkjær, not to mention the quality of Sampdoria, who created several gilt-edged chances of their own.

Next week, Hellas travel to Torino to face yet another serious title contender; a team that has the best attacking record in the league (14 goals scored compared to Verona's 13) and are now just a single point behind Hellas in the title race, having enjoyed back-to-back victories against AC Milan and Juventus. It promises to be yet another memorable encounter between the two in-form teams in the league this season. It is if too early, of course, to be talking about a possible championship decider but the clamorous Italian media is already raising the stakes.

9A GIORNATA

Ascoli 1-1 Napoli
Atalanta 1-0 Lazio
Avellino 0-0 Milan
Como 1-0 Cremonese
Inter 1-0 Udinese
Juventus 1-2 Torino
Roma 2-1 Fiorentina
Verona 0-0 Sampdoria

CLASSIFICA

Verona	**15**
Torino	14
Inter	12
Sampdoria	12
Milan	11
Fiorentina	9
Roma	9
Atalanta	9
Como	9
Avellino	9
Juventus	8
Udinese	7
Napoli	7
Lazio	6
Ascoli	4
Cremonese	3

10a Giornata

25 November 1984

THIRTEEN-YEAR-OLD BARBARA Salazer is one of the lucky ones. She's got a season ticket and never misses a home game. Even better, her dad organises a supporters' bus, so she goes to all the away games as well. She's a funny, curious, scrawny little girl. She's also football daft and idolises her father. And why not? He takes her to all the games! She's captivated by the ultras, their habits and eccentricities, their colours and pageantry, their occasional tendency to overdo things. Of course, there aren't many 13-year-old girls on the terraces but she doesn't care. No one does. Rich or poor, old or young, Left or Right. It really doesn't matter.

On the way to Torino, Barbara's father hijacks the bus. He 'politely threatens' the driver, insisting they make a detour to the Basilica of Superga so they can pay their respects to the legends of the *Grande Torino*.[27] Respects paid, they reboard the bus and make the short journey to the Stadio Comunale di Torino. When they're not busy being obnoxious, football fans can be surprisingly pious.

Since winning the Serie A title in 1976, Torino have been a formidable force in Italian football, consistently finishing

---

27 On 4 May 1949, a Fiat G.212 Italian Airlines flight carrying the Torino football team (popularly known as the *Grande Torino*), crashed into the retaining wall at the back of the Basilica of Superga, which stands on a hill on the outskirts of Turin. All 31 of those on board were killed. On the day of the funerals, half a million people took to the streets of Turin to bid a final farewell to the players. The following season the other top Italian teams were each asked to donate a player to Torino so they could compete. Such was the shock surrounding the plane crash, the Italian team travelled by ship for the 1950 FIFA World Cup in Brazil.

in the top five in the championship and regularly making it to the latter stages of the Coppa Italia. After a slight slump in the early 1980s, they are now back at their best, with the reappointment of legendary championship-winning coach Luigi 'Gigi' Radice at the start of the current season.

In 1975 – after spells at Monza, Treviso, Cesena, Fiorentina and Cagliari – Radice settled in Torino, where he would spend the next five years resurrecting the spirit of the *Grande Torino*. Along with Trapattoni, he is credited with blending the fluidity of Dutch-style 'Total Football' with the pragmatism of the more defensive Italian approach. A pioneer of the full press (applying pressure on the player in possession in *all* areas of the pitch), according to the Italian daily newspaper *Il Foglio*, Radice was 'one of the best coaches our league had between the 70s and 80s'.

In his very first spell with Torino (the 1975/76 season), Radice won the Italian championship, Torino's first since the Superga tragedy, which earned him the *Seminatore d'oro* award for best coach of the season. In the following three campaigns, his side finished second, third and fifth. But then tragedy struck. On 17 April 1979, Radice was involved in a car crash on the Autostrada dei Fiori, the motorway that connects Genoa with Ventimiglia in France. A truck travelling in the opposite direction crashed through the central reservation and struck the car the Torino coach was travelling in. Radice was seriously injured but survived. His passenger, former team-mate Paolo Barison, was killed.[28]

In February the following year, with his team struggling in the relegation zone, Radice was sacked. For a man who had given so much, it was a brutal dismissal. Despite some tough times, Radice remained a revered and respected figure in Turin and, in the summer of 1984, after spells with Bologna,

28 Paolo Barison won the 1962 championship and the 1963 European Cup at Wembley against Eusébio's Benfica with AC Milan (playing alongside the likes of Cesare Maldini, Giovanni Trapattoni, José Altafini, Gianni Rivera and Luigi Radice). He made nine appearances and scored six goals (the last at the 1966 England World Cup) with the national team.

AC Milan, Bari and Inter, he returned to Torino, where president Sergio Rossi and sporting director Luciano Moggi were constructing a team capable once again of competing for silverware. With the arrival of players of the calibre of Júnior, Giuseppe Dossena (another 1982 World Cup winner), Walter Schachner and Aldo Serena, Radice was determined to bring the good times back to Torino. Nicknamed *Sergente di ferro* (the Iron Sergeant) for his abrupt and disciplined approach, in reality he was a consummate professional who loved his job and cared deeply about his players. He and Bagnoli were cut from the same cloth. Both were born in 1935 and they played together in the AC Milan youth team, since when they had enjoyed a healthy professional rivalry. Prior to their crucial 1984 meeting, they have already encountered each other four times as coaches, with three victories for Radice and just one for Bagnoli.

Following his decision to choose Verona over Cesena in 1981, Bagnoli earned immediate promotion with Hellas Verona. After the decisive game against Pescara at the tail end of the 1981/82 season (a goalless draw at the evocatively named Stadio Adriatico), the team dinner that evening was a jubilant affair. After yet another toast, Roberto Tricella, already nicknamed 'Gerry' for his ability to imitate Jerry Lee Lewis, performed a hilarious impression of Bagnoli, mimicking the taciturn coach's half-time pep talk as his team were losing 2-1 against Lazio two weeks previously. Tricella, with his legs apart and hands thrust deep in his pockets in the manner of Bagnoli, glared at the players: 'Cavasin, go and sit down!' 'Volpati, shut up! And stop attacking!' 'Guidolin, sit down!' Then, after an even longer silence, he exploded into a barrage of angry exclamations in Bagnoli's Milanese dialect, followed by a rousing incitement to victory. The players erupted in fits of laughter. Even Bagnoli managed a wry smile!

Having grown up in the Inter youth system, Roberto Tricella made just a handful of appearances for the *Nerazzurri,* before signing for Verona in 1979. With the club then struggling in Serie B, Tricella soon established himself as a familiar presence in Verona's starting XI. Lean, elegant and rangy, Tricella had the preppy good looks of an undergraduate and by his second season in Verona he was already the club's captain, aged only 23. On the eve of a match against Roma at the beginning of the 1982/83 season, the Hellas team were granted an audience at the Vatican with Pope John Paul II. When introduced to Tricella, His Holiness expressed surprise that one so young could be captain.[29] But his unassuming good nature and softly spoken manner belied a quiet determination and keen footballing intelligence.

Tricella's much-applauded imitation of Bagnoli at the end-of-season dinner was funny – but, more than that, it was a tribute to the extraordinary personality of Osvaldo Bagnoli and his legendary impact in the dressing room. Hellas went on to win that crucial match against Lazio 3-2, with two decisive goals from Mauro Gibellini. For Tricella, that after-dinner performance also marked his coming of age from the timid young Inter reject who had arrived at Verona in 1979 to the confident and quietly charismatic captain who led his team to promotion as champions of the notoriously competitive Serie B.

In the third game of the 1982/83 season, Tricella scored his first goal in Serie A in a memorable victory against Juventus. Though Paolo Rossi scored a late consolation goal for Juve, Tricella's piledriver, which flew past legendary goalkeeper Dino Zoff, was enough to secure three points. It was a pivotal victory and a massive turning point for newly promoted Hellas. After consecutive defeats against Roma and Inter in the opening two games of the season, voices were already beginning to circulate that Bagnoli wasn't cut out for Serie A. That goal by Tricella and that victory against Juve in the third game of the season marked the beginning of a remarkable 17-game unbeaten run and quashed any suggestion that Bagnoli was out of his depth. It also propelled the newly promoted Hellas to the very top of the table. That game also saw Fanna's first goal for Hellas Verona since signing from Juve earlier in the

---

29 Following the blessing that Pope John Paul II bestowed upon the team on 18 September 1982, Hellas Verona went on a 17-game unbeaten run.

summer. His emotional celebration was a release of all that pent-up frustration at a club who had so unceremoniously discarded him.

Now, with three seasons in Serie B and two in Serie A under his belt, Tricella is a key defensive lynchpin in a well-drilled Hellas team. He has matured into his role as *libero*, hoovering up defensively and probing decisively on the counter-attack. 'Bagnoli taught me to play without the ball,' says Tricella. In fact, his form is so good that he is now being spoken of as a possible successor to Baresi in the national team. An astute tactical presence and respected leader on and off the pitch, Tricella is helped and protected in that role by his friend, Domenico Volpati, with whom he has formed a close-knit and effective partnership, each capable of leading the team in moments of difficulty.

This is one such moment, as Hellas arrive in Turin without Mauro Ferroni, who will remain on the sidelines for the next couple of months. Elkjær is also missing through injury. In their places, Bagnoli shifts the versatile Volpati back a gear, giving him the unenviable task of restraining Schachner, and rewards Franco Turchetta with his first start of the season up front alongside Galderisi. In better news, Di Gennaro returns to his familiar place in the heart of the Hellas midfield.

Both teams are in impressive form going into this game. With impressive victories against Napoli (3-0), AC Milan (2-0) and Juventus (1-2) and with 14 points on the board, *Il Toro* are just a single point behind Verona. A victory for either side today will put them at the top of the table. Torino have a well-balanced team that blends youth and experience and, unlike Juventus, Inter and Napoli, are not dependent on a single player for goals. They have Aldo Serena (who would go on to win three *Scudetti* with Juventus, Inter and Milan), Austrian international Walter Schachner and Brazilian legend Júnior – an offensive trio which has already contributed nine goals this season.

Leovegildo Lins da Gama Júnior, more commonly known as Júnior, is one of a clutch of genuine Brazilian icons drawn to Italy in the summer of 1984.[30] Nicknamed '*capacete*' (the Portuguese word for helmet) because of his distinctive afro hairstyle, Júnior was a right-footed left-back who had won four Brazilian league titles in the fabled red and black hoops of Flamengo. He was a player of such talent and charisma that Pelé once called him his idol! With his hair and bristling handlebar moustache, the Brazilian icon was instantly recognisable – and that was before he even touched the ball. One of the most intelligent players of the era, he had a velvet touch and incredible vision, coupled with a fierce determination and deadly accuracy from set pieces. When he arrived in Torino, he insisted on playing in midfield and the positional change seemed to suit him. The flamboyant afro of his youth had thinned and he had allowed his moustache to grow into a scraggy beard but his class remained undiminished.

This morning, a long convoy of 43 buses and more than 100 cars set off from Verona for the three-hour drive west to Turin. With heavy fog forecast, many more fans take the train. In total, more than 5,000 Hellas fans arrive at the Stadio Comunale and, while a sense of nervous euphoria is building up amongst the travelling fans, the players seem relaxed, sporting for the first time the club's official tailoring: grey vicuña trousers, a tartan jacket, a blue shirt and matching tie. According to an agreement reached at the beginning of the season, each player will receive 1m lire (net) for each point gained in the standings. When the total exceeds the 26-point ceiling, that bonus will double to 2m. And if Verona are still at the top of the standings at that point, the bonus will rise to 3.5m lire per point. In addition to the 10m lire the players have already received for qualifying for the next round of the Coppa Italia, it's a tidy package, which perhaps explains why they look so flush as they soak up the pre-match atmosphere at the Stadio Comunale. Even the problem with the cold showers at the training ground seems to have been fixed!

---

30 Between 1979 and 1992, Júnior made 74 appearances for Brazil and appeared in both the 1982 and 1986 World Cup finals. In 1985 he would be voted Serie A player of the year.

Today, national coach Enzo Bearzot is amongst the guests in the stands, from where he will follow the duel between Torino's Giuseppe Dossena and Verona's Antonio Di Gennaro, rivals for Italy's coveted No.10 jersey. Another interested spectator is Giovanni Agnelli, the ex-president of Juventus, who, if reports are to be believed, would like to see Briegel and Tricella at his former club.

The match pits the best defence in the league (Hellas, with just three goals conceded) against the best attack (Torino, with 14 goals scored). Unbeaten Verona against an in-form Torino, who have lost just once, against Cremona. A makeshift Verona, missing Ferroni and Elkjær, against a full-strength Torino. It's Briegel v Júnior. Di Gennaro v Dossena.

In a game that lives up to its pre-match billing, it's Briegel who breaks the deadlock with a 20-metre howitzer midway through the first half. Just four minutes later, Torino equalise thanks to a Dossena header at the back post, following some elusive footwork and a lingering cross from Walter Schachner. While Torino begin the second half in search of a winner, it's Verona, in a devastating counter-attack, who score through Marangon. Galderisi is released down the left and Marangon is on hand for the cut-back to bundle the ball past Torino keeper Silvano Martina. With 30 minutes remaining, Bagnoli immediately responds by introducing Luigi Sacchetti for his first appearance of the season, greeted by thunderous applause from the travelling supporters. Once again, fortune smiles on Verona, as Garella puts his body on the line to deny Torino an equaliser. But as well as discipline, organisation and determination, Verona's second-half performance displays customary flashes of attacking flair. It's a style of football that the Italians like to call *verticalizzazione* but is executed with such pace and precision that it leaves opposition defenders straggling. Hellas ride their luck, with the crossbar and the post coming to Garella's rescue on more than one occasion. Final score at the Comunale: Torino 1 Hellas Verona 2.

For some, it's the greatest game in the club's history – certainly a massive result in what was already being billed in some quarters as a title decider. The newspapers tomorrow morning will describe it as one of the greatest matches in recent years, with Tricella and Briegel singled out for praise. With just two points for a victory, a three-point lead at this stage of the season is seismic. With 15 goals scored and just four conceded, Verona once again boast the best attacking and defensive records in the league. Even without Ferroni and Elkjær, they have demonstrated the value of their small but perfectly formed squad, with Bruni, Turchetta and Sacchetti providing excellent cover.

For captain Roberto Tricella, this is the moment when he realises that Verona are capable of something special, though he doesn't say so publicly. If it's possible to achieve such a victory and still be angry, somehow Bagnoli manages it. When he finally emerges from the away dressing room in a fetching check jacket and pullover combo, it is with the long face of someone who has just lost a game rather than won one. He accuses his opponents of unfair play and the referee of bias. It is, Bagnoli insists, still premature to speak about a *Scudetto.* If anything, Galderisi is even more scathing of the referee's performance: '[T]he referees protect Maradona, but then [...] they caution me and Fanna. You've all seen the *Granata*: they hit like hell. Do you want to see my leg? It's full of bruises and what was the result? I got booked!' Marangon, author of one of Verona's goals, strikes a different tone: 'We can't hide it anymore. This Verona is worthy of the championship. We say it quietly but we can't hide anymore. We showed it in Turin.' For Torino, Júnior is phlegmatic: 'Verona had two chances and took advantage of them. Games like this have no logic. But it's true, we played at a lower level than in the matches against Milan and Juve. Briegel was very good, for his goal, but also lucky.'

Elsewhere, Sampdoria continue their excellent run of form with a victory against AC Milan at the San Siro thanks to a Trevor Francis penalty kick, while Inter draw 1-1 in Florence and Juventus win 3-0 at Udinese thanks to a Michel Platini double. Napoli's victory at the San Paolo is overshadowed by a serious incident when Cremonese defenders Sergio Paolinelli and Mario Montorfano collide. Both require emergency medical treatment and Montorfano is resuscitated on the pitch before being transferred to hospital along with his team-mate.[31] Off the pitch, it is another violent Sunday, with the most serious incidents occurring in Ascoli, Milan and Bergamo, where the police made numerous arrests.

However you interpret today's Torino–Verona game, there is no doubting its historical significance. It's the first time Hellas have ever won in Turin. It also marks a turning point in the season. Hellas are three points clear at the top. They can no longer dismiss speculation about a championship run. There is still a long way to go but you can now at least whisper it: could Verona actually win the *Scudetto*?

Next week, Hellas host *Il Barone*'s AC Milan at the Bentegodi. Although Milan trail Verona by six points, it will be another stern test for Bagnoli's men, with Mark Hateley and Ray Wilkins bringing some English steel and guile to proceedings.

---

31 Both players made a full recovery.

10A GIORNATA

Ascoli 0-0 Roma
Atalanta 3-3 Avellino
Fiorentina 1-1 Inter
Lazio 3-2 Como
Milan 0-1 Sampdoria
Napoli 1-0 Cremonese
Torino 1-2 Verona
Udinese 0-3 Juventus

CLASSIFICA

Verona	**17**
Torino	14
Sampdoria	14
Inter	13
Milan	11
Fiorentina	10
Avellino	10
Juventus	10
Roma	10
Atalanta	10
Napoli	9
Como	9
Lazio	8
Udinese	7
Ascoli	5
Cremonese	3

11a Giornata

2 December 1984

RELENTLESS RAIN and arctic temperatures have enveloped Verona for the last 24 hours. Winter has arrived. On days like this, the gently looping Adige becomes a surging torrent of churning brown water, carrying a deluge of debris as it loops through the ancient city on its way east to the impassive Adriatic. A family of ducks can't decide whether to revel in the surging torrent or mourn the loss of their nest as the river breaches its lower banks. In Piazza Brà, a giant metallic shooting star, the biggest of its kind in the world, has just been installed. It soars 70m high and is 82m long, with points that extend some 22m. Built with 80 tons of steel and 2,500 bolts, it is supposed to be a one-off but will become an annual feature of Verona's Christmas landscape.

On this bleak first Sunday of Advent, 41,870 have flocked to the Bentegodi. Today's adversary, the once-mighty AC Milan, have spent several seasons in the footballing wilderness, including two spells in Serie B, as recently as 1983. A significant rebuilding project is now under way and the *Rossoneri* have begun the season with a seven-game unbeaten run (three victories and four draws), including their first victory in a Milan derby for six years, thanks to a powerful header by their towering English striker – a goal that is already being mythologised in the red and black half of Milan.

Twenty-two-year-old Mark Hateley signed for AC Milan from Portsmouth on 28 June 1984 for a reported £1.5m, having scored 22 goals in 38 appearances in the English second tier. His Italian adventure has started well, with his five goals so far putting him amongst the league's top scorers (alongside

Galderisi and Serena), but his time in Milan will always be remembered for that derby goal against Inter. Despite being marked by World Cup-winning defender Fulvio Collovati (a player who left AC Milan in favour of Inter when the *Rossoneri* were relegated to Serie B for the second time in three seasons), Hateley soared above him and powered a header into the top right corner, past the legendary Inter goalkeeper Walter Zenga. In the very next match, however, Hateley suffered a significant knee injury, the true extent of which seems to have been the subject of some dispute. Though he has returned to light training, he is not expected to play against Verona.[32]

Hateley is by no means the only AC Milan player on a fast-track to footballing immortality. In a crowded field, *libero* Franco Baresi is remembered as the greatest Italian defender of all time and in the 1984/85 season, he is barely midway through his 20-year playing career with Milan. Mauro Tassotti, Filippo Galli and Alberigo Evani will go on to form the backbone of a Milan rearguard that, within just a few years, will dominate the Italian game for the next decade to come playing alongside a certain Paolo Maldini, who will make his Serie A debut later this season, and Alessandro Costacura a few years later.

Ray Wilkins is another new face in Italy, having arrived in the summer of 1984. With a wealth of experience at both Chelsea and Manchester United (he had been handed the captain's armband at Stamford Bridge at just 18 years old and was Manchester United's player of the season in 1983/84), AC Milan paid a reported £1.5m to bring the English midfielder

---

32 In fact, it will be three months before Hateley next appears on the scoresheet, scoring back-to-back goals against Udinese and Fiorentina in January 1985. By the end of his first season in Milan, Hateley had managed just seven goals in 21 appearances. In the 1985/86 season, he went one better and scored eight goals in 22 league appearances, plus four in both the Coppa Italia and the UEFA Cup. By then, a charismatic media and property mogul named Silvio Berlusconi had taken an interest in the club, and with him would come the investment that would propel the Milan giants to the most successful period in the club's history. Off the pitch, Hateley experienced a degree of professionalism and preparation unlike anything he had ever known before, including being flown back to Milan from international fixtures on Berlusconi's private jet.

to Italy. Wilkins is the kind of player that coaches love. He is calm, reliable and has a profound tactical intelligence – such that coach Nils Liedholm will often fondly observe that, with Wilkins on the pitch, it feels like his team are playing with 12 men.

Liedholm, known affectionately as *Il Barone* (The Baron), is one of the most successful managers in the history of the Italian game, having coached in the top tier for more than four decades, winning titles with AC Milan in 1979 and Roma in 1983. With the latter, he successfully implemented the innovative new zonal marking system, a revolutionary shift from Italy's traditional *libero* or man-marking systems. In five seasons at Roma, between 1979 and 1984 (his second spell with the club), Liedholm only finished outside the top three once and that was in 1980, his first season in charge, when Roma finished in a respectable, if unspectacular, sixth place. His coaching style had an impact on one young player in particular from that period, a young midfielder named Carlo Ancelotti who, of course, would go on to become one of the greatest coaches in the history of the game.[33]

Aside from having one of the most innovative and experienced coaches in the business, AC Milan boast state-of-the-art training facilities at the Milanello sports centre. Inaugurated in 1963, it would be substantially modernised during the Berlusconi presidency and represented the first dedicated training facility of its kind in the world. A far cry from anything available in Verona, where training took place on the rudimentary back pitches behind the stadium and the showers, as Bagnoli regularly reminded us, were freezing cold!

With Baresi in his prime and Maldini about to make his breakthrough, it is an AC Milan team built on the strongest foundations but it will take the arrival of a Dutch trio in 1987

---

33 Ancelotti, the most successful manager in UEFA Champions League history, would subsequently say that Liedholm was the coach he learned the most from.

for the Milan giants to once again compete for silverware.[34] The Berlusconi-inspired future is bright for AC Milan but, in December of 1984, they aren't yet ready to mount a serious title challenge. In fact, after an unbeaten start to the season, their first defeat of the campaign came on matchday eight at Torino and was followed by a draw against Avellino and another narrow home defeat against Sampdoria.

Verona, of course, remain unbeaten. They are not, however, regarded as unbeatable. Once again, they are without two key players, defender Mauro Ferroni and striker Preben Elkjær Larsen, with the versatile Domenico Volpati once again deputising at full-back. The notorious Bentegodi playing surface is a deep battlefield green and the heavy rain has rendered the underfoot conditions almost unplayable. This is a battle that will be won and lost in the middle of the park, where Bagnoli has selected a robust midfield unit in the shape of Bruni, Di Gennaro, Briegel and Sacchetti, the latter of whom is making his first start of the season. Fanna and Galderisi lead the attack in a formation designed to contest everything and concede little.

True to form, it's a bruising encounter played with a heavy ball which frequently gets stuck in the clawing pools of mud and rain.

Even players with the technical ability of Fanna and Briegel are frustrated by the worsening conditions. While Verona create a number of chances with their trademark vertical through balls, it is the conditions that defeat them rather than the close attention of the Milan defence, with the ball getting held up in the mud on more than one occasion. Once again, though, Verona are impeccable at defending their area and Milan are limited to a couple of speculative long-

34 Berlusconi's AC Milan would finally win the *Scudetto* in 1988, before embarking on a period of dominance in the early 1990s during which they would win three Italian championships in a row as well as back-to-back European Cups in 1989 and 1990. That formidable squad, with its reliance on the defensive partnership of Baresi and Maldini, had its roots in the 1984/85 season, augmented of course by the arrival of Rijkaard, van Basten and Gullit.

range efforts. Unsurprisingly, given the conditions, a turgid first half ends goalless.

In the second half, it's once again Verona who dominate, pushing for a goal as conditions deteriorate even further. From a Fanna corner, a scrappy ball finds its way through a scramble of players and eventually falls to Di Gennaro, who bundles it into the net. Goal!!! While the linesman appears to confirm the goal, referee Mauro Mattei has other ideas. Offside! And so, under leaden skies, the battle of attrition finishes goalless. A second dropped point at the Bentegodi, following the draw against Sampdoria, but Hellas remain unbeaten.

With the match official taking centre stage today, it's time to say something about referees. Of course, bad refereeing decisions are sometimes exactly what a game needs. A sense of injustice can galvanise a team and, more importantly, the fans, rallying them to a cause and providing a common enemy. A bad decision can intensify that sense of 'us against the world', accentuating the notion that there are powerful forces at work conspiring to defeat us. *Soli contro tutti*, as the Veronese like to say (alone against everyone).

In Italy there is little stigma or shame attached to rule-breaking. Indeed, the opposite is often true – certainly on the football pitch. Whether it be skipping a queue or filing a tax return, the only rules that are sacrosanct relate to food and coffee! In football, cheating (or bending the rules to your advantage) is applauded. *Cattiveria* (nastiness) and *furbo* (cunning) are seen as positive characteristics on the football pitch. Coaches will often complain that their team wasn't sufficiently *cattivo*. '*Dobbiamo essere più cattivi*' (we have to be nastier) is a common complaint.

Anyway, in the 1984/85 season, something strange happened in Italian football. Referees were, for the first and only time, allocated at random. In 1926, the Viareggio Charter (Italian football's constitution) established a committee to oversee referee selection. Throughout the 1930s, 40s and 50s, to avoid the possibility of malpractice, the authorities didn't announce in advance which referee had been allocated to each match. Of course, clubs and officials found ways to subvert the system and by the 1950s, the process had fallen into disrepute. In 1958, lists were issued in advance to the clubs and the press and the bigger clubs found ways to influence selection and blacklist unfavourable referees. For decades, the perception prevailed that the big clubs had the match officials in their pockets. Following the *calcioscommesse* betting scandal of the early 1980s (also known as '*Totonero*'), which resulted in AC Milan and Lazio being relegated to Serie B, the Italian football authorities decided to try and clean up the tarnished image of the game. The situation reached a head after the controversial back-to-back championships won by Juventus at the expense of Roma and Fiorentina in 1981 and 1982 respectively. Ahead of the 1984/85 season, a ballot system was introduced, the draw taking place in public to avoid any possible accusations of corruption.

One of the measures introduced was the random allocation of referees. Proposed by the league with an almost unanimous vote and reluctantly accepted by the referees' association, the new system was complicated and, in fact, not entirely random. Under the new system, Serie A and Serie B games were divided into bands of 'match difficulty', with each band assigned by the designator a number of referees equal to the number of matches, plus one. After that, the draw was made band by band. This more random system undoubtedly gave referees a certain liberty. They were under less pressure and could perform without fear of retaliation or the risk of professional repercussions. Of course, the big clubs hated it. Their 'psychological power' over referees was diminished by the increased randomness of the draw.

Regardless of the system in place, controversial decisions, like the offside decision against Verona in favour of the bigger club, continued to occur. Verona's sporting director Emiliano Mascetti was characteristically diplomatic in his post-match assessment of the referee's performance, insisting that he had been unable to see if Di Gennaro was offside from his position on the bench, magnanimously giving the referee the benefit of the doubt.

Bagnoli was less diplomatic. In fact, with the newspapers acting as a willing intermediary, the Verona coach was declared to be 'at war' with the referees. 'There's always something that goes against us,' he complained bitterly to the press. Di Gennaro was also mystified by the decision to annul his goal: '[I]t was a difficult match. Whoever managed to score would win the game. I didn't understand why my goal was disallowed. The linesman ran towards the centre, then I asked him [the referee] for an explanation and he didn't respond. Too bad. It was a beautiful goal and really important.'[35]

Franz Beckenbauer, coach of the West German national team, had been observing the match from the stands. Afterwards he complimented both the quality of football on display and Briegel's contribution. Perhaps he, too, was just being diplomatic – the match was far from a classic!

Elsewhere, Torino recovered immediately from their defeat against Verona by beating Avellino 1-3, while Sampdoria failed to take advantage against a struggling Lazio (2-2) and Inter snatched a late winner against Napoli (2-1).

The following weekend, on the day of the Immaculate Conception, Italy were to host Poland in a friendly in Pescara. The match would see Antonio Di Gennaro start and coach Enzo Bearzot use Hellas captain Roberto Tricella, winning his first cap, and team-mate Pierino Fanna as substitutes. Three Hellas Verona players in the national team was unheard of and spoke volumes of the confidence that Bagnoli had given his players. As Italy secured a 2-0 victory, Di Gennaro grabbed a late second. Bearzot was so impressed with the Hellas midfielder that he declared his intention to build Italy's World Cup team around him.

With just four games remaining until the mid-point of the season, Hellas had games to come against Lazio, Como,

---

35 Today's match official, Maurizio Mattei, was an experienced and well-respected referee who would go on to have a long and illustrious career as refereeing administrator in Italy. He died on 12 February 2021 at the age of 78 at the COVID centre in Civitanova Marche where he had been hospitalised after testing positive for COVID-19.

Atalanta and Avellino. It appeared to be a favourable run that gave Hellas a tantalising opportunity to be crowned '*Campione d'inverno*' (winter champions) for the first time in the club's history. *That* would be something to celebrate.

11A GIORNATA

Avellino 1-3 Torino
Como 0-0 Atalanta
Cremonese 1-1 Fiorentina
Inter 2-1 Napoli
Juventus 2-2 Ascoli
Roma 2-1 Udinese
Sampdoria 2-2 Lazio
Verona 0-0 Milan

CLASSIFICA

Verona	**18**
Torino	16
Inter	15
Sampdoria	15
Roma	12
Milan	12
Fiorentina	11
Atalanta	11
Juventus	11
Como	10
Avellino	10
Lazio	9
Napoli	9
Udinese	7
Ascoli	6
Cremonese	4

12a Giornata

16 December 1984

SEVENTEEN-YEAR-OLD SERGIO 'Chicco' Guidotti was at school one Saturday morning in November 1978 when there was a knock on the classroom door. 'Telephone call for Guidotti,' the school janitor announced. Expecting the worst, Chicco went to the secretary's office to take the call. It was his mother, who informed the startled youngster that he'd been called into the squad for Verona's game against Lazio the next day. Chicco was a promising young defender in the Hellas youth team. The call-up to the first team came completely out of the blue.

The youngster rushed home to wait for Saverio Garonzi,[36] Hellas Verona's colourful club president, who was driving to Rome to join the rest of the squad already in the capital. For

---

36 Saverio 'Don' Garonzi was a colourful character, a local tycoon whose life merits a book of its own rather than just a footnote. In the mid-1960s, he became president of Verona. In 1968, with Nils Liedholm leading the coaching staff, Verona returned to Serie A after a ten-year absence, where they remained for six consecutive seasons. On 20 May 1973, the last day of the championship, Verona beat Milan 5-3, handing the championship to Juventus – sparking the myth of 'Fatal Verona'. At the end of the 1973/74 season, Verona were demoted to last place following the verdicts in the Telefonata trial, following a phone call between Garonzi and former Verona player Sergio Clerici. Garonzi was suspended for three years, and Hellas were condemned to Serie B.

On the evening of 29 January 1975, Garonzi was kidnapped in front of his home in Borgo Trento. He was eventually released on 4 February near Bergamo after paying a ransom of one billion lire. At Verona's next match against Como, an exhausted but relieved Garonzi received a hero's welcome. After stepping down as president of Hellas he subsequently became a leading figure in the development of an emerging team from a suburb on the outskirts of Verona called Chievo. He died on 25 March 1986, after falling from the roof of a showroom at his Fiat dealership.

Chicco, it was a dream come true. Since he was five years old, his father had taken him to the Bentegodi and he had progressed through the club's youth section all the way to the *primavera* (youth team). Bundled into the back of the president's Fiat 130, in a journey of around six hours, the timid schoolboy barely said a word. He arrived at the hotel in Rome to find the rest of the squad had gone to the cinema (a pre-match ritual in those days). The next day, at just 17 years old, he found himself sharing a changing room with the heroes of his childhood – above all, the legendary Emiliano Mascetti.

Chicco made his first-team debut a few months later against Catanzaro, the first of two Serie A appearances in the 1978/79 season. The following season, he made a single appearance as Hellas struggled in Serie B. Then, in the 1981/82 campagn, 20-year-old Chicco made eight appearances under new coach Osvaldo Bagnoli, playing alongside the likes of Roberto Tricella and Domenico Penzo as Hellas earned promotion back to the top tier.

Ultimately, it was Chicco's father, Celestino, who would have a bigger impact on the history of the club. In 1945, spotting a niche in the market, Celestino Guidotti opened a driver and vehicle licensing agency in Verona. His business thrived and, in 1960, when Innocenti, one of Italy's best-known car servicing and repair companies and manufacturer of the popular Lambretta range of scooters, was granted a manufacturing licence to produce iconic British models like the Morris Minor, Austin Allegro, Mini 90 and Mini 120, Celestino was offered a dealership in Verona. He became one of the most well-known and respected businessmen in the city.

By the late 1970s, long-serving club president Saverio Garonzi (another car salesman) had had enough. The football club was in crisis, with just 15 points on the board at the end of the 1978/79 season. After 12 years at the helm, he wanted out. With a new president (Giuseppe Brizzi), new coach (Fernando Veneranda) and new playing staff (former Inter and Juventus striker Roberto Boninsegna, former Bologna captain Tazio

Roversi and a promising young defender named Roberto Tricella), the 1979/80 season started promisingly enough. Verona looked stable in the upper echelons of the second tier and an immediate return to the top flight seemed possible. Then, midway through the season, their form slumped and Hellas finished in a disappointing 13th place. At the end of the season, captain Emiliano Mascetti announced his retirement. The loss of such an influential figure marked the end of an era. But his departure would leave space for the emergence of a new leader on the pitch.

Celestino Guidotti was a passionate football fan, a passion he shared with his son, Chicco. He was also a shrewd and respected businessman. By now, he was on the Hellas board and, in March 1980, he led a consortium to take over the club and assume the presidency. With a prominent nose and oversized spectacles, Guidotti was a familiar face around the city. Popular with fans, on matchdays he was always ready with a playful word or comment for the press. He was also a regular guest at supporters' club functions, a familiar and popular figure at club dinners and social events, where he would often be the last to leave. At the beginning of the 1980/81 campaign, Guidotti appointed Giancarlo Cadé as first-team coach. An ex-Atalanta player, Cadé had two previous spells coaching Hellas, the second of which included the famous 5-3 victory against Milan in 1973 which cost the *Rossoneri* the *Scudetto.*

Despite the changes, 1980/81 was another challenging season in Serie B for Hellas, who spent much of the campaign hovering above the drop zone. In the end, they avoided relegation thanks only to a series of draws in the second half of the season and to the frailty of their relegation rivals, Vicenza, Taranto, Monza and Atalanta, who were relegated to C1. Once again, young Tricella was the club's most consistent performer, making 37 league appearances. In fact, it was a Tricella assist in the last game of the season against SPAL that earned Verona the point they needed to stay up. Without that crucial point in the last game of the season, the future for the club would have been very different.

At the beginning of the 1981/82 season, four significant things happened: Adidas became the club's official kit supplier; an official sponsor, the Japanese electronics company Canon, was announced for the first time in the club's history; Ferdinando Chiampan (entrepreneur and importer of the Canon brand for Italy) took a financial stake in the club; and Osvaldo Bagnoli was appointed coach.

The impact was immediate. With 21 points on the board by the midway point in the season, only Varese and Pisa were in front. In the second half of the campaign, Hellas did even better, accumulating 27 points and securing a first-place finish. Two strikers emerged as protagonists in Verona's revival – Domenico Penzo, with 16 goals, and Mauro Gibellini, with 13. New signings Claudio Garella (from Sampdoria) and Antonio Di Gennaro (from Perugia) also made important contributions alongside club captain Roberto Tricella.

Meanwhile, club president Guidotti's son, Chicco, remained on the fringes of the squad, making eight appearances for the team that won promotion in 1982. But his father's role at the club put the youngster in a difficult position. Those who knew no better assumed the youngster owed his place in the team to the fact that his dad was president, not realising that Chicco's involvement as a player preceded his father's as president. Chicco's first encounter with the club's new coach at the start of the season was reassuring. 'I don't care who your father is,' Bagnoli told him, 'I'll judge you on how you play.' For an anxious teenager, these were words that stayed with him for the rest of his life. Chicco made his last appearance for Hellas on 25 April 1982, just as the club's fortunes were looking up. The following season, he was released to a local Serie C side. His dream at Verona was over but he would remain a lifelong Hellas fan and an instrumental figure in preserving the history of the club and the well-being of former players who had fallen on hard times. And he would never forget that day the janitor hauled him out of class for that game against Lazio.

In the winter of 1984, Hellas Verona are a club on the up but these are turbulent times for Società Sportiva Lazio.

Caught up in the *Totonero* illicit betting scandal, the Roman club had been relegated to Serie B in 1980. In 1983, the legendary ex-player Giorgio Chinaglia returned from New York as the club's majority shareholder and he has invested heavily to return the club to its former glories. Despite the significant investment, his first season at the helm was another disappointing one for Lazio, who only avoided relegation thanks to a last-minute draw against Pisa in the final game of the 1983/84 season.

There is little so far to suggest that this season will be any different. With just two victories (against Cremonese and Como), Lazio's biggest problem has been a lack of consistency. The crisis for the *Biancocelesti* began almost immediately. Coach Paolo Carosi was sacked in the aftermath of a 5-0 humiliation at Zico's Udinese on matchday two. His replacement, Juan Carlos 'Toto' Lorenzo, the legendary Argentinian coach, returned for his third stint at the club after a 13-year hiatus. With draws against Inter, Napoli, Roma, Sampdoria and Ascoli, Lazio are no pushover, despite having suffered a series of humiliating setbacks already this season. They are, however, a far cry from the team of hotheads and raw talent, epitomised by the gun-toting striker Giorgio Chinaglia, which won an historic *Scudetto* ten years ago.[37]

For Lazio, the one possible source of inspiration is a young Danish striker named Michael Laudrup. In the 1982/83 season, he scored 24 goals in 38 appearances for Danish side Brøndby, earning the title of Danish player of the year. He was just 18 years old and already attracting the attention of some of the biggest clubs in Europe, with Juventus leading the charge. The Turin giants paid an unprecedented $1m US for his signature (a Scandinavian record at the time) before immediately releasing him to Lazio on a two-year loan deal so that he could gain experience in Italian football. The Dane made his debut against Bagnoli's Verona on 12 September

37 In a tragic footnote to Lazio's historic 1974 *Scudetto*, Luciano Re Cecconi, one of the stars of that team, was shot and killed in a practical joke that went terribly wrong.

1983. Lazio soon found themselves 4-0 down but it was the Danish winger who salvaged some pride for the visitors, scoring two late consolation goals. In his first season in Italy, he scored eight goals in 30 appearances. This season, things haven't gone quite so well and Laudrup has managed just a solitary league goal (against Como on 25 November).[38]

With Ferroni and Elkjær once again unavailable, Hellas are also without the suspended Briegel. This means that Bagnoli has selected an all-Italian team for the first time this season, with Sacchetti[39] replacing the German Panzer in midfield and winger Franco Turchetta, born in Latina and a lifelong Lazio fan, proudly wearing the No.11 shirt of Hellas Verona. Turchetta had spent most of his career with Varese in Serie B when he joined Hellas in the summer of 1984. Deputising for Galderisi and Elkjær, this is the chance he has been waiting for.

Perhaps surprisingly, this is a match that many predict Hellas will lose, as Bagnoli's pre-match comments to the *Corriere della Sera* acknowledge: 'I know very well that Italy has been waiting for our defeat for months. Lorenzo [Lazio coach Juan Carlos Lorenzo], a famous prophet, says that Lazio will win the match. I will limit myself to one promise: Verona, even without the foreigners, will not lose our place as league leaders. And a league leader has the duty to play to win.' Of his injury list, Bagnoli makes no pre-emptive excuses: '[O]ur absences are serious but the true soul of my team is represented by Di Gennaro, Fanna and Tricella. These three players represent

---

38 That strike against Como would be Laudrup's only goal in Serie A in the 1984/85 season. In the summer of 1985, his loan spell at Lazio came to an end and he moved to Juventus where he won the Italian championship in 1986. In four seasons he would make 152 appearances for the Turin giants, scoring 36 goals. He then became a European champion with Johan Cruyff's Barcelona, where he made 226 appearances and scored 55 goals over five seasons, winning La Liga four times, as well as the Copa del Rey, Supercopa de España, the European Cup and the UEFA Super Cup.

39 Midfielder Luigi Sacchetti came close to winning a historic *Scudetto* with Fiorentina in 1981/82, only losing out to Juventus in the last 15 minutes of the season thanks to a controversial Liam Brady penalty.

the backbone, the axis of our game, both in attack and in defence.'

If Di Gennaro, Fanna and Tricella represent the soul of the team, Tricella is its leader. Eight days ago, the Verona captain made his first appearance for the national team in a friendly against Poland, coming on as a half-time substitute for the legendary Giuseppe Bergomi.[40] It's a remarkable achievement for a player who was languishing in the depths of Serie B just a few seasons ago. Garella, meanwhile, also has something to prove, returning once again to the Olimpico to face Lazio, the club where he endured so much ridicule.

With Volpati still covering for the injured Ferroni in defence, Luciano Bruni makes another start in Verona's midfield. A promising young player who was even tipped to succeed the great Giancarlo De Sisti at Fiorentina,[41] Bruni won the 1978 Torneo di Viareggio (the prestigious international tournament for the best youth teams in the world) and made his Serie A debut the same year. But during the 1980/81 season, he suffered a serious injury (torn ligaments) which forced him to take a long break and, in October 1981, was sold to Pistoiese, where he made 17 appearances. After another year in Serie B (with Reggiana, for whom he made 28 appearances and scored two goals in the 1982/83 season), he arrived at Verona in 1983, making 14 appearances and contributing two goals from midfield in his first season. Another of Verona's diminutive midfielders, Bruni measures in at just under 1.7m (around 5ft 6in).[42]

It's a lively first half, with Hellas dominating possession but clearly missing the pace, power and impact of Briegel and Elkjær. The breakthrough comes 15 minutes into the second

---

40 Tricella would go on to make 11 appearances for his country, mainly in friendlies.

41 Nicknamed 'Picchio', Giancarlo De Sisti, in a professional career that spanned 20 years, won a league title, the Coppa Italia (twice), a Coppa Mitropa and a Coppa delle Fiere, as well as the European Championship with the *Azzurri* in 1968.

42 Earlier in his career, Bruni had been rejected by scouts from AC Milan, Inter and Napoli precisely because of his lack of physical stature.

half, thanks to a move that looks like it's come straight from the training ground. Di Gennaro, Sacchetti, Bruni and Galderisi combine. A neat one-two between Bruni and Galderisi dissects the Lazio defence and the diminutive Hellas striker bundles the ball in with a deflection off Podavini, adding to the sense of confusion in the Lazio rearguard. Even Elkjær, despite carrying a lingering injury, leaps from the bench with joy when Nanu scores.

With 20 minutes remaining, Turchetta makes way for Dario Donà, a rare appearance for the young midfielder, who was playing with Bologna in Serie C1 last season. A precocious talent, he was scouted by AC Milan in 1981 but played just two matches for the club, both in the Coppa Italia. His career stalled when, instead of joining the club's pre-season retreat, the 19-year-old went AWOL for ten days with his girlfriend. Luigi Radice, AC Milan's famously strict coach, was furious and Donà's days in Milan were numbered. A few months later, he was released to LR Vicenza, from where he would subsequently find his way to Bologna.[43]

In the dying minutes, Bagnoli gives Marangon's younger brother, Fabio, his Serie A debut in place of the injured Fontolan. Final score, Lazio 0 Hellas 1. For Verona, it's another well-earned, if unspectacular, two points on the road. It's also the first time they have won away to Lazio in 15 years. Perhaps the most remarkable thing to take from the victory, however, is the fact that it has been achieved by an all-Italian team. When given the chance, those players on the fringes of the squad (Bruni, Turchetta and Donà) have demonstrated that they have the quality and unity of purpose to deliver.

Hellas Verona remain unbeaten and have taken 20 of the 24 points available to them so far this season. In the tunnel after the match, Lazio coach Juan Carlos Lorenzo spots Bagnoli

---

43 Dario Donà married his childhood sweetheart, Patrizia, for whom he sacrificed his career at AC Milan. He went on to play for Catanzaro, Reggiana and Ancona in the second and third tiers before hanging up his boots in 1990. He worked in logistics and recently retired. He lives in Treviso, where he spends his free time gardening.

and offers his hand. 'Congratulations,' he says, 'you really have a great team.' Bagnoli, usually so serious and reserved, lights up with a slightly embarrassed smile and replies: 'Thank you, Mister. Coming from you, that's a big deal.' Galderisi, meanwhile, observes that Verona are 'capable of winning anywhere, even without three starters'. For Laudrup, its yet another disappointing performance and he expresses his clear frustration after the game, saying: 'I've had enough. We can't go on like this. They all take it out on me but they never give me the ball. I've run 10km for nothing. On the pitch, it takes 11 players to make a team [...] [Verona] – that's a football team where everyone fights for each other. That would really be the ideal club for me.'

Elsewhere, Inter take maximum points on the road against Cremonese, Torino beat Como 3-1, Roma overcome Napoli 1-2, while Fiorentina and Juventus fight out a goalless draw. It is a series of results that maintains Verona's two-point cushion over Torino. Next week, on the last Sunday before Christmas, Hellas will be on the road again, this time to face a tough Como side, as they look to bring the year to a close at the top of the table.

12A GIORNATA

Cremonese 1-2 Inter
Fiorentina 0-0 Juventus
Lazio 0-1 Verona
Milan 2-2 Atalanta
Napoli 1-2 Roma
Sampdoria 1-0 Avellino
Torino 3-1 Como
Udinese 1-1 Ascoli

CLASSIFICA

Verona	**20**
Torino	18
Inter	17
Sampdoria	17
Roma	14
Milan	13
Fiorentina	12
Atalanta	12
Juventus	12
Como	10
Avellino	10
Lazio	9
Napoli	9
Udinese	8
Ascoli	7
Cremonese	4

13a Giornata

23 December 1984

THERE'S SOMETHING about a city on a lake. History. Splendour. Romance. Como has it all. One of the most evocative settings in all of Italy. Hills that have been inhabited since the Iron Age. The birthplace of the ancient writer Pliny the Younger and his uncle, Pliny the Elder, not to mention Pope Innocent XI, one of 13 popes who share that pontifical name with varying degrees of self-awareness. The magnificent duomo, one of the most famous in Italy, built between 1457 and 1485, is a blend of gothic and renaissance splendour, executed in glistening marble. Passing through the side portal, with its magnificent relief of the Flight into Egypt, the interior boasts masterpieces by Gaudenzio Ferrari and Bernardino Luini, contemporaries of Leonardo da Vinci, but these can be 'hard to see in the dim light', warns our handy 1982 travel companion. Of course, Como also has a football team.

Throughout the 1960s and much of the 1970s, Como 1907, to give the club its official title, shifted restlessly between Serie B and Serie C. Finally, in 1975, once again under the technical stewardship of Giuseppe Marchioro, and with the contribution of a rising star named Marco Tardelli, a second promotion to Serie A finally arrived. Despite the best efforts of players such as Alessandro Scanziani and penalty-taking goalkeeper Antonio Rigamonti, Como were in the top flight for just a single season. A brief dalliance in Serie C1 was followed immediately by two consecutive promotions in 1979 and 1980, with Como returning to Serie A for the 1980/81 season. With a completely revamped squad, including the tenacious defender Pietro Vierchowod, the son of a Ukrainian Red Army soldier from Starobilsk,[44] Como finished just above the relegation zone in 13th place. The following season, however, they finished at the bottom of the table, returning to Serie B.

In the 1982/83 Serie B campaign, Como found themselves competing in the play-offs with Catania and Cremonese in their bid to bounce straight back up to Serie A. It wasn't to be. In 1984, Como did return to the top flight, where they would remain for the following five championships, making it the most successful period in the club's history.

Now, having fought so hard for their place in the top tier and with a steely determination to preserve it, coach Ottavio Bianchi and sporting director Sandro Vitali have assembled a tough team that concedes little at home. Como are a blend of emerging talent from the youth sector and seasoned professionals with Serie A experience, supplemented by West German attacking midfielder, Hansi Müller, an international team-mate of Briegel's, and Swedish centre-forward Dan Corneliusson. Como are undefeated at home this season and haven't conceded a single goal at the Stadio Giuseppe Sinigaglia, thanks in no small part to the form of 26-year-old goalkeeper Giuliano Giuliani.

So, as Hellas travel to the town on the lake, they can expect to find an obstinate opponent. A club more accustomed to the grind of Serie B than the glamour of Serie A, a squad lacking in star quality but boasting a formidable home record. Elsewhere, the key fixtures on matchday 13 are all taking place within a 50km radius, with Torino facing Atalanta in Bergamo and Inter hosting Sampdoria at the San Siro.

On the eve of the game, the Hellas players appear on a Christmas special of *Premiatissima*, the popular Saturday night variety show. As well as being presented with the '*Coppa Premiatissima*', the team join hosts – crooner Johnny Dorelli and Ornella Muti (best known for her role as Princess Aura in

---

44 Pietro Vierchowod would go on to make 115 appearances for Como followed by brief spells with Fiorentina and Roma (where he won the *Scudetto* in 1983) before settling at Sampdoria where he made 358 appearances, winning the historic *Scudetto* in 1991.

the cult 1980 science fiction film *Flash Gordon*) – in a cheesy rendition of 'White Christmas'. Earlier in the week, Hellas played a friendly against Treveigliese, winning 2-1 with goals from Galderisi and Turchetta. More significantly, Elkjær made a second-half appearance, a good sign that the Dane is on the mend.

The other good news is that Briegel returns to face Como. Bruni and Sacchetti retain their places to protect playmaker Di Gennaro in midfield and, with Elkjær not yet deemed fit enough to reclaim his place, Fanna is once again deployed as a striker alongside Galderisi. Domenico Volpati (who made 69 appearances for Como) returns to his more familiar role in the Hellas midfield, while Silvano Fontolan, another former Como stalwart, with 248 appearances on the lake, returns in defence. At over 6ft (1.83m) tall, Fontolan is one of the defensive foundations upon which Verona's success this season has been built. Except for a single season at Inter, the towering defender spent his entire career yo-yoing between Serie A and Serie B with Como. Bagnoli first encountered him back in the mid-1970s, when he was a youngster at Como. In 1983, he persuaded Fontolan to come to Verona, where he would be reunited with former team-mates Domenico Volpati and Mario Guidetti. It proved to be another shrewd acquisition, as the ex-Como defender would go on to make 143 Serie A appearances for Hellas, demonstrating once again Bagnoli's knack of identifying players with the right characteristics and temperament for his team.[45] Bagnoli, when asked how he identified players for his squad, explained: 'I browse the Panini almanac and look for midfielders who can score three or four goals a season.' While Fontolan didn't fall into that category, he was a solid and reliable defender.

---

45 Referred to in the media as '*La quercia di Garbagnate*' (the oak of Garbagnate) after the commune of Milan where he's from, in a tawdry blemish on an otherwise exemplary professional career, in March 1988, following a UEFA Cup tie against Werder Bremen, Silvano Fontolan tested positive in a drug test, though he protested his innocence, claiming to have taken a medical prescription to treat bronchitis.

Another crucial aspect of the environment that Bagnoli created was the club's annual summer retreat in Cavalese. Nothing too luxurious but an important opportunity for the players to bond, relax and make final preparations for the forthcoming season. At the end of the 1984 retreat, Bagnoli gathered his players together and announced his starting XI. The others would play, he explained, in the event of injuries or suspensions, so they must always be ready. This was his way. To speak plainly and clearly, never behind the players' backs. The result was a close-knit group of players who each understood and accepted their role within the squad. Even those players on the fringes of the team were ready to perform when called upon to do so, Luciano Bruni being a case in point. After a few seasons on the fringes of the Fiorentina squad, the combative midfielder was released to Pistoiese before settling in Reggiana, where he was plucked by Hellas in the summer of 1983. In his first season in Verona, he made 14 Serie A appearances and scored two goals. In the first half of the 1984/85 season, he had made just a handful of appearances but had never let his team-mates down.[46]

Everyone who ever encountered him agreed that Bagnoli was a truly exceptional individual but not without his eccentricities. A man of exceptionally few words, often just a look was enough. When he spoke, his players listened. 'He didn't', as ex-player and local journalist Gianluca Tavellin explained, 'mess with the heads of his players.' His messaging was clear and simple and he could be disarmingly direct. But he also gave responsibility to his players and, when preparing for a match, he wanted to hear everyone's opinion. Sometimes, he even let Volpati take training. On the pitch, he enabled his players to express themselves and play without fear. For

46 Luciano Bruni had a promising early career, but one that was punctuated by injuries. When his playing career ended in 1995, he enjoyed success as a youth coach, winning the prestigious Viareggio tournament, which he had also won as a player with Fiorentina. At the time of writing, Bruni lives in Ostuni in southern Italy. On 29 October 2024, he joined the travelling Hellas Verona fans in the *curva* at Lecce. Like all the legends from that season, he remains a highly revered figure in Verona.

creative players like Di Gennaro and Fanna, and strikers like Galderisi and Penzo, this approach was transformative. Their undoubted qualities weren't suffocated as they had been elsewhere. Though he gave them the confidence to thrive, he wasn't without his faults. 'If you passed him in the morning, he wouldn't say hello,' remembers Chicco Guidotti. 'It was nothing personal. He wasn't being rude. It was just his way. He was shy with an extremely reserved character.' This was a characteristic that 18-year-old Gianluca Tavellin, son of club legend Guido Tavellin, also observed as a member of the youth team in the 1984/85 season. One day, Gianluca greeted Bagnoli in the corridor and the coach completely blanked him! It wasn't because he was rude or even shy – it was just how Bagnoli interpreted his role. It was, Gianluca explained, a kind of mask. Outside of the immediate football environment, Bagnoli could be extremely good company and very funny but, as a coach, he preferred to maintain a certain aura.

Reserved, nurturing and loyal, Pierino Fanna, who shares the same sign of the Zodiac (Cancer) with Bagnoli, had this to say about his former coach: 'A great personality but also introverted, a man of few words.' After the trials and tribulations of the Juventus changing room, Bagnoli's was exactly the kind of straightforward and pragmatic approach that Fanna needed. The two men understood each other almost immediately.

For the new arrivals, it was clear that Bagnoli was miles ahead of other coaches they had worked under. Back then, football coaches were exactly that – coaches. Bagnoli had few backroom staff and was extremely hands-on. He prepared, organised and ran his own sessions. The only assistance he had was from the goalkeeping coach, Antonio 'Toni' Lonardi. Bagnoli did everything else himself. He knew how to manage the changing room, which in those days would typically involve just 16 players, plus two apprentices from the youth team. Sergio Guidotti, one of those young players during Bagnoli's first season, observed an immediate surge in the quality of training and pre-match preparation, with a greater focus on athletic preparation, alongside a more innovative tactical approach. The results were immediately visible on the pitch in a team that ran more than the others but also had a clear shape and identity. Bagnoli was also ahead of his time in terms of understanding and analysing his opponents. His game management was exceptional – making minor corrections and adjustments depending on the flow of the game. At half-time, he had the ability to say three things that could change the course of a match.

Notwithstanding his success as a coach, Bagnoli remained a simple, modest and straightforward person, taking the bus to training or sometimes even cycling. He treated everyone the same – from the young players breaking through to experienced World Cup winners. When he spoke, it was in a gruff dialect, a coarse blend of Milanese and Veronese that not all his players could understand, even the Italians! Domenico Volpati had a particularly close relationship with him: 'I've had many good coaches but Bagnoli is unique. A man of great acuity and technique who really taught us how to play football. A true friendship ties me to him. Even today I can't call him by his first name. I call him Mister, like in the days of the championship. We often met when he came to ski here with me in Cavalese. What a chat: between us there is mutual respect and esteem. But it's true that with some people just a glance is enough.'

Bagnoli believed in letting his players enjoy and express themselves on the pitch and in playing them in their favoured roles. His was a vertical style of football. He favoured a 4-2-1-3 formation that combined defensive solidity with offensive directness. With three passes, he wanted his team to be in front of goal. It wasn't exactly a long-ball game but what might more accurately be described as a 'play forward fast' philosophy.[47] There was little in the way of lateral passing or patient build-

---

47 Play forward fast is a term I first heard used by Scottish analyst and podcaster John Walker. Although it may be interpreted as a euphemism for a long-ball game, in the case of Bagnoli in the 1984/85 season, it was executed with precision and quality and generally involved retaining possession but progressing the ball up the pitch as quickly as possible.

up from the back. Instead, the objective was to get the ball to the '*punta*' (the most advanced player on the pitch) as quickly as possible.

When Hellas were promoted to Serie A in 1982, Bagnoli found himself competing against some of the most experienced, innovative and successful footballing coaches in the history of the Italian game – Luigi Radice at Torino, Nils Liedholm at AC Milan, Sven-Göran Eriksson at Roma, Rino Marchesi at Napoli and Giovanni Trapattoni at Juventus. Each was capable of winning the Italian championship – indeed, most of them already had: Radice once as a player (with AC Milan in 1962) and once as a coach (with Torino in 1976); Liedholm four times as a player (with AC Milan) and twice as a coach (with AC Milan in 1979 and Roma in 1983); Eriksson had lifted numerous trophies across Europe as a coach and would finally lift the *Scudetto* with Lazio in 2000; Marchese came close to leading Napoli to their first *Scudetto* in 1981. Then, of course, there was 'Trap'. He had already won the *Scudetto* five times with Juve and would go on to win it twice more with Inter.

Today, at Como, Bagnoli faces Ottavio Bianchi, an up-and-coming coach who has worked his way up through the divisions with the likes of Siena, Mantova, Triestina and Atalanta, before having a crack in Serie A with Avellino and now Como. He is destined to achieve great things at Napoli, who he will join at the end of the season, but for today his objective is to keep another clean sheet and maintain Como's unbeaten record at home.

As the game kicks off, Verona, in yellow, immediately seize the initiative, dominating the opening skirmishes but, in the 19th minute, Bruni is injured and Bagnoli is forced to adjust. Turchetta enters to play on the right, while Fanna switches to the left, with Sacchetti providing cover in the centre. The change in shape shifts the balance of the game as Verona struggle to adjust and Como look to capitalise.

In the second half, Verona once again dominate but lack the energy, penetration and power to break down a stubborn Como defence. Only once, with just a few minutes remaining, do Hellas come close to breaking the deadlock and giving the 10,000 travelling fans something spectacular to celebrate, Fanna and Briegel combining to deliver a long ball to Di Gennaro, whose attempted overhead kick forces Giuliani into a miraculous save.

And so it ends as a bland 0-0 draw, the fifth of the season for Hellas, but another significant result. With a tired and depleted squad, Bagnoli is pleased with the result: '[A] draw was fine for us. It helps us overcome this unfortunate period. We managed to get points despite experiencing a series of injuries. Think of Ferroni, think of Elkjær. Think of Bruni, who got injured right here.'

Elsewhere, Torino draw in Bergamo, Roma struggle to overcome last-placed Cremonese, eventually winning 3-2, while Juventus show Maradona that his Napoli are not yet ready for greatness with a convincing 2-0 victory. The most important fixture is played in Milan, pitting Castagner's Inter against Bersellini's Sampdoria. Altobelli and Rummenigge ease Inter to a 2-0 victory, a sure sign that the *Nerazzurri* have shaken off their initial torpor and are now pursuing Verona, drawing level with Torino on 19 points.

Back in Como, the late afternoon shadows are lengthening across the stadium as the winter sun fades behind the hills that surround the lake. A few Verona fans stick around to enjoy the lakeside surroundings and take a stroll around the town. With a few lire in their pocket, they might even buy a local silk scarf, an early Christmas present or souvenir of a match to forget in a championship that will go down in history. As they travel back to Verona later that evening, news begins to trickle through of a major incident in a tunnel between Florence and Bologna. Details are sketchy but rumours suggest a possible terrorist attack on the Naples to Milan passenger train.[48]

---

48 At 7.08pm on Sunday, 23 December 1984, a bomb exploded in a second-class carriage of a Rapido 904 service from Naples to Milan. The train was packed with passengers travelling home for the Christmas holidays. Sixteen were killed and 266 injured. Although various right-wing groups claimed responsibility for the bombing, the Mafia would subsequently be found guilty of the atrocity.

As Christmas 1984 beckons, a charity single written by pop stars Bob Geldof and Midge Ure to raise money for the famine in Ethiopia has just entered the UK singles chart at No.1, where it will remain for five weeks. Hellas Verona are also at No.1. Unbeaten – with eight wins and five draws – they have 21 points on the board and are two points clear of their closest rivals. There are still five months to go. Formidable rivals in the form of Inter, Torino, Sampdoria, Roma, AC Milan and Juventus are all within striking distance, waiting for the inevitable slip-up. But Bagnoli's men have proven themselves to be compact, versatile and resolute and, with Elkjær and Ferroni ready to return early in the new year, they can look forward to 1985 with some optimism.

At the club Christmas dinner, Tricella has organised gifts for everyone, from the youth players and the bag man to the coach and the club president. Gianluca Tavellin still has the little silver elephant that the players gave him that Christmas. In Cavalese, a smaller group of players, staff and wives gather to celebrate new year. As the clock chimes midnight, Pierino Fanna proposes a toast. '[T]his is our year', he declares. 'It's now or never.'

13A GIORNATA

Ascoli 0-1 Milan
Atalanta 0-0 Torino
Avellino 1-0 Lazio
Como 0-0 Verona
Inter 2-0 Sampdoria
Juventus 2-0 Napoli
Roma 3-2 Cremonese
Udinese 2-2 Fiorentina

CLASSIFICA

Verona	**21**
Inter	19
Torino	19
Sampdoria	17
Roma	16
Milan	15
Juventus	14
Fiorentina	13
Atalanta	13
Avellino	12
Como	11
Udinese	9
Lazio	9
Napoli	9
Ascoli	7
Cremonese	4

14a Giornata

6 January 1985

IN ITALIAN folklore, the Befana is an old witch who delivers gifts to children on the eve of the Epiphany. While the Epiphany is an unashamedly Christian celebration, primarily commemorating the visit of the Magi to the Christ child, the Befana is a pagan-like figure linked with the nativity story. According to the traditional retelling of the myth, soon after the Star of Bethlehem appeared in the night sky, a humble housekeeper (the Befana) was visited by the Three Wise Men, who had lost their way trying to find the stable in Bethlehem to visit the baby Jesus. They asked the housekeeper for directions and even invited her to join them on their sacred journey but she was too busy working and declined the offer. She would come to regret her decision and pursued the Wise Men with her broom and a basket of gifts for the holy child. But she would never find them and her search for the Christ child has continued ever since, flying on a broomstick and slipping down chimneys and into the homes of sleeping children. With ember eyes, sharp feline teeth, a cutting tongue and a sooty face from the chimneys she descends, she wears rags and a headscarf and carries a sack full of gifts – toys or sweets for the good children, cinder or coal for the naughty ones. The Befana is shy and rather grumpy, and doesn't like to be disturbed, so children should avoid being seen by her.

In 1977, the Italian government, in an attempt to stimulate a flagging economy, cancelled Epiphany as a national public holiday. The move didn't go down well and most Italians continued to celebrate the holiday anyway, calling in sick from work or school or simply not showing up. For the children of Verona, the Befana evokes a strange combination of hope and fear. Hope that their dreams will be fulfilled. Fear that they may not. For fans of Hellas Verona in 1985, the new year brings that exhilarating fusion of emotions as we approach the midway point in the season and the dreams of the past turn into the fears of the future.

On 6 January, after a month's absence (Verona's last home game was against AC Milan on 2 December), football finally returns to the Bentegodi. In the build-up to the game, Bagnoli is asked whether he thinks his players have indulged too much during the Christmas break, appearing on *Pronto, Raffaella?*, a daytime talk show hosted by Raffaella Carrà, 'the queen of Italian television', then on *Sport Sette*, a light-entertainment sports programme, then on Canale 5 for Christmas carols and, finally, suffering a humiliating defeat, albeit in a friendly, against Serie B side Padova, before finally escaping to the mountains. The philosopher coach dismisses such talk, insisting to the *Corriere della Sera* that he is more concerned about the degree of praise coming his team's way – 'Verona the best team of 1984, Di Gennaro at the top of certain rankings, Garella the best of the Italians, Bagnoli a magician ...' – before pointing out that his team still haven't won anything. That may be true but they are certainly on the brink of something spectacular. The only problem is the evidence which points towards the 'spectacular' being a collapse in the second half of the season.

There is an argument that Bagnoli's teams tend to earn fewer points in the second half of the season. It is certainly true that in his first season with Hellas in Serie A, they dropped from second to fourth place. But, then again, they also reached the final of the Coppa Italia, losing in Turin against Juventus. It is also certainly true that Verona's recent form has been far from spectacular. Three of their last five games ended in goalless draws, with narrow victories against Torino and Lazio, not to mention that 5-0 humiliation in the friendly against Padova. Could the bubble be about to burst?

At this midway point in the season, a victory against Atalanta today would seal Verona's place as 'winter champions' and silence some of the critics who are beginning to cast doubt on the Bagnoli project. Bagnoli, himself, admits that such an achievement exceeds even the rosiest pre-season predictions. With characteristic modesty, the credit, he insists, rests entirely with his players.

Like Hellas, Atalanta owe their name to the ancient Greeks. Atalanta, in Greek mythology, was a renowned and fleet-footed huntress and it is her image that adorns the club's jersey. They have experienced a turbulent few years, plunging to the third tier in 1981, before bouncing straight back as champions of Serie C1 in 1982. The Bergamo club then spent a season in the second tier before earning promotion in 1984 as Champions of Serie B. Like Lazio, Atalanta lack strength in depth but, in a midfielder named Roberto Donadoni, they have nurtured a promising young talent for which the football club would one day become synonymous.[49]

In the summer of 1984, Atalanta sought to strengthen their squad with the arrival of experienced players from AC Milan (goalkeeper Ottorino Piotti), Avellino (Carlo Osti) and Sweden (Glenn Peter Strömberg and Lars Larsson). The famous *Nerazzurri* academy is also beginning to churn out talented players like Marco Pacione, Marino Magrin and Donadoni. Atalanta also have two ex-Hellas players in the shape of defender Carmine Gentile (88 appearances and two goals for Hellas Verona) and midfielder Sauro Fattori (28 games and four goals in *gialloblù*). Humiliating defeats on the road, against Juventus (5-1) and Fiorentina (5-0), in the opening phase of the championship have given way to a degree of consistency that has seen *La Dea* go unbeaten all season at Bergamo's Stadio Comunale. It is an unexceptional squad (with the exception, perhaps, of young Donadoni) but Atalanta have

---

49 Roberto Donadoni would make 123 appearances for Atalanta before joining Milan in 1986 for ten billion lire. He would go on to win six *Scudetti* and three European Cups with the Milan giants and feature in two World Cups (1990 and 1994).

enjoyed victories against Cremonese, Napoli and Lazio and taken hard-earned points from, amongst others, Inter, Roma, AC Milan and Torino. Eight points now separate the two teams and, if Verona are to silence their critics and confirm their status as serious title contenders at the midway point in the season, this is a game Hellas are expected to win. But, with 13 points on the board, Atalanta are no pushover.

For Hellas, Ferroni and Elkjær remain on the sidelines. Volpati is deployed at right-back, with a formidable-looking midfield composed of Bruni, Di Gennaro, Sacchetti and Briegel, while Fanna plays alongside Galderisi up top. Though the sun is shining, dappling the east stand in pleasant winter sunshine, it's bitterly cold in Verona as a minute's silence is observed ahead of kick-off for the victims of the terrorist attack on the Naples–Milan train.[50] On a compact murky brown playing surface, Atalanta start brightly, earning four corners in quick succession, but with little concrete to show for their efforts. Gradually, Hellas begin to impose themselves, dusting off any lingering Christmas cobwebs, dominating midfield and creating a string of chances for Fanna, Di Gennaro and Galderisi.

With ten minutes remaining of the first half, Hellas take a well-deserved lead – a shot drilled low and hard from distance by Bruni for his first (and only) goal of the season. In the second half, Atalanta push for an equaliser. They may lack world class talent but, in Roberto Soldà, they have an offensive-minded *libero* and a hard-working midfield that covers miles without ever stopping. Nine minutes into the second half, Donadoni enters. And, with five minutes remaining, it's the talented youngster who provides the spark that ignites the Atalanta comeback, as Stromberg and Pacione combine and Garella is, for once, slow and awkward as he sprawls helplessly in the mud; 1-1.

With just a few minutes remaining, Soldà ends up on the deck in a seemingly innocuous off-the-ball incident. The

---

50 As the search for the perpetrators continues, the death toll has reached 16.

linesman steps in and, in the general confusion that follows, both Galderisi and the Atalanta defender are sent off. For his involvement in the incident, Galderisi can expect little but coal from the Befana and for Hellas it seems that the illusion of a team capable of winning the championship may well have burst. With two consecutive draws, one either side of new year, the sceptics are circling. A well-earned point for Atalanta. For Verona, cause for concern?

While Bruni has orchestrated things well in midfield and contributed a wonderful goal, Briegel and Fanna both have off days. The prolonged absence of Elkjær and Ferroni is not helping. Tino Guidetti, Verona's usually chipper president, is not happy with the result, telling the *Corriere della Sera*: '[M]aybe the cold affected our players. The fact is that they didn't play as usual. We threw away a truly golden opportunity. We were too naive.' Then someone reminds him that Verona are still clear at the top of the table and he rediscovers his habitual smile.

Elsewhere on matchday 14, Inter and Roma contest a goalless draw and it's also honours even between Sampdoria and Juventus (1-1) and Torino and Fiorentina (2-2). In that eagerly awaited face-off between Junior (Torino) and Sócrates (Fiorentina), Junior responded better to the freezing temperatures (which rose from minus 11 degrees Celsius in the morning to minus five by kick-off), crowning an outstanding performance with a well-taken penalty. Sócrates, having just returned from the smouldering heat of Rio de Janeiro, continues to disappoint and is substituted midway through the second half. Meanwhile, Lazio's encounter with AC Milan is postponed, the victim of freezing temperatures and heavy snowfall in the capital. In short, none of the chasing pack have been able to capitalise on Verona's dropped point.

Verona look fragmented, fragile and predictable. The absence of key players? A Christmas hangover? Unrealistic expectations? They haven't won at the Bentegodi since 28 October. Has the bubble finally burst? With two tricky away trips to come (against Avellino and Napoli), Hellas wouldn't be the first outsider to experience a winter collapse. Despite taking just two points from Como and Atalanta, it isn't time to panic but is, perhaps, a moment to re-evaluate what is possible. Hellas remain unbeaten and are still two points clear of Torino and Inter. But, with hungry predators from the media and the footballing establishment circling, can the hope of a city that is finally daring to dream overcome the fear that success is merely illusory?

14A GIORNATA

Como 2-1 Avellino
Cremonese 2-0 Ascoli
Inter 0-0 Roma
Lazio 0-1 Milan
Napoli 4-3 Udinese
Sampdoria 1-1 Juventus
Torino 2-2 Fiorentina
Verona 1-1 Atalanta

CLASSIFICA

Verona	**22**
Torino	20
Inter	20
Sampdoria	18
Roma	17
Milan	17
Juventus	15
Fiorentina	14
Atalanta	14
Como	13
Avellino	12
Napoli	11
Udinese	9
Lazio	9
Ascoli	7
Cremonese	6

15a Giornata

13 January 1985

THE 6.9 magnitude earthquake struck at 7.34pm on Sunday, 23 November 1980. The first violent shock was followed by 90 devastating aftershocks that left 2,483 dead (including 27 children in the orphanage of Sant'Angelo dei Lombardi), at least 7,700 injured and 250,000 homeless. In nearby Balvano, 100 worshippers were killed when a medieval church collapsed during Sunday Mass. Fifty-nine trillion lire (equivalent to €151bn in 2020) was spent on reconstruction and international aid arrived from West Germany ($32m) and the United States ($70m). Much of it would be siphoned off by the Camorra, the powerful organised crime group which decided that this was the right time to enter the construction industry. By early 1985, the wounds, physical and mental, were still healing and the landscape remains scarred, though Avellino itself was now a modern and largely rebuilt city and the football team had done more than their fair share in that rebuilding and recovery process. In fact, the devastating earthquake coincided with a golden age for US Avellino 1912 under the presidency of the entrepreneur and politician, Arcangelo Iapicca, and the technical guidance of coach Paolo Carosi. From promotion to Serie A in 1978 to relegation to Serie B in 1988, no team in southern Italy (apart from Napoli) has spent longer in Serie A.

Small and compact, the Stadio Partenio could nonetheless be an extremely intimidating place to play. Of 150 games played there in that ten-year spell in Serie A, Avellino won 63, drew 60 and lost just 27, scoring 172 goals and conceding 110. AC Milan played there eight times in that period, drew three and lost five, with other upsets involving Juventus and Inter.

The renowned Italian journalist Gianni Brera described the Avellino of the 1980s to *Domenica Sportiva* in this way: '[T]here is a team in Italy that plays like Brazil, with the scent of authentic food and fields in bloom. A team, however, that is not Brazilian; it is called Avellino. This team plays football masterfully, without feeling inferior to anyone and without showing any boastful sense of superiority. Humble and hard-working, and at the same time noble, as only true aristocrats can be. This team, Avellino, is the most beautiful provincial football team in Italian history.'

Ahead of Verona's visit in January 1985, journalists at the *Corriere della Sera* – perhaps with too much time on their hands as they speculate whether the game will go ahead or not – have been testing a theory that larger players are more comfortable on heavy pitches. With this in mind, and with the help of data provided by the *Almanacco del calcio* published by Panini, they have calculated the average weight of each team in Serie A. With Hellas Verona weighing in as the heaviest squad in Serie A (averaging 74.8kg or around 11st 11lb a player), Roma are the lightest (just 71.7kg or around 11st 4lb a player). Verona's superiority in this department owes much to the imposing bulk of Briegel. Weighing in at 92kg (roughly 14st 7lb), the athletic German is the biggest player in the league. To anyone who has seen him in action this season, it is obvious that '*il Panzer*' barely carries an ounce of fat on his towering Teutonic frame. While it's an interesting theory that covers a few column inches, there must surely be more relevant factors behind Verona's success this season!

In Avellino, snow shovellers have been working for two days to clear the pitch, which until Thursday was covered in more than 60cm of snow. All week, Italy has been shivering in arctic conditions, with temperatures in Florence plummeting to a bone-chilling minus 23 degrees Celsius. With the symbolic title of 'winter champions' at stake, the pitch, it goes without saying, is in a terrible condition. The snow has been cleared but rising temperatures have turned the surface into a vast muddy brown bog. To make matters worse, Bagnoli has a depleted squad of just 14 to choose from, with Ferroni and Elkjær both still out with injury. Galderisi is suspended after his red card the previous weekend and even the young midfielder Antonio Terracciano is unavailable.[51] Without a recognised striker, Bagnoli has to completely re-invent his attack, opting for Fanna and Turchetta up front. On top of the injuries, Verona have an abysmal record at the Stadio Pertenio. They have played in Avellino four times in Serie A and lost on all four occasions, conceding eight goals and scoring only one. The Argentine striker Ramon Angel Diaz and local boy Fernando De Napoli, a product of the Avellino academy and destined to become a pillar of Maradona's Napoli and the Italian national team, are the biggest threats in the Avellino team.[52]

Avellino dominate the early exchanges and, with 32 minutes on the clock, the hosts take a well-deserved lead thanks to an unfortunate deflection off Volpati from a Diaz shot. This seems to be the wake-up call Verona need. Just a few minutes later, Sacchetti sets up Di Gennaro but his shot is lopsided. Barely two minutes later, however, and the *Gialloblù* equalise. Bruni plays a speculative ball into the area and the green and white defence is static as Luciano Marangon arrives first and scores. It's a rare goal for the defender, another of the unsung heroes of the Hellas Verona team.

An unsung hero maybe but Marangon also has a certain reputation as a womaniser with a taste for the high life.

---

51 Terracciano would have to wait until 1987 to make his debut in Serie A (on 20 September 1987 against Avellino). In his first season in Serie A (1987/88), he made 11 appearances in the championship, which rose to 15 the following year. He would spend the remainder of his career alternating between Serie B and Serie C1, for clubs such as Triestina, Capri and Mantova. His son, Filippo Terracciano, made 39 appearances for Hellas Verona between 2021 and 2024 before being signed by AC Milan in January 2024 for €4.5 million. At the time of writing, the versatile 21-year-old midfielder has made six Serie A appearances for Milan.

52 A regular in the Napoli team that won four major trophies in four seasons between 1986 and 1990, Fernando De Napoli won another *Scudetto* with AC Milan as well as the Super Coppa and the UEFA Champions League.

'Everyone thinks I'm a playboy. Who knows why they gave me this fame? Maybe because I'm separated but for four years I've been in a relationship with a dear Neapolitan girl and I'm getting married again soon,' he explained to the *Corriere della Sera*. He came close to winning the *Scudetto* with Napoli in 1981. With just five games to go, they were clear favourites for the title but on 26 April, they suffered an unexpected home defeat against an already relegated Perugia. In the end, they had to settle for third place behind Juventus and Roma, who fought out a bitter battle until the end, the recriminations of which would rumble on for decades to come. Marangon then signed for rivals Roma, where he made 26 appearances before joining Hellas in 1982. Despite his off-pitch reputation, on it Marangon brings a steely determination and drive, forming the perfect counterpoint to Pierino Fanna's flair on the opposite flank. In his first two seasons in Verona, Marangon made 53 Serie A appearances without finding the net. Now, midway through his third season, Verona's Casanova has finally scored!

In the second half, Avellino continue to dominate and create several chances, twice hitting the woodwork. Six minutes from the end, just as Verona think they might escape with a draw, substitute Angelo Colombo ('*il Rummenigge della Brianza*') unleashes an incredible shot ('*il colpo della Domenica*') from 40 yards that leaves Garella stationary as it flies into the top corner. With just minutes remaining, Hellas are unable to respond, shocked it seems by the realisation that a 14-game unbeaten run is finally coming to an end.

Avellino's Peruvian winger Geronimo Barbadillo is undoubtedly the man of the match, though questions must be asked about whether Fontolan was the best choice to mark him. Angelo Colomba (even though he only played for one half) has clearly won his duel with Di Gennaro, while Ramon Angel Diaz, recovering from a strain, and the young Fernando De Napoli also perform well. For Verona, it is a disappointing performance and result. In a usually dependable midfield, only Bruni can claim pass marks, while Briegel seemed to struggle in the heavy conditions. Although Garella was hardly at fault for either goal, he will be disappointed to have conceded twice. Up front, while Fanna was willing, Turchetta was almost non-existent.

On the day, Avellino were simply the better team and Bagnoli concedes as much in his post-match remarks: '[T]he home team won because they fought with greater conviction and determination.' The conditions played a part and Hellas were once again without three key players but Bagnoli is never one to make excuses: '[O]f course, the pitch was very heavy but this fact does not in any way diminish the victory of Avellino who, in any case, played on the same pitch and in the same conditions.' Fanna admits to having struggled on the heavy pitch: '[W]e suffered a lot from the conditions but, on top of that, there were also the absences of three regulars.'

For Garella, it's the first time all season he has conceded more than a single goal: '[I]t's too early to talk about the championship. For now we just have to forget, and quickly, this defeat that shattered our invincibility and we have to react, starting next Sunday against Maradona's Napoli.'

Elsewhere, Torino lose to Roma at the Olimpico, thanks to a Roberto Pruzzo goal, AC Milan are beaten by Como at the San Siro, while Inter draw against Ascoli. So, despite the defeat, Hellas are crowned 'winter champions'. For an unfancied provincial club, it is a genuinely historical moment. Twenty-two points – eight wins, six draws and only one loss. As well as the most points on the board, Hellas Verona also have the best defensive record in the championship, with just seven conceded.

For those fans who have made the long trip south, the journey home in treacherous snowy conditions provides the opportunity to reflect on the significance of today's results. For Emiliano Mascetti, Verona's general manager, there isn't even time for that; the flight from Avellino is an adventure in itself, as the aeroplane carrying the team eventually lands in Verona at two o'clock the following morning.

With just two points from the last three games and a daunting away trip to Napoli to come, Bagnoli's men are experiencing their first major crisis of the season. If it's any consolation, the team leading at this point in the season has won the *Scudetto* 12 times in the last 17 seasons. Furthermore, Inter have failed to fully capitalise on Verona's slump, although they have moved to within a point of the league leaders for the first time since matchday two. Torino have also failed to take advantage, losing to Roma, and remain two points adrift. Roma, on the other hand, are the ones to watch, having reduced the gap at the top from seven points two months ago to just three at the midway point in the season. For Verona, being crowned 'winter champions' is a seismic achievement. The greatest in the club's history. But brace yourself. There are aftershocks on the way.

15A GIORNATA

Ascoli 1-1 Inter
Atalanta 0-0 Sampdoria
Avellino 2-1 Verona
Fiorentina 0-1 Napoli
Juventus 1-0 Lazio
Milan 0-2 Como
Roma 1-0 Torino
Udinese 2-0 Cremonese

CLASSIFICA

Verona*	**22**
Inter	21
Torino	20
Sampdoria	19
Roma	19
Milan	17
Juventus	17
Atalanta	15
Como	15
Fiorentina	14
Avellino	14
Napoli	13
Udinese	11
Lazio	9
Ascoli	8
Cremonese	6

'Winter champions'

16a Giornata

20 January 1985

ON TUESDAY, 15 January 1984, something extremely unusual happens in Verona. It snows! A thick white blanket covers the city and the outlying areas, slowing traffic and delaying trains. The city's airport is shut down and schools and offices are closed. Snowploughs are deployed and the city's fleet of buses are fitted with snow chains as thousands of tons of salt are spread over the cobbled streets and pathways. Children are seen skiing across Piazza Brà, as mounds of snow are piled up on verges and roadsides. Arctic conditions prevail for the rest of the week as the players do their best to train in sub-zero temperatures on snow-covered pitches, while fans contemplate the long, perilous journey south to face Maradona's Napoli.

As the cold snap continues, the vexed question of whether Italy should introduce a winter shutdown is rehashed in the media. Tino Guidotti, president of Verona, is sympathetic to the idea, telling *Corriere della Sera*: 'I approve of the proposal. I think it makes a lot of sense and our league must consider it seriously.'

Last Sunday afternoon, despite the intense cold, a small crowd had gathered at Piazza Brà to listen to the unmistakable voice of Roberto Puliero from the loudspeakers on the balcony of the studios of Radio Adige. With his harmonious blend of the Venetian dialect and the euphoria of a Brazilian radio commentator, his live commentary is as close as many fans will get when the game is being played 700km away at the other end of the peninsula. For once, when Avellino retook the lead in the 84th minute, even Puliero was lost for words. Within minutes Piazza Brà emptied, as a thousand dreams suddenly evaporated into the night.

All week, the pressure has been mounting as newspapers and commentators rush to declare the Hellas 'miracle' is over. Emiliano Mascetti, Verona's general manager, acknowledged as much in his comments to the press earlier in the week: '[W]ell, at least with this defeat we have made many people happy. For some time now, every Saturday, even in the newspapers, they have been preparing our funeral.' As Hellas prepare for a second trip south in the space of just a week, it is worth remembering that the shadow of Vesuvius is not a happy hunting ground for Hellas Verona, with defeats the previous season on the road at Napoli and Avellino, and the first defeat of the current season coming at Avellino. Waiting in the wings to capitalise on Verona's apparent dip in form are an Inter team that contains half the Italian national side, plus Rummenigge, and the smart money is now moving decisively in that direction. After a slow start, Juventus are finally beginning to gain some momentum, spurred on by a morale-boosting victory against Liverpool in the European Super Cup.[53] Despite having a strong-looking squad to choose from, AC Milan still haven't found their best form, hampered by the absence through injury of their talismanic English striker, Mark Hateley. The Fiorentina of Passarella and Sócrates lack depth and consistency, while Maradona's moment at Napoli has not yet arrived. Roma are now performing well but, with a young and inexperienced coach in Sven-Göran Eriksson, few expect them to make a serious title challenge this season. Verona have put on a good show but, alongside Torino and Sampdoria, they don't have what it takes to win a championship. That, at least, is the conventional wisdom.

---

53 The UEFA Super Cup was played on 16 January 1985 at the Stadio Comunale in Turin between Liverpool, winners of the 1983/84 European Cup, and Juventus, holders of the 1983/84 Cup Winners' Cup. Juventus won 2-0 thanks to a brace from Boniek, the first time an Italian club had ever won the cup.

In Napoli, too, the tension has been building all week. Captain Giuseppe Bruscolotti, sent off in September at the Bentegodi, has spoken of revenge. Maradona has referred to unpleasant memories that must be erased. On the eve of the match, Bagnoli leaves the team's hotel in Napoli to buy a newspaper and encounters a group of irate Napoli fans who reproached him 'for what we did in Verona'. The coach protests: '[I]n Verona, we only won. We didn't do anything else.'

Despite the freezing conditions the match goes ahead. The San Paolo is packed. Eighty thousand expectant fans, in a marine blue that matches the churning Gulf of Naples, singing in unison: '*Oi vita, oi vita mia!*' No one parties like the Neapolitans! But, hovering just above the relegation zone, they have little to celebrate. With an ageing, mediocre squad, Napoli are not yet a team to fear. After losing to Verona in the opening game of the campaign, their season has lurched from one disappointment to the next, with defeats against Torino, Atalanta, Inter, Roma and Juventus. In fact, they are only now finding their best form of the season, with back-to-back wins against Udinese and Fiorentina, their only other victories this season coming against Como and Cremonese.

For Verona, playing in their all-yellow away kit, Ferroni and Elkjær are still only deemed fit enough to be on the bench, once again limiting Bagnoli's options in defence and, more importantly, up front. But at least Galderisi is back. Once again, the big question is who will mark Maradona. With Briegel being given licence to roam, Bagnoli has suggested that the task will fall to someone else this time (or is this just more *pretattica* from the wily coach?)

On a turgid and muddy pitch that is cutting up badly, the first 20 minutes are played out in midfield. Both teams are understandably cautious, neither wishing to risk losing ground in the standings. Then, in the 21st minute, Fanna crosses for Galderisi, who beats Castellini from close range. Goal! But the cries of offside are immediate and spontaneous and the referee is quick to concur, leaving Galderisi to throw punches in the mud.

Napoli respond immediately with an attack of their own. Bertoni plays a nice one-two with Caffarelli, who deftly pokes the ball past the on-rushing Garella. But once again the linesman is quick to raise his flag for offside and the referee has no choice but to disallow the goal. The first half ends with a strike from Walter De Vecchi that grazes the post. With neither side mastering the appalling conditions, it's finely balanced as the referee blows his whistle for half-time.

In the second half, Bagnoli demands more from his team, while Maradona is once again neutralised by Briegel and Tricella. It turns out that Bagnoli was bluffing when he said that Briegel wouldn't be marking Maradona – once again, the big German has relished the task. As Fanna comes close, Verona look composed, confident and solid, creating several decent chances in the murky conditions. But, with barely ten minutes of the second half played and with Napoli still thirsting for revenge, the Hellas midfield begins to wilt. The hosts sense an opening and begin to apply some pressure of their own.

With Roma now ahead at Avellino, Inter winning at Atalanta and Juve also in front at Como, a defeat now could change the course of Verona's season. It's at this point that Garella emerges, once again, as the star of the show. In the 59th minute, he performs a miracle to deny Maradona from a free kick. Two minutes later, Paolo Dal Fiume tries from distance but Garella is once again on the ball. In the 64th minute, in an attempt to break the *Azzurri* siege, Bagnoli introduces Elkjær in place of Di Gennaro, who is struggling in the heavy conditions. The Dane takes his place in attack alongside Galderisi, leaving Bruni in the playmaker's role, but the Dane lacks match sharpness and fails to make an impact. His mere presence, however, is enough to give his team-mates a boost and his opponents pause for thought.

Then, with 11 minutes remaining, comes the decisive moment of the match. Referee Pairetto blows for a foul by Briegel on Maradona. The position isn't ideal. Central, yes, but fully 30 muddy metres from Garella's goal. In an instant, the entire crowd is on its feet chanting Maradona's name. The stocky Argentine grasps the ball, as if there is any doubt that he'd be taking it, and places it carefully on the indicated spot. Deep in concentration, he takes a long run-up and strikes hard with his left foot. The ball thunders over the wall and dips ferociously towards the top corner. But, as it hurtles towards goal, Garella also begins to fly. He extends his left arm, reaches out with a finger and somehow tips the ball over the crossbar. Another remarkable save from a keeper who is enjoying the form of his life. Final score: Napoli 0 Garella 0.

Post-match, Bagnoli is uncharacteristically dapper in an overcoat, check jacket and matching tie and handkerchief combo, offset by his trademark baker boy hat – a nod to his working class roots. In his caustic remarks, he is his usual stubborn and contrary self, as he robustly plays down Garella's performance. Bagnoli doesn't like superstars. For him, football is a team game. With a goal apiece ruled out for offside, a draw at the San Paolo against Maradona's Napoli is a good result for Verona. The other positive for Hellas is the return of Elkjær. Although still clearly lacking match sharpness, his mere presence was enough to alter Napoli's approach to the game. Briegel, perhaps lacking the linguistic skills to be more nuanced, tells the *Corriere della Sera*: 'Verona played well and next Sunday we will be alone in the lead again, because we will play at home, while Inter will play away. Napoli has improved a lot compared to the first leg but Maradona, he only took the two free kicks.' As for Maradona, it was another difficult result to accept: '[A] well-prepared team [Hellas Verona] but Inter are stronger. There's not nine points' difference between Napoli and Verona.'

Meanwhile, in Udine, at a bitterly cold Stadio Friuli, a 16-year-old defender makes his debut for AC Milan as a second-half substitute. It will prove to be the first of 902 appearances by Paolo Maldini for the club he will lead into one of the most successful periods in its history. But that is in the future. Today, the Milan giants have to settle for a 1-1 draw.

Elsewhere, Inter narrowly beat Atalanta, while Torino can only manage a draw against Ascoli. Roma beat Avellino thanks to a Roberto Pruzzo penalty, while Sampdoria fall one point behind the chasing group, drawing in Cremona. For the first time all season, Verona's lead at the top of the table comes down to goal difference, as Inter, ominously, draw level on 23 points.

While the Verona players and fans are making the long journey home from Napoli, 7,000km miles away in a private ceremony in the North Entrance Hall of the White House, US president Ronald Wilson Reagan is being sworn in for the second time as temperatures in Washington plummet to a blistering minus 32 degrees Celsius.

For Verona, the winter campaign in the south is over. They are no longer alone at the top of the table. Next week, Bagnoli's men will finally return to the Bentegodi to host Ascoli, a surmountable adversary, while their closest rivals, the *Nerazzurri*, face a tricky trip to Avellino.

16A GIORNATA

Ascoli 2-2 Torino
Cremonese 1-1 Sampdoria
Fiorentina 3-0 Lazio
Inter 1-0 Atalanta
Juventus 2-0 Como
Napoli 0-0 Verona
Roma 1-0 Avellino
Udinese 1-1 Milan

CLASSIFICA

Verona	**23**
Inter	23
Roma	21
Torino	21
Sampdoria	20
Juventus	19
Milan	18
Fiorentina	16
Atalanta	15
Como	15
Napoli	14
Avellino	14
Udinese	12
Ascoli	9
Lazio	9
Cremonese	7

17a Giornata

27 January 1985

'BAGNOLI, WHAT do you think of Dirceu?' That infamous grimace cracks across the coach's face. It's summer 1982, Hellas Verona have just been promoted and the board is considering a range of options to strengthen the squad ahead of the new season in Serie A. Most coaches would be delighted by the prospect of working with a bona fide Brazilian legend but that grimace suggests that Bagnoli is less convinced. In fact, he has already promised that role to someone else and, for the principled coach, his word is his bond.

Francesco 'Guido' Guidolin was the captain of the Hellas team that had just earned promotion with Bagnoli and the loyal coach had no reason to discard him at this point. Serious, humble and tactically intelligent, Guido is a team player, not unlike Bagnoli himself. 'So where would I play him?' the coach responds bluntly to the enquiry about Dirceu. 'I've already got Guido.'

What Bagnoli really wanted was a striker. But he wasn't involved in the decision to bring Dirceu to Verona. 'The team is already assembled and the role is already filled,' he explained to the *Corriere della Sera*, 'but, if you want to give him to me as a gift, I'll take him.' Speaking many years later to the *Cronaca di Verona*, Guidolin, now a football pundit and commentator after a long managerial career, remembers Bagnoli's loyalty: 'When I read those words, I understood how great Bagnoli was but not because they were about me. Because that was the sense of the team, it was a message that had a meaning for everyone: the group always comes first. He knew that Dirceu was infinitely better than me but first of all came respect, gratitude, recognition for his players. It's a lesson I will never forget.'

Back in that balmy summer of 1982, as peace was returning to a remote archipelago in the South Atlantic Ocean[54] and Hellas Verona were contemplating life in Serie A, Bagnoli's team were on retreat at the Hotel Los Andes in Castello, a typical mountain village in the Val di Fiemme, one of the principal valleys of the Dolomites.[55] That summer, the squad had already been boosted by the arrival of Pierino Fanna, Domenico Volpati, Luigi Sacchetti and Luciano Marangon. Despite Bagnoli's reservations, Dirceu was another new face at the summer *ritiro* that year, replacing Francesco Guidolin, who was on his way to Bologna.

After his performances at the 1978 World Cup, Dirceu was considered one of the top players in the world. In 1979, he signed for Atlético Madrid, where he made 82 appearances and scored 26 goals in three seasons, before joining Hellas Verona at the age of 30. He may not have been Bagnoli's choice but his eye-catching signing led to a sharp spike in season ticket sales. Two thousand fans even turned out to welcome him to his first training session on the back pitches behind the Bentegodi.

In the 1982/83 season, Hellas Verona surprised everyone. Seemingly unaffected by the leap in category and thanks in no small part to the acquisition of experienced match-winning players such as Fanna and Dirceu, the *Gialloblù* took Serie A by storm. The Brazilian midfielder made an impressive 47 appearances in his first season in Italy, including ten starts in a run that would see Hellas reach the final of the Coppa Italia. Every time he touched the ball, the stadium rose to its feet in expectation. Aside from the Brazilian, one other player stood out as the goalscoring protagonist of Verona's resurgence under

---

54 On 2 April 1982, Argentine military forces invaded the islands known in Spanish as Islas Malvinas. On 14 June, the Argentines surrendered, and British governance was once again restored to the Falkland Islands.

55 It is typical for Italian football teams to spend part of the summer break in *ritiro* (retreat) in the mountains where the air is fresh, the temperatures are mild and the possibilities for mischief are limited.

Bagnoli in the 1982/83 season – Domenico Penzo, who scored 22 goals, 15 in the championship and seven more in the Coppa Italia. Fans obviously liked what they saw, as average gates that season surged to more than 31,000.

After a memorable 2-1 victory against Juventus on matchday three (with goals from Fanna and Tricella), Hellas went on a 17-game unbeaten run that ended in late February with a deflating 3-0 thrashing away to Avellino (the southerners would become something of a bogey team for Hellas). Despite that chastening slip-up, it was the kind of form that demonstrated that Bagnoli's team could compete at the very top of the Italian game. In the end, Verona finished in fourth place to earn, for the first time in the club's history, a coveted spot in the UEFA Cup. In fact, the 1982/83 campaign could have ended even better. As the season was reaching its climax, Hellas were just a single point behind Inter and two behind Juve. With a little more self belief and composure, they might even have mounted a serious challenge for the championship. But, with narrow away defeats at Catanzaro and Cagliari in March, it wasn't to be. A fourth-place finish in Serie A, though, was still an impressive achievement for a newly promoted club and Verona's best-ever finish.

The cup run also ended in disappointment, losing in the final to Juventus. Verona went 2-0 ahead at the Bentegodi, with goals from Penzo and Volpati. A third was ruled out in dubious circumstances as a number of fans, perhaps prematurely, invaded the pitch as the final whistle sounded. In the return leg three days later at Torino's Stadio Olimpico, it was Juventus who dominated. Paolo Rossi opened the scoring after just eight minutes but the Turin giants just couldn't consolidate their lead. Newly promoted Hellas were just ten minutes away from an historic cup final victory! Then, with just nine minutes remaining, Michel Platini grabbed a late second to take the tie into extra time. Deep into the additional period, with penalties looming, it was the Frenchman who snuck in at the back post for a last-minute winner that broke Veronese hearts. That cup final would mark the end of the line for some of Verona's most influential players. That summer, Dirceu moved to Napoli, Domenico Penzo[56] to Juventus and Emidio Oddi, a tough and underrated full-back, to Roma. On the other hand, Giuseppe Galderisi, who had already won two championships as well as that disputed cup final with Juventus, would soon be heading in the opposite direction.

Today, Dirceu, one of the protagonists of that season, returns to Verona in the black and white of Ascoli. It's not quite the hero's welcome you might expect. Dirceu is uncharacteristically angry and outspoken. The home fans will whistle mercilessly at him throughout the game but he expects that. They did the same last year when he was playing for Napoli. He had a fantastic season in Verona but, for him, those memories are tarnished by the brusque nature of his departure and the prolonged contractual dispute that now seems destined to end up before the courts. 'Verona was my first Italian team, my Italian first city,' he explains to the *Corriere della Sera* on the eve of the game, 'but it was also the first to betray me.'

And, so, there is a bitter undercurrent surrounding Dirceu's return to the Bentegodi today. The disgruntled Brazilian implies that the reason Bagnoli has been so incensed by all the attention Garella has been getting is because he doesn't like superstars in his team. 'As soon as a player rises above the others,' Dirceu says, 'Bagnoli gets angry. He talks about the collective all the time. He is a man who tends to crush the technical personality of the players. Can there ever be a coach

---

56 One of seven siblings, Domenico Penzo was born in Chioggia near Venice in 1953. His father was a fisherman and, after leaving school at the age of 14, Domenico worked as a carpenter, then a mechanic, before pursuing a career in football, eventually coming to the attention of Roma in 1974. He spent a few seasons in the lower leagues before helping Brescia secure promotion to Serie A in 1980. He joined Verona in 1981, a key component of the team that earned promotion in 1982, scoring 14 goals in 31 appearances. In the 1982/83 season, playing as a lone striker, he scored 15 goals in Serie A, just one behind Platini, who won the *Capocannoniere* title. In the Coppa Italia he scored seven times in 13 appearances, including a decisive goal against Milan in the quarter-final, and a goal in Verona's 2-0 home win in the first leg of the final against Juventus.

who gets angry because his goalkeeper saves everything? Well, there is – Bagnoli.' It's a crushing assessment by a former player but is there any truth in it? Or is this just another pre-match mind game or, worse, the bitter grievances of a jilted player?[57]

After last weekend's match against Napoli, prominent radio commentator Enrico Ameri attributed Verona's success to the undeniable heroics of Garella.[58] Bagnoli took exception to this characterisation and sought to play down Garella's overall impact on the game, insisting that it was an effective team performance and even suggesting that the goalkeeper would have had to have been asleep not to have saved a well-struck Maradona free kick. A bitter spat ensued, which inevitably resulted in one of those verbose and self-righteous statements issued by 'the fans', a leaflet with a headline that will become a mantra for the club: '*FORZA VERONA: Siamo soli contro tutti* (BE STRONG VERONA: We are alone against everyone).'

Adding to the pressure in the Verona camp is the growing feeling amongst commentators and pundits that the Verona bubble is about to burst. On the eve of the match, several national newspapers point out that in each of the last two seasons, Hellas have accumulated just 14 points in the second half of the campaign. To add to the sense of foreboding, Ferdinando Chiampan, the Canon executive bankrolling Verona's current renaissance, was involved in a serious car crash during the week and is expected to wear a plaster cast for 30 days.

In the modern game, Sir Alex Ferguson is considered the master of mind games but, in stoking up grievances with

---

57 After a single season with Verona, Dirceu went on to play for Napoli, Ascoli, Como and Avellino. He played in three World Cups for Brazil and earned 44 caps in an international career that spanned 13 years. Dirceu died in 1995 at the age of 43, the victim of a road traffic accident in Rio de Janeiro.

58 Ameri was an important Italian sports journalist and radio commentator, considered the heir of Nicolò Carosio, the official commentator of the Italian national team for over 30 years, who retired in 1971. Ameri was the leading voice on the popular radio show *Tutto il calcio minuto per minuto* from 1960 to 1991 and one of the most respected radio commentators in Italy.

the national media, perhaps Bagnoli is playing the same game. Creating a siege mentality, a collective state of mind in which the team believes itself to be under attack from external forces, can strengthen the sense of unity and foster a greater determination towards achieving a common goal. The 'us versus them' mentality can be particularly powerful in football, as most players thrive on a certain degree of confrontation. However, it is unsustainable in the longer term and can ultimately be counter-productive, as José Mourinho has discovered in recent years. Knowing when to go on the offensive and when to relent is crucial, as such a strategy can be mentally fatiguing and negate the personal or collective responsibility necessary for constant improvement at elite level. Whether it comes naturally to him or not, instigating a siege situation at this crucial juncture in the season has helped Bagnoli to get the best out of his team, emerging from a pivotal period in the season with the players galvanised, the fanbase activated and, most importantly, his team still top of the table.

Mind games or not, Claudio Garella has unquestionably been Verona's most important player so far this season. The charismatic goalkeeper has conceded just seven goals in 16 games, with several outstanding man of the match performances (most notably away to Roma and Napoli). At the glamorous coastal resort of Sanremo, the Verona keeper has just picked up an award for best goalkeeper of the season so far.

On the eve of the match, Dirceu is defiant: '[W]e lost ten games but we could have won nine. We will fight to the death again. I am convinced that we will save ourselves [from relegation].' To do so, Ascoli need to take points from Verona today. Since losing 3-1 to Hellas in the second game of the season, they haven't won a single match in the championship. After an appalling start in which they gathered just two points from seven games, coach Carlo Mazzone was fired and replaced by the Yugoslav Vujadin Boškov. They have, nonetheless, accumulated nine points thanks to a series of low-scoring draws, including against Torino, Inter, Juve and Napoli, but are still languishing deep in the relegation zone. Hellas, meanwhile, haven't won since 16 December against Lazio and need to get back into the habit of winning, as external voices continue to sow doubt in the camp.

At the Bentegodi, the playing surface has been covered with tarpaulins to provide some protection from the intermittent rain and snow, while earlier this morning groundstaff were out with shovels, doing their best to drain the worst patches of mud and sludge from the heavy pitch. Elsewhere, the ramifications of last week's arctic conditions are rumbling on, with Cremonese on the receiving end of a hefty 10m lire fine from the football authorities because one of their fans hit the referee with a snowball!

More than 30,000 expectant fans are now packed into the Bentegodi as kick-off approaches. Hellas, once again in their familiar blue with yellow pinstripes, are still without Ferroni and Elkjær, who take their places on the bench – more in hope than expectation. Meanwhile, Ascoli have packed their midfield and are playing with a lone striker, providing space for Verona's full-backs to exploit, while the undeniable class of their Brazilian midfielder gives Bagnoli something to think about as he delivers his brusque last-minute instructions.

In the 28th minute, Galderisi breaks the deadlock, reacting first to a rebound from a spectacular long-range Sacchetti effort that appeared to have crossed the line. Only minutes later, it's once again Sacchetti who seizes the initiative, stealing the ball from Dirceu as the Brazilian dithers inside his box and unleashing a right-footed shot to double the home side's lead. With playmaker Di Gennaro once again finding form, it is a dominant Verona who could be three or four up by the interval. While Briegel is back to his assertive best, combining well with Galderisi and Di Gennaro, Garella is a distant observer for large swathes of the match, protected as ever by the imperious marshalling of Roberto Tricella. Bruni puts in a solid performance that demonstrates his growing maturity, while Sacchetti, deputising for Elkjær, has put aside the injury troubles that kept him on the sidelines for so long.

In short, Verona, like a well-oiled machine, are back to their fluid, direct, offensive best.

To crown a morale-boosting performance, the 79th minute sees the long-awaited return of ex-Sampdoria defender Mauro Ferroni after two and a half months on the sidelines. The popular player is greeted with rapturous applause as Briegel makes way. But the near-frozen turf is unforgiving and, after his first sprint, Mauro freezes. The entire bench stands up as one and Bagnoli reels off a series of muttered expletives as the masseur rushes on to tend to the stricken defender. Ferroni's comeback has lasted barely 180 seconds!

Finally, a clear and convincing victory, two goals, two points and a clean sheet. Remarkably, it's Verona's first win since 16 December. The only cloud for Verona is the recurrence of the injury to Ferroni. With another international break scheduled next week, at least the unfortunate defender has time to recover.

Post-match, Bagnoli speaks of using the 15-day break to 'detoxify' – a veiled reference to the negativity that has been circulating in recent weeks and, perhaps, an indication that the 'siege' around his team is now being lifted. While Bagnoli takes flight, leaving a throng of bewildered journalists in his midst – heading to the mountains with his wife – his senior players, Di Gennaro, Fanna, Garella and Tricella, reiterate the message that the siege is over – that normal service has been resumed. The resounding victory and convincing performance against Ascoli have repelled the negativity that has engulfed the club in recent weeks. As Pierino Fanna explains: '[I]t's no use disguising it. If we hadn't won against Ascoli, we would have had to say goodbye to certain dreams.' With two points and supremacy restored, the veil of pressure has lifted.

Elsewhere, Inter's goalless draw at the Partenio is disrupted by the bizarre spectacle of a German Shepherd entering the field of play and briefly bringing the game to a halt. Turin narrowly beat Cremonese (1-0), while Roma and Sampdoria are also involved in goalless draws, against Como and Napoli respectively. For Roma, their draw extends their unbeaten run to 12 games.

Hellas have survived the siege, the extreme cold and January's tricky run of fixtures. They have suffered and ground out hard-fought results in far-flung places. The winter isn't over and February will bring fresh challenges but Verona will face the coming battles with a renewed sense of unity and purpose. Their lead is narrow but they can no longer deny that they are serious title contenders. They must learn to cope with the added pressure that status brings.

17A GIORNATA

Atalanta 1-1 Juventus
Avellino 0-0 Inter
Como 0-0 Roma
Lazio 1-4 Udinese
Milan 1-1 Fiorentina
Sampdoria 0-0 Napoli
Torino 1-0 Cremonese
Verona 2-0 Ascoli

CLASSIFICA

Verona	**25**
Inter	24
Torino	23
Roma	22
Sampdoria	21
Juventus	20
Milan	19
Fiorentina	17
Como	16
Atalanta	16
Avellino	15
Napoli	15
Udinese	14
Ascoli	9
Lazio	9
Cremonese	7

18a Giornata

10 February 1985

WITH FOUR goals in ten thrilling second-half minutes to add to four in the first half, this was one of the greatest games of the Bagnoli era. For the sceptics, both inside and outside the camp, it was a pivotal moment that finally convinced them that Hellas might actually have what it takes to become champions of Italy. It is a match that will be remembered as one of the most thrilling in the club's history. And, in this golden age, Hellas fans have had no shortage of drama in recent years.

Early in the 1983/84 campaign, the Bentegodi experienced that most rare of occasions – a European night. In fact, the Bagnoli era is still fondly remembered for those '*notti magiche*', those magical European evenings under the floodlights that, to date, have never been repeated. The European adventure that season was the stuff of legend. The UEFA Cup, Europe's second-tier club football competition, saw the likes of Real and Atlético Madrid, Bayern Munich, Spartak Moscow, Nottingham Forest and Inter Milan competing against lesser-known footballing entities like Drogheda United, Austria Memphis, Inter Bratislava and St Mirren. In the first round, Hellas drew Serbian giants Red Star Belgrade, one of the most successful football teams to emerge from the Balkans and who had a respectable, if unspectacular, European pedigree. In the first European match ever played at the Bentegodi, Hellas emerged with a narrow one-goal victory, with dead-ball specialist Pierino Fanna scoring a 36th-minute penalty.

The return leg was epic in every sense. More than 90,000 packed into the Stadion Rajko Mitić, nicknamed the 'Maracanà', that Wednesday evening in Belgrade, including

500 Hellas fans who had made the 900km journey east in seven chartered coaches and a vast convoy of cars.[59] Red Star went 1-0 up from a penalty after some questionable Hellas defending. Verona's equaliser was an early goal of the season contender as Luigi Sacchetti dinked the ball over the head of his marker before volleying into the top corner from 25 yards.

In the second half, Red Star restored their lead with a powerful header from a set piece that left Garella with no chance. Just five minutes later, Fanna broke through following a defensive error by Red Star, teeing up Giuseppe Galderisi, who finished with a delightful chip. It was Galderisi who grabbed the winner for Hellas with a wonderful individual effort, effortlessly evading three defenders before once again chipping over the helpless Red Star keeper, sealing a famous European victory in Belgrade. Broadcast live across Italy on RAI TV, for many fans it remains the greatest game in Verona's history. For those lucky enough to have been there, it was quite simply the best away trip of their lives. After the game, dozens of Hellas fans gathered outside the away changing room waiting for the players to emerge. Giuseppe Galderisi gleefully flung himself among them before being launched into the air in raucous celebration. Back at the hotel, even Bagnoli was observed to crack a wry smile, while Billy Pattaro, a chef from the Veronese plain, a region famed for its rice production, prepared a celebratory meal of *risotto al tastasal*, a local speciality.

A month later, the Bentegodi hosted little-known Sturm Graz of Austria. After the heroics of Belgrade, expectations were high. But, despite a promising start, things didn't go as planned. Fanna put Verona 1-0 up after just 12 minutes but, barely five minutes later, the Austrians grabbed a well-worked equaliser from the edge of the box. Then, on 26 minutes, a stunner from long range gave Graz the lead. With the half-time whistle approaching, Galderisi seized on a loose ball inside the box to equalise going into the break. With Marangon sent off

---

59 Attendance figures that evening are variously reported as between 75,000 and 90,000.

and Verona playing with ten men, the second half would end goalless. In fact, Galderisi's effort would be the last goal of the tie.

Five thousand Hellas fans travelled to Austria, and, in a compact stadium, it was the visitors who seemed to be making most of the noise. The match, however, ended in a disappointing goalless draw, resulting in the Austrians progressing on the away goals rule. Hellas were undefeated in Europe but were eliminated due to a lack of experience, two away goals and an inability to break down a stubborn Austrian defence. The fleeting European dream was over but the memories would last forever.

Meanwhile, on the domestic front that season, Hellas progressed to the final of the Coppa Italia for the second consecutive season. This time, Verona's opponents were Nils Liedholm's high-flying Roma. Once again, Hellas faced the challenge of playing the first leg at home. Roma opened the scoring with a crucial away goal, while Verona grabbed a late equaliser through Massimo Sturgato. In the return leg, Roma took the lead thanks to a 27th-minute Mauro Ferroni own goal. Once again, Verona were unable to snatch that vital away goal. For Roma, it was the conclusion of a memorable season in which they finished second in the league and were beaten finalists in a seismic European Cup Final against Liverpool.[60] For Verona, it was more disappointment for a team that had proved it could compete with the best but just didn't seem to have what it took to secure silverware. Notwithstanding the lack of trophies, by the end of the 1983/84 season, Bagnoli had constructed what local journalist Matteo Fontana has recently described as '*lo spogliatoio di ferro*' (an iron changing room), with a group of hard-working, committed and ambitious players. A

---

60 The 1984 European Cup Final took place on 30 May 1984 at the Stadio Olimpico in Rome. It was Liverpool's fourth European Cup final (having won the competition in 1977, 1978 and 1981). It was Roma's first time in the final. Liverpool took the lead in the first half through a Phil Neal goal, but Roberto Pruzzo equalised for Roma just before half-time. With the scores still level at full time and after extra time, the match went to a penalty shoot-out which Liverpool won to claim their fourth European Cup.

towering presence in that changing room that season was a Scot known locally as '*Lo Squalo*' (the shark).

In 1981, after successful spells with Leeds United and Manchester United, combative Scottish centre-forward Joe Jordan signed for AC Milan. In his first season in Italy, he scored just two goals in 20 appearances as Milan were relegated for only the second time in the club's history. He fared better in the second tier, scoring ten goals in 30 league appearances, earning immediate promotion with the *Rossoneri* as champions of Serie B. Instead of renewing with Milan, however, Jordan took a gamble and signed for Hellas Verona, who had just finished fourth in the 1982/83 Serie A campaign, securing a coveted place in the UEFA Cup in the process.

With his wealth of experience and combative style, Jordan was seen as the perfect foil for the up-and-coming young talents of Maurizio Iorio and Giuseppe Galderisi, who were fast and agile but lacked power, strength and experience. The two diminutive Italian strikers were thought to be incompatible and the local newspaper, somewhat unkindly, referred to them as '*Puffi al tritolo*' (Smurfs on dynamite). Jordan, nicknamed 'Jaws' due to an incident early in his playing career that caused him to lose his front teeth, was seen as exactly the kind of physical and streetwise veteran they needed to bring out the best in them. Although he wore dentures, he was in the habit of taking them out to play.

Like many Brits who preceded him, Jordan's time in Italy would ultimately end in disappointment. For Hellas, he played just 24 games, including 12 in the league, and scored just two goals – one in the league, the other in the cup. He is, nonetheless, widely credited with passing on his valuable experience to Iorio and Galderisi and other young players at the club.[61] Italian clubs were only permitted two foreign players

---

61 Until the arrival of Liam Henderson in 2018, followed by Josh Doig four years later, Jordan was the only Scot to have ever played for Hellas Verona. Despite his short stay and limited impact on the pitch, he is still fondly remembered in the city by team-mates and fans alike and was even trackside alongside Liam Henderson as Hellas earned promotion in 2019.

and, with the arrival of Briegel and Elkjær in the summer of 1984, there was no room in the squad for '*Lo Squalo*'.

Today, after sitting out a significant stretch of the season with a thigh strain, Jordan's replacement, Preben Elkjær, is finally ready to make his comeback against Udinese. The Dane scored in his second Serie A game against Ascoli and then again in the 2-0 home victory against Juventus, the famous goal – scored at the end of a mazy run during which he lost his right boot – earning him the nickname '*Cenerentolo*' (Cinderella). Since then, he has spent several months on the sidelines.

For many kids growing up in Verona in the 1980s, Elkjær was their hero. Matteo Fontana was an awkward, shy and studious kid, his backpack invariably full of textbooks. He also loved football and played on the street with the kids from his neighbourhood. Elkjær was his superhero.[62] Seventeen-year-old student Alessandro Fiorio remembers Elkjær's incredible strength: 'Perhaps not beautiful to look at from an aesthetic point of view but absolutely stubborn and concrete.' He was also funny – he always seemed to have a joke ready – and his Danish-Italian accent endeared him to kids like Alessandro. He stood out because, in an era of rigid professionalism, he didn't always follow the rules – he even liked to smoke! But most of all, Elkjær was just crazy – a characteristic that the Veronese value above all else, as the popular nursery rhyme proclaims: *Venesiani gran signori, padovani gran dotori, visentini magna gati, veronesi tuti mati.*[63]

Elkjær isn't the only one making a big comeback today. Zico, after three and a half months on the sidelines, also returns to Udinese's starting line-up. Even with the Brazilian's prolonged absence, Udinese boast one of the most prolific attacks in the league (Edinho, Carnevale and De Agostini) and a goalscoring

---

62 Matteo Fontana's biography of Elkjær, *Elkjær Sindaco!* was published in 2020.

63 This popular nursery rhyme translates as: 'Venetians are great lords, Padovans great doctors, Vicentini [people from Vicenza] eat cats, Veronese are all mad.'

record (25 goals scored) just behind Torino (on 26). With one of the worst defensive records in the league, however, they are hovering perilously close to the relegation zone.

Back in late September, when the temperature was still in the high 20s and Hellas were little more than plucky upstarts enjoying a promising start to the season, Verona eked out a narrow 1-0 victory against Udinese at the Bentegodi thanks only to a 59th-minute Galderisi penalty. On a heavy pitch, today's match will undoubtedly be another physical encounter, with Bagnoli opting for a muscular and offensive 4-3-3 formation, with a midfield of Di Gennaro and Briegel built around the in-form Sacchetti. Though they expect a battle against Zico's Udinese, few could anticipate the epic nature of what is about to unfold.

With early goals from Briegel (a header from a trademark Fanna free kick) and Galderisi (the striker is once again first to react from a rebound off the goalkeeper following a long-range Briegel effort), Hellas are 2-0 up after just ten minutes. Then comes the moment of the match and, indeed, one of the most memorable moments of the entire season. A long clearance on a pitch that is cutting up badly finds Elkjær on the halfway line. He shrugs off his defender and accelerates towards the box, leaving another sprawling defender in his wake. As the goalkeeper rushes out towards him, Elkjær pulls off an audacious lob. A remarkable finish! With 20 minutes played, Hellas are already three up and have witnessed another Elkjær goal that will live long in the memory. The Great Dane is back!

Udinese continue to create chances but without success. In fact, it's Verona who score again on the break but Tricella's finish is eventually ruled offside. In the 41st minute, Fanna is hit hard by an opposing defender and forced to hobble off, making way for Bruni. Then, on the stroke of half-time, Udinese pull one back from a well-struck Edinho free kick, leaving Garella justifiably furious with his porous defensive wall.

In the second half, two more goals (from Andrea Carnevale and Massimo Mauro) in the first 14 minutes complete an epic Udinese comeback, with the momentum shifting decisively in favour of the home side. For the *Gialloblù*, these are the most challenging moments of the season. How have they squandered a three-goal lead? Have they thrown away the championship? Is this a turning point in a season that has already exceeded expectations?

Verona respond. Elkjær (who else?) grabs a second in the 61st minute before Briegel (of course!) completes the rout two minutes later. On a heavy pitch, it's not always been pretty but it is the direct, offensive, spirited football that we have come to associate with Hellas Verona and, once again, the two foreign signings have proved decisive.

In his post-match interview, Bagnoli admits that he's never seen a match quite like it. Many years later, in an interview with *L'Arena*, Elkjær offered his thoughts on the significance of the game: '[W]hen you win games like that, it means you are strong, both mentally and as a team. From that day, I thought we could win the championship.'

It was a game that Zico would remember for decades to come as well. In an interview 35 years later with *L'Arena* journalist Simone Antolini, the great Brazilian offered his personal recollections of the game: '[W]e were 3-0 down. Then we came back. Then Verona came back. Such a great team. We lost, of course. But it's okay to lose games like that. You don't experience it as a defeat. That was the essence of football. The football that I liked so much. I believe that Verona, at that time, represented the most beautiful expression of Italian football.'

Elsewhere, at the San Siro Inter beat Lazio 1-0 thanks to a late and unstoppable Gianpiero Marini volley, while Torino suffer a 2-1 defeat in Naples (a Júnior free kick cancelled out by a Maradona penalty and well-worked Caffarelli winner). Roma's 1-1 draw with Atalanta brings them to 23 points, while Juventus reach 22 points with a narrow 2-1 victory against Avellino thanks to two Platini goals.

So, Verona have preserved their supremacy at the top of the table and Elkjær has scored two on his comeback. Briegel has also chipped in with a brace. After a long, hard winter, everything seems to be coming together at just the right moment. The previous week's international break provided Verona's players with the time and space they needed to recover, physically and mentally.[64] And that's just as well, because next week Hellas host Inter at the Bentegodi. With the Milan giants just a single point behind Hellas, it is another match that could determine the outcome of the championship.

---

64 Italy travelled to Dublin for a friendly where they beat Ireland 2-1 with goals from Rossi (penalty) and Altobelli. But it was Antonio Di Gennaro, Hellas Verona's outstanding playmaker, who orchestrated things in midfield.

18A GIORNATA

Ascoli 2-0 Sampdoria
Cremonese 0-1 Milan
Fiorentina 2-1 Como
Inter 1-0 Lazio
Juventus 2-1 Avellino
Napoli 2-1 Torino
Roma 1-1 Atalanta
Udinese 3-5 Verona

CLASSIFICA

Verona	**27**
Inter	26
Roma	23
Torino	23
Juventus	22
Milan	21
Sampdoria	21
Fiorentina	19
Atalanta	17
Napoli	17
Como	16
Avellino	15
Udinese	14
Ascoli	11
Lazio	9
Cremonese	7

19a Giornata

17 February 1985

IT'S CARNIVAL season in Verona and, on a chilly Sunday afternoon in mid-February, the Bentegodi is expectant. The battle for the championship is now surely between Associazione Calcio Hellas Verona and Football Club Internazionale Milano. As fate would have it, Hellas and Inter now come face to face, with both teams peaking at just the right moment. Inter are unbeaten since that derby defeat back in October when Mark Hateley's towering header sealed the victory for city rivals AC Milan. Since then, the *Nerazzurri* have been on an 11-game unbeaten run. Hellas haven't been quite as convincing in recent months, although back-to-back victories, including their dramatic 5-3 victory away to Udinese, and the return of talismanic striker Preben Elkjær Larsen, suggest that the *Gialloblù* have rediscovered their mojo just when it matters most.

It's David and Goliath. Metropolitan versus provincial. The industry and work ethic of Milan against the charm and romance of Verona. A clash of styles, with Hellas direct and offensive, while Inter are cautious and compact. Inter's away form this season has been less than convincing, having won just once (against Cremonese), drawn six and lost one. Hardly the match-winning form of a team with championship pretensions. At the Bentegodi, Hellas are unbeaten in eight games this season, with five wins and three draws.

On paper at least, Inter have a superior squad. They have what many regard as the strongest attacking duo in the world in Altobelli and Rummenigge and strength and experience in depth, as well as a convincing track record at the Bentegodi.

In 13 encounters in the post-war period, Inter have won eight and drawn three, scoring 21 goals and conceding just 13. But Verona have been ahead since the first day of the championship. This season, it is Inter who have been chasing. And Rummenigge? Well, he's only found the net four times in Serie A this season, all four goals coming at the San Siro. While his transfer from Bayern Munich was met with enormous fanfare in both Germany and Italy, it is fellow West German international Briegel who has had the greater impact so far this season, with Rummenigge struggling to adjust to the demands of the Italian game. 'Kalle', as the German striker is commonly known, is desperate to increase his tally and to score on the road: 'I absolutely need to score, on this occasion I could score my first away goal. I want to score, I know that the most important thing is to win but I also know how important it is for me to be a goalscorer again,' he tells the *Corriere della Sera* on the eve of the game. But, for an out-and-out striker like Rummenigge, it's not easy to find space in the box, where he's often double-marked by tenacious Italian defenders. Of course, the face-off between the two illustrious Germans adds another dimension to this encounter and, while the media would have us believe that this is some kind of 'Homeric duel' between the two Teutons of the championship, the truth is that, while they may not exactly be best friends, they are international team-mates with a great mutual respect. While Rummenigge is the superstar striker, it is the former left-back, Briegel, who has scored six goals already this season. 'It's easier for me playing from deeper,' Briegel explains to the *Corriere della Sera*. 'I'm less well marked. In fact, I'm the one who's doing the marking [...]. Rummenigge always has an opponent on his back.'

Back in October, Hellas returned from Milan with a precious point from their encounter with Inter. A similar result today would consolidate their place at the top of the table. And, with two formidable defences, it's certainly going to be another tight game. In fact, in the build-up, Briegel predicts a goalless draw. Elkjær, who scored two last Sunday against Udinese after two months on the sidelines and then another decisive one on Wednesday in the cup against Genoa, is also forecasting a draw: 'I always want to win but, this time, a draw would be fine with me,' he concedes to the *Corriere della Sera*.

The cup tie on a freezing cold Wednesday evening in Genoa – made all the worse by a bitter arctic wind – was a distraction that Bagnoli's threadbare squad could have done without. Bagnoli made what limited changes his scant resources would allow him, with Garella, Fanna and Di Gennaro making way for Spuri, Turchetta and Bruni, but it was an otherwise familiar-looking line-up that came away from Genoa's Stadio Luigi Ferraris with a slender one-goal advantage to take into the return leg in two weeks' time. It was another morale-boosting victory and more invaluable game time for Elkjær, helping him return to match fitness. Meanwhile, on Friday, at the city's annual carnival parade, lorries were adorned with giant papier-mâché renderings of Bagnoli, Garella and company and the intoxicating spirit of the carnival lingers on throughout the weekend.

Inter are at full strength, relying on the solidity of their defence but also on the impact of Rummenigge, who is trying to rediscover the kind of form that made him an international phenomenon. For Verona, Ferroni remains on the injury list, where he is joined by Sacchetti, one of the unsung stars of the campaign so far. Elkjær and Briegel are back at their rampant best and Di Gennaro's form is such that he has forced his way into the heart of the Italian midfield. Fanna, Tricella and Galderisi are also enjoying the form of their lives and are not far behind him in the race for international recognition.

In Ferroni's absence, the task of subduing Rummenigge falls to the ever-versatile Domenico Volpati. Asked on the eve of the game if he fears the great German champion, Volpati responds calmly: '[F]ear? No. Professional respect? Yes.' Volpati has studied the German closely. Anticipating his quick movements in confined spaces, feints, dribbling, sprints and shooting ability, Volpati sets out his approach: '[Y]ou have to sit off him at a reasonable distance and only press him in the last 20 metres.' His team-mate, Ferroni, has given him some advice: 'Elastic marking … don't get too close to him because he can push you easily with the physical strength of his legs and torso. You should, instead, try to anticipate him.' Bruni, who has been quietly effective so far this season, will deputise for Volpati in midfield, while, in Sacchetti's place, there is a rare start for Dario Donà, the unassuming midfielder who arrived in Verona after his career went off track following his indiscretions at AC Milan. He is given the unenviable task of marking Liam Brady, one of Europe's most gifted playmakers.

Inter full-back Ricardo Ferri has the equally unenviable task of containing Elkjær. Ahead of the game, he spoke of the three qualities that make the Dane so difficult to defend: an unpredictable change of pace; an incredible capacity to dribble; and a devastating directness. The only way to defend against him, Ferri believes, is to anticipate his movements and never give him a metre of space. Two contrasting approaches for dealing with two outstanding offensive players. Time will tell how effective these strategies are.

With a capacity of just 38,000, there's a thriving black market for tickets. In fact, the Bentegodi could have sold out two times over for today's match. A convoy of German fans has made the ten-hour journey by bus from Kaiserslautern, including 27 personal guests of Briegel. Rummenigge has a contingent of his own making the shorter journey down the Brenner Pass from Munich. During the week, 250 tickets were stolen from a city centre outlet and touts are now hawking tickets for up to 130,000 lire a pop, while official sales have generated an estimated 655m lire for the Hellas coffers.

With kick-off rapidly approaching, rumours begin to circulate that a flu bug swept through the Verona camp last night. Might this be just the break the *Nerazzurri* have been hoping for? Meanwhile, on the streets and piazzas around the stadium, 600 *carabinieri* have been deployed, with police dogs patrolling the turnstiles and two helicopters circling ominously overhead. But, with vibrant colours and cheerful face masks painted in yellow and blue, the carnival atmosphere lingers. The police, however, are taking no chances and have prohibited fans from entering the stadium with masks, fearing that they might be used to hide the faces of hooligans. As the atmosphere intensifies, a few violent skirmishes break out between rival sets of fans, leading to dozens of arrests.

Inside the stadium, as kick-off looms, flags, flares, balloons and an anarchy of noise erupt from opposing ends. The stadium. A seething cauldron of contradictions. One of the few places where you can scream and shout and yell abuse one minute and hug a complete stranger standing three rows in front of you the next! Today, there is even a bare-footed novice from the College of San Bernardino in the *Curva Sud* wearing the habit of Saint Francis. He has a prayer card of Saint Francis of Assisi in his hand and will pray conspicuously during the match. At half-time, he surreptitiously places a 1,000 lire bet that Verona will win!

In the tunnel before kick-off, a sweating and nervous-looking Briegel concedes that a draw would be an acceptable result. Elkjær is more forthright: 'I always want to win. I'm not afraid of Inter.' And this attitude sums up what the two great foreigners bring to the team (beside their undoubted quality on the pitch) – a fierce determination to win and a healthy lack of respect for their opponents, regardless of who they are. While their Italian team-mates have been brought up to fear and respect the big beasts of Italian football, Briegel and Elkjær are outsiders. They have no such preconceptions. That mentality is clearly contagious. As the smoke from the pre-match pyrotechnics slowly begins to fade, there is no sense that Verona are playing for a draw, launching a series of vertical surges deep into the Inter half. In fact, it is Inter who look nervous in these opening exchanges.

The first real flash of danger comes in the 29th minute when Elkjær, well-marked by Ferri, controls the ball on his chest on the edge of the Inter area and, with a spontaneous acrobatic volley, blasts high over Zenga's crossbar. Barely five minutes later, the Dane again comes close, this time with a header from a magnificent Tricella cross. Galderisi, as usual, is making a nuisance of himself and has two penalty claims denied.

But a team of Inter's quality are capable of absorbing such pressure and seizing the opportunity when it comes. And, sure enough, with just five minutes of the first half remaining, Mandorlini releases Brady, who launches a long ball forward which Fontolan heads directly into the path of the oncoming Altobelli, who strikes first-time on the rise from just outside the 18-yard box, leaving Garella helpless as the ball slips in under the crossbar and finds the top corner. Verona 0 Inter 1.

In the remaining six minutes of the first half, Verona twice come close to equalising, first through Galderisi and then Briegel, while, at the other end, Inter threaten to double their lead. Despite the flurry of chances at either end, Inter preserve their narrow advantage going into the break.

Three minutes into the second half, a Fanna corner finds Di Gennaro at the front post and he flicks it on for an unmarked Briegel to head home from inside the six-yard box; 1-1! For anyone counting, it's the 300th goal of the Serie A season so far. Briegel sets off towards the Hellas fans, a savage mix of joy and fury as he celebrates the equaliser and his victory in a personal duel with the champion of champions, Karl-Heinz Rummenigge.

Garella pulls of one of his trademark 'miracle' saves with his feet, while Zenga also has to improvise at the other end as Elkjær comes close to snatching a late winner. So, a pulsating contest ends in a draw. With Briegel and Rummenigge embracing. With both sides ruing missed changes and having relied on defensive fortitude and goalkeeping brilliance. Above all, it ends with one question unanswered: who will win the *Scudetto*?

After the match, Beppe Bergomi, Inter's World Cup-winning defender, is less than charitable towards Elkjær. 'No one noticed what he did to me on the pitch,' he complains. 'He insulted me, made faces at me and finally kicked the ball at me. That's his way.'

Rummenigge is the last player to emerge from the changing rooms into the prison-like corridors of the Bentegodi (he 'likes a long shower'), approaching journalists with his customary gentle and distinguished air. Clean shaven and immaculately dressed in shirt and tie, speaking in precise Italian, he has the air of a Hollywood star. Briegel, meanwhile, is dressed in a blue overall as if he's been working on the stadium's water system. Unlike Rummenigge, who in just a few months has worked miracles with his Italian, Briegel speaks extremely slowly. One. Word. Per. Minute. His entire vocabulary consists of about 30 words. 'Languages aren't my strong point,' he explains with a smile. 'I speak better with my feet.'

Elsewhere, AC Milan win 3-2 against Juve, with Ray Wilkins emerging as the matchwinner, dictating the pace of the game, organising his team-mates and coming close to a first goal since arriving in Italy in the summer. Notwithstanding the missed opportunity, it is the Englishman's best performance so far in the red and black stripes of Milan. In Genoa, Roma collapse against a Vialli-inspired Sampdoria, who win 3-0, leaving Ancelotti, who has a violent argument with Souness and is reprimanded at length by the match official, to blame injuries for the poor performance and result. Torino immediately return to winning ways by beating Udinese 1-0, thanks to a goal by Schachner, bringing the *Granata* back to within three points of Verona, while Inter still trail the leaders by a solitary point.

With 11 matches left to play, it is still far too early to make any rash predictions about the destination of the title. Besides, Verona now have to go to Turin to play Juventus, while Inter host Torino in what could be yet another decisive day in the championship race.

19A GIORNATA

Atalanta 2-2 Fiorentina
Avellino 2-0 Cremonese
Como 1-1 Napoli
Lazio 0-0 Ascoli
Milan 3-2 Juventus
Sampdoria 3-0 Roma
Torino 1-0 Udinese
Verona 1-1 Inter

CLASSIFICA

Verona	**28**
Inter	27
Torino	25
Sampdoria	23
Milan	23
Roma	23
Juventus	22
Fiorentina	20
Napoli	18
Atalanta	18
Avellino	17
Como	17
Udinese	14
Ascoli	12
Lazio	10
Cremonese	7

20a Giornata

24 February 1984

THINGS JUST haven't clicked for champions Juventus in the league this season. The Turin giants have, however, progressed to the quarter-final of the European Cup, thanks to a convincing 6-2 aggregate demolition of Grasshoppers, with the first leg against Sparta Prague to come on 6 March. Though their primary focus this season has been on European glory, *La Vecchia Signora* still pose an ominous threat in the league, despite losing narrowly to AC Milan last weekend. Entering the final third of season, and with 22 points on the board, Juve are six points adrift of Verona. If they are to keep any championship hopes alive, this is a match they have to win.

Despite their superior form this season, Verona's track record against Juve leaves no room for complacency. In 13 matches contested in the post-war period, Juventus have won 11, with the remaining two fixtures ending in draws. Another cause for concern is the absence of one of Verona's most influential players this season, the German panzer, Hans-Peter Briegel.

Last weekend, Briegel and Rummenigge faced each other as adversaries at the Bentegodi. This weekend they are team-mates for West Germany in a crucial World Cup qualifier against Portugal in Lisbon. The international fixture coincides with the Serie A Sunday afternoon kick-off slot, leaving the Germans forced to choose between club and country. Arriving late in Portugal, Briegel drives 300km to participate in a practice match on the eve of the qualifier but arrives just as the game is finishing. He gets changed anyway and, after a long day spent travelling, trains alone that evening.

Second-placed Inter, who host third-placed Torino, will also be without their German *wunderspieler*, Karl-Heinz Rummenigge, who has travelled to Lisbon for the international. Both Hellas and Inter made representations through the West German national team coach, the legendary Franz Beckenbauer, to have the game brought forward by 24 hours so the players could return to Italy in time to play on Sunday. While the Germans were sympathetic, the Portuguese swiftly rejected the proposal. So, Hellas will face Juventus without Briegel. And Inter will host Torino without Rummenigge. It's a farcical situation that secs Verona without one of their most influential players in one of the most challenging fixtures of the campaign.

While Briegel is in Portugal, some estimates suggest that as many as 10,000 Hellas fans have made the trip to Turin, with 50 specially chartered buses to transport 3,000 fans to the Piedmont capital. Another 1,000 or so will take the train, with the remainder travelling by car. As the massive convoy departs, a major police operation is under way to ensure the safety of those travelling and prevent altercations between rival sets of fans, with up to 1,000 police and security officers deployed in and around the stadium itself. At a stadium constructed in the 1930s and originally known as the Stadio Municipale Benito Mussolini, Hellas have never won against Juventus and have drawn on only two occasions.

On the eve of the match, Bagnoli concedes that he would, for once, settle for a draw. The *Bianconeri*, meanwhile, are still smarting from the 2-0 humiliation earlier in the season (remember Elkjær's shoeless goal?) and the Italian champions are determined to set the record straight. After all, it is not too late for Juventus to launch a late title challenge of their own. Two points for the home side today could change the dynamics of the title race going into the final third of the season.

Legendary striker Paolo Rossi has declared himself reborn after his stunning goal at the San Siro against Milan (his third of the championship), insisting that if *La Signora* are to peak for the European Cup they must also remain focussed in the league. To come away with anything from today's match, Verona must also subdue the league's top scorer and winner of the Ballon d'Or two seasons in a row.

In the two and half seasons since he arrived in Turin, Michel Platini has played 77 matches, scored 49 goals and won a league title. In both previous seasons, he has been Serie A's top scorer, with 16 in 1982/83 (ahead of Inter's Altobelli and Verona's Domenico Penzo, who scored 15), while last season, with 20 goals, he narrowly beat Zico, who netted 19. This season, the Frenchman is, once again, leading the rankings with 13 goals scored so far.

For Hellas, Fanna and Galderisi return to their former stomping ground, having made a decisive impact on the same fixture back in October. The first of the two goals in that victory came from a Galderisi header from a Fanna cross. While it would be overstating it to speak of revenge, there is no doubt that there is a certain rancour amongst Verona's former Juventus contingent. Even in the build-up to today's game, Trapattoni appears to cast doubt on Galderisi's ability, even accusing him of diving. Galderisi is offended by such comments, pointing out that the Juventus coach never made such complaints while the striker was playing for him. Despite such pre-match polemics, Galderisi has nothing but fond memories of his time in Turin, having joined Juventus as a 14-year-old, before bursting on to the scene with six goals in 16 fleeting appearances, including a memorable hat-trick against AC Milan. Despite showing such promise, Galderisi was soon discarded by *La Signora*, joining the pantheon of waifs and strays who eventually found their way to Bagnoli's Verona.

Without Briegel, Sacchetti and Ferroni (the latter of whom are also missing through injury), Bagnoli must once again improvise. In a five-man defence, he deploys both the Marangon brothers, Fabio on the right and the more experienced Luciano on the left, with Volpati and Fontolan alongside captain Tricella in the middle. Like Fanna and Galderisi, the Marangon brothers are also discarded products of the Juventus youth system. Twenty-eight-year-old Luciano spent several years at Juventus but never started a game (appearing on the bench just once in a cup match in Amsterdam). His younger brother, 23-year-old Fabio, played just once for Juve, in May 1980 against Fiorentina. Since arriving together at Verona, they have shared just a few minutes together on the pitch, in the fixture against Lazio in Rome. Finally, the brothers have the chance to start together against their former club, the champions of Italy.

In midfield, Bagnoli asks Di Gennaro to check the runs of Boniek. Donà is dropped in favour of Bruni, while Fanna will shift between the left and right flanks and Elkjær and Galderisi will provide the firepower up front. It's a solid 5-3-2 formation that provides defensive solidity and a compact midfield but also the possibility to hit their opponents on the counter-attack. On the bench, in addition to the usual Spuri, Donà and Turchetta, Antonio Terracciano and Andrea Matteoni from the youth team make up the numbers.

Juventus begin briskly, determined to seize the initiative. After 11 minutes, Cabrini makes a run on the left flank and a cross which Paolo Rossi meets with a high volley, forcing Garella to parry. Two minutes later, Tardelli forces himself into the area and unleashes a perfect diagonal shot. Garella sticks out a foot and, somehow, deflects it wide.

Meanwhile, in Milan, Torino have taken a 13th-minute lead against Inter thanks to a delightful Giancarlo Corradini volley. But Verona's two-point lead at the top of the table barely lasts 15 minutes. In the 28th minute, Inter equalise through Fulvio Collovati, restoring the gap between first and second to just a single point.

With some encouragement from Bagnoli, the *Gialloblù* finally begin to exert themselves on the game. With Elkjær dropping deep, Verona regain a semblance of control in midfield as half-time approaches. Neither side, however, is able to gain an advantage and it remains goalless at the interval.

Three minutes into the second half, Garella is finally beaten from a Cabrini free kick but the post comes to his rescue. Maybe, for once, Lady Luck is smiling on Verona in

Turin. Then, in the space of just five second-half minutes, the referee disallows two goals, the first by Tricella (for the second time this season) from a set piece and the second by Boniek for offside. Despite the drama, Hellas seem more settled now and continue to press. In the 61st minute, Bodini denies Galderisi. Then, with barely 15 minutes remaining, Juve take a deserved lead with a header from an unmarked Briaschi. Juventus 1 Verona 0. As things stand, with it currently even at the San Siro, Inter will draw level with Verona at the head of Serie A.

From the restart, Verona are immediately on the attack, probing for an equaliser that would restore their superiority at the top of the table. Seizing on a misplaced Platini pass, Bruni finds Di Gennaro, who has time to take aim before unleashing a banger from outside the box, leaving Bodini flailing as it thunders into the top-right corner. Juventus 1 Verona 1. It is, arguably, the greatest goal of Di Gennaro's career. Though Enzo Bearzot, the pipe-smoking Italian national team coach, is in Lisbon to observe Germany's World Cup qualifier against Portugal, he has already identified Di Gennaro as the player who will lead the national team's midfield and, with goals like that, it is easy to understand why.

Meanwhile in Milan, Inter have a penalty. World Cup winner and prolific striker Alessandro Altobelli steps up to take the spot kick. It's a gilt-edged chance for the *Nerazzurri* to go top of the table for the first time this season. It's the 77th minute and this could be the turning point of the entire campaign. Hellas have been in front since the very first game of the season against Napoli, while Inter have spurned several opportunities to close the gap. Chances don't come much better than this. A late penalty at the San Siro, with one of the greatest Italian strikers of his generation poised to take it. But Altobelli's low shot lacks both power and precision. Martina guesses correctly and parries!

Back in Turin, Di Gennaro and Tricella form a defensive shield around the Hellas penalty box, while Juve introduce the creative talents of Beniamino Vignola. Bagnoli immediately takes counter-measures by replacing the spent Fabio Marangon with the more aggressive Donà, who is given clear instructions to suppress Vignola. The contest effectively ends here, with Juve unable to breach a resolute Verona rearguard.

As Garella leaves the field, Platini compliments him on an outstanding performance. For the Verona keeper, who began playing football as a kid in Turin, it couldn't get much better – being complimented on his performance by one of the greatest No.10s to ever wear the black and white stripes of Juventus. Volpati is also satisfied with his performance, telling the *Corriere della Sera*: 'Controlling Platini wasn't easy. I'd tried several other times and I knew that it would have been suicidal to mark him tightly. I waited for him, I followed him, I battled with him and I think I managed to suppress him. The fact that he, a proven goalscorer, didn't score, proves my point. But what matters most is the performance of the entire team. We proved to be an effective group, even with three key players missing.' Marco Tardelli is generous in his praise for Hellas, who he concedes played 'an outstanding game, demonstrating that they are a great team'. For Juve's legendary coach, Giovanni Trapattoni, it is 'a massive missed opportunity' for Juventus.

In Milan, it finishes 1-1, with boos ringing out across the San Siro. Altobelli's missed penalty represents another squandered opportunity for Inter. Elsewhere, Verona's next two opponents, Roma and Fiorentina, both lose. In Rome, Liedholm's AC Milan overcome the *Giallorossi* at the Olimpico, thanks to a goal by Virdis, while Fiorentina crumble against Sampdoria, beaten 3-0 with Salsano scoring one and Trevor Francis netting a brace. In Lisbon, meanwhile, Briegel is the star of the show while Rummenigge watches from the stands as West Germany defeat Portugal in their World Cup qualifier to go top of their group.

Fine margins can determine championships. So, too, can Garella's feet, Altobelli's missed penalty, Platini's misplaced pass and a wonderful moment of individual magic by Di Gennaro. While the Verona playmaker will take the plaudits for his spectacular goal, another heroic performance by Garella should not go unrecognised. The Verona keeper made numerous saves with his legs, backside, arms and even his hands to deny a Juventus onslaught led by Tardelli and Cabrini. Nor, too, should the contribution of Volpati, who kept Platini in check, the diligent performances of the Marangon brothers and Fontolan, who tempered Briaschi, notwithstanding the well-placed header that gave the Italian champions a fleeting advantage. Roberto Tricella, meanwhile, has underlined his status as the likely heir to Scirea, while Bruni once again let no one down.

In his post-match press conference, held on Monday rather than immediately after the game, when tensions were still high and his mood risked getting the better of him, Bagnoli refers to 'an anomalous championship'. Of the four teams, he explains, who were competing for the *Scudetto* at the beginning of the season (Inter, Roma, Juventus and Fiorentina), only Inter are still in the running. The others have been superseded by Verona, AC Milan, Torino and Sampdoria.

Many years later, when Bagnoli was asked by a reporter at what point he thought Hellas could win the championship, he responded with a smile: 'After the match in Turin with Juventus.' With ten games remaining and Inter trailing by just a single point, there is still a long way to go. But Verona have weathered another storm against one of the most formidable teams in the history of the Italian game; a result that leaves *La Signora* six points adrift. Only Inter, it seems, can mount a credible title challenge at this point.

20A GIORNATA

Ascoli 2-2 Avellino
Cremonese 0-0 Atalanta
Fiorentina 0-3 Sampdoria
Inter 1-1 Torino
Juventus 1-1 Verona
Napoli 4-0 Lazio
Roma 0-1 Milan
Udinese 4-1 Como

CLASSIFICA

Verona	**29**
Inter	28
Torino	26
Sampdoria	25
Milan	25
Juventus	23
Roma	23
Fiorentina	20
Napoli	20
Atalanta	19
Avellino	18
Como	17
Udinese	16
Ascoli	13
Lazio	10
Cremonese	8

21a Giornata

3 March 1985

FALCÃO HAS played his last game for Roma. Now in his fifth season in the Italian capital, the Brazilian's salary may be the highest in the league (reportedly more than 1bn lire a year) but injuries have taken their toll on the 31-year-old this season and his relationship with club president Dino Viola has reached breaking point. On 16 December, the Brazilian scored the opener against Napoli at the San Paolo as Roma went on to win 2-1, a result that consolidated their place in the top five going into the Christmas break. But it was only his fourth appearance of the season and it proves to be his last.

After that game against Napoli, Roma went on a six-game unbeaten streak (three victories and three draws), propelling them to within just two points of Verona, only for them to lose heavily to Sampdoria (3-0) and then, last weekend, narrowly (0-1) to AC Milan at the Olimpico. As well as suffering two consecutive defeats, Roma haven't scored in their last two fixtures and the team that won the *Scudetto* just two seasons ago and reached the European Cup Final against Liverpool last season now finds itself six points adrift of the league leaders.

Back in October, Hellas clinched a hard-won point in Rome thanks only to a truly outstanding performance by Garella. Notwithstanding Roma's current difficulties (including the absence of their talismanic Brazilian), today promises to be yet another testing encounter for Verona at the Bentegodi. The gladiatorial clash of two of Italy's great Roman cities has had an added frisson in recent seasons, a period that will be remembered if not as a *Pax Romana*, then certainly as an unprecedented golden age. On 23 January 1983,

47,896 fans packed into the Bentegodi, the highest recorded attendance in the stadium's history, as the two in-form sides fought out a tense 1-1 draw. Roma would go on to win the league that season, while newly promoted Hellas surprised many by finishing fourth.

While the name Marcantonio may suggest a link with ancient Rome, the origins of the Stadio Marcantonio Bentegodi are, in fact, to be found in the 19th century. A classically educated physician and philanthropist, Marcantonio Bentegodi was a man with a simple idea: to make sport accessible to all. Born in Verona on 25 April 1818, the doctor spent a lifetime promoting sports among young people in the city. In his will, he left a quarter of his estate to a sporting foundation to continue to fund physical education facilities for young people in the city. For his contribution to grassroots sports in the city, his name would be immortalised in street names, sports clubs and, of course, the stadium.

The first Stadio Bentegodi was constructed in 1910 and is commonly remembered as *Vecchio Bentegodi* (or *Vecio Bentegodi* in Veronese dialect, meaning 'old'). It was the venue for the matches of various city football teams, including Bentegodi Verona (who used it from 1919 to 1928) and Hellas (who used it from 1910 to 1914). At the beginning of the 1928/29 season, after the merger between Hellas and Bentegodi, the simple playing fields of Piazza Cittadella (located just behind Piazza Brà) were transformed into the Stadio Bentegodi, taking advantage of financial incentives available at the time for the construction of sporting infrastructure. Verona's first season in Serie A was played here in 1957/58 but by 1963, a new facility was required.

Inaugurated on 15 December 1963, the new Stadio Bentegodi was originally designed to seat up to 40,000 spectators but, due to security restrictions and a decades-long slump in demand, attendances rarely rose above a half or even a quarter of that capacity. Designed by the engineer, Leopoldo Baruchello, to replace the old municipal structure of the same name, the new design consisted of three levels of overlapping staircases and an eight-lane athletics track. The first semi-covered stadium in Italy at that time, the utopian 1960s vision was to create a bold, communally owned multi-purpose arena for the city.

That inaugural game at the new Bentegodi was a Serie B derby between Verona and Venezia. Amidst the festivities, a slice of *pandoro*, the local sweet bread popular at Christmas and New Year, was distributed to the spectators, while a bouquet of flowers was offered to the handful of women in attendance. On the pitch, things didn't go according to plan, with players complaining that the fans were too far away from the action and critics even blamed the new stadium for the team's failure to earn promotion that season!

One of the most pleasing aspects of the stadium from an atheistic point of view (perhaps the only pleasing thing) is that it is a single entity stadium (a bowl), unlike classic English stadiums of the era that were a ramshackle collection of seemingly unconnected stands. By the 1980s, however, the Bentegodi was beginning to show its age as the utopian dream of the 1960s began to crack under the harsh neon lights of the new decade. The numerous bars around the stadium were vital communication hubs for the fans. For away games, lists of names were gathered on a sheet of paper. With no mobile phones, for 100 lire you could buy a *gettone* (token) to make a quick five-minute call.

While English fans of the early 1980s were busy cultivating a reputation for hooliganism, culminating in the tragic events of the Heysel Stadium disaster of May 1985, Italian fans can hardly claim innocence. Verona, at this point, were not particularly renowned for the behaviour of their fans, perhaps because they didn't have a European platform and had spent so long in the lower leagues, where there was less visibility. By the mid-1980s, that was beginning to change. In fact, Hellas Verona were one of the first Italian football clubs with a fully organised fanbase, modelling themselves on the English casual scene of that era.

The dominant fan group in the Bentegodi's notorious *Curva Sud* was the historic *Brigate Gialloblù*. Officially established in November 1971 at the Bar Olimpia in the Borgo Venezia neighbourhood of the city by a pair of 16-year-old students, the *Brigate* was soon at the forefront of the Italian ultra scene. The *Brigate* was a familiar presence at away games, too, with their distinctive banner (the first model had a stylised skull as its symbol) and vocal support. Organisationally, it was still erratic, but the *Brigate*'s activities were typical of Italian fan groups of that era: drums, cymbals, scarves and the appearance of the first crude customised banners. In 1974, a rival group, known simply as the Ultras, was established. Its symbol was a skull with two crossed bones behind it but this was later replaced by an eagle perched on a Celtic cross with a four-rung ladder inside, an enduring symbol of the Della Scala family ('scala' in Italian means ladder).

With relegation to Serie B in 1979, the group lost some of its shine and began to make headlines for the wrong reasons, with violent scuffles with AC Milan and Vicenza fans, whose teams were also languishing in Serie B that season. During this period, the symbol of the *Brigate* became a simplified version of the city's historic coat of arms, a ladder with three rungs, an emblem that endures to this day. Success on the pitch in the 1980s brought with it many new recruits to the terraces. After years of political activism and domestic terrorism, the 1980s witnessed a general withdrawal ('*il riflusso*') from politics and political activism. Political parties and trade unions began to lose members and influence and electoral turnout declined as the political movements and ideologies that had shaped the post-war and Cold War landscape – communism and anti-communism, fascism and anti-fascism – began to lose their appeal. For many disaffected young men, that void was filled by football and, more particularly, the lure of the *curva*.

For the *Brigate*, mass long-distance trips began again (at least 5,000 Veronese invaded Rimini in 1982) and, with them, violent clashes with opposing fans. That period also marked the emergence of a bitter rivalry with Napoli, characterised by provocative banners, insulting chants and the occasional violent skirmish. This period also saw the introduction into the stadium of giant flags that completely covered the terraces, the prolific use of smoke bombs, firecrackers and fireworks and increasing violence, leading to more draconian measures to lock down stadiums and segregate opposing sets of fans.

The composition of the *Curva Sud* during these so-called 'golden years' was certainly younger than in previous eras, with more and more teenagers coming from the towns and villages of the province, some from as far afield as Trentino, Rovigo, Mantua and Brescia (including a large group from Sirmione). While the demographics were certainly younger, there remained a hardcore of 'veterans' from the 1970s. The new generation shaped a more aggressive style of support, with the *curva* divided into various sub-groups but united in their support for the team. In the 1970s, although certain factions were openly aligned with a certain political point of view, the Curva Sud somehow managed to maintain an outwardly apolitical stance. In the 1980s, in line with wider societal trends, explicit political symbols began to appear and the direction was overwhelmingly to the right. Starting in 1983, the banners of the 'Verona Front' (a group established by members of the neo-fascist Youth Front) and the '*Gioventù Scaligera*' appeared in the *curva*, while flags with Celtic crosses – and sometimes even swastikas – also appeared. Despite these tendencies, the stadium generally remained a colourful and welcoming place, with a politically mixed fanbase that also included left-wing groups (such as the 'Rude Boys').

Despite the occasional violent outburst, most members of the *Brigate* expressed their aggression in words only. For many young fans, wearing the scarf was a simple statement of identity as they searched for a cause to define themselves by. From lawyers to bricklayers, doctors to the long-term unemployed, the *curva* was predominantly a male-dominated world, with many fans leading a double life as respectable citizens during the week and violent hooligans at the weekend. For some, the *curva* even provided a stepping stone into the murky world of municipal politics. But fanatics and troublemakers were in the minority. Most fans, like 13-year-old Barbara Salazer, were simply entranced by the thrill of the game and the fervour of the stadium. On matchday, Barbara would have lunch at home with her family and then get a lift with her dad or jump on her Ciao Piaggio (a two-stroke moped) with a friend. Sometimes, she walked the 3km dirt track from her house with her friends in the Santa Lucia neighbourhood to the stadium, chatting and chanting all the way.

In the week leading up to the Roma match, Hellas secured a place in the Coppa Italia quarter-finals with a 2-1 victory (3-1 on aggregate) against Serie B side Genoa, thanks to two second-half goals from Antonio Di Gennaro. The cup run provided a rare start for reserve goalkeeper Sergio Spuri, as well as Dario Donà and Franco Turchetta. Otherwise, it was a familiar-looking Hellas line-up, reflecting Bagnoli's limited options in reserve. While Verona return to the Bentegodi for the second time this week to face Roma, Inter will spend Sunday afternoon on the shores of Lake Como, while AC Milan, looking for their fourth consecutive victory, host Napoli. Torino travel to Rome to face Lazio, while Sampdoria host Udinese and Juventus welcome Cremonese. With just a single point between first and second, it's another massive day in a title race that no one saw coming.

Deputising for Roma's absent Falcão, a talented young midfielder named Giuseppe Giannini has emerged as one of the breakthrough players of the season. While the Brazilian was crowned the 'Eighth King of Rome', the young Italian midfielder will in time become known as '*Il Principe*' (The Prince), a precursor to the great Francesco Totti; but that is all in the future.[65] For Verona, Briegel returns after his trip to Portugal, while Ferroni is on the bench after suffering a relapse of his troublesome knee injury.

Though the long cold winter is now in the past, it's been raining in Verona for several days and the Bentegodi pitch is, once again, heavy and bordering on the unplayable.

---

65 Giuseppe Giannini would go on to make 437 appearances for Roma and 47 for the national team.

A young Osvaldo Bagnoli during his early coaching days with Como in the 1970s.

Exciting young Danish prospect, Preben Elkjær Larsen, with FC Köln in 1976.

Hans-Peter Briegel looks on in despair as Paolo Rossi celebrates a penalty in the 1982 World Cup Final which Italy win 3-1.

Claudio Garella denies Antonio Cabrini as Hellas beat Juventus 2-1 in Turin. A resurgent Hellas would finish the 1983/84 season in sixth place.

Briegel and Maradona in one of numerous encounters for club and country (1 January 1981)

The ever-dependable Domenico Volpati faces down Juventus striker Zbigniew Boniek in February 1985.

A pensive-looking Pierino Fanna during a training session with Juventus in 1979.

Giuseppe Galderisi in action for Italy against Argentina at the 1986 World Cup.

In 2017, Osvaldo Bagnoli receives a place in the Italian Football Hall of Fame alongside Ruud Gullit, Antonio Conte and Alessandro Del Piero.

The bond between the group remains strong. Here Bagnoli, Fanna, Volpati and Tricella celebrate the 30th anniversary in 2015.

In August 2022, the Curva Sud commemorates the death of legendary goalkeeper Claudio Garella with the words 'The Great Claudio Garella. Bye Champion of Italy'.

Unsurprisingly, given the conditions, it's a sluggish first half that passes without major incident, both sides seeming content to settle for a draw. In Genoa, meanwhile, Sampdoria's Trevor Francis is knocked out following a 31st-minute clash with Udinese defender Cesare Cattaneo. As Francis lies unconscious on the ground with blood pouring from a wound above his left eye, the desperate response of his team-mates and opponents alike indicates immediately that something serious has happened. Francis is urgently stretchered off to the changing room to be resuscitated, while fellow Briton Graeme Souness races into the stands to find the Englishman's wife. 'For a few moments, we feared the worst,' Sampdoria doctor, Professor Andrea Chi, later explains. 'Francis seemed to be in a serious condition. He was unconscious for four or five minutes and the masseur Marchi and I had to give him mouth-to-mouth resuscitation. Little by little, however, he began to recover.'

Back in Verona, an increasingly tense and bad-tempered encounter is playing out. For the home side, the only real moment of inspiration in the first half comes in the 44th minute when Di Gennaro hits the crossbar from a free kick.

In the dressing room at half-time, Bagnoli delivers a rousing dressing down: 'You can't beat Roma with a foil and not even with a sword, so let's draw the sabre!' Hellas emerge in the second half suitably inspired, as Bruni, Fanna and Briegel step up a gear and Galderisi almost scores following a corner in the 48th minute. In the 54th minute, Buriani brings down Nanu with a clumsy challenge from behind but referee Casarin denies a strong penalty claim. Five minutes later, Fanna misses with the goal at his mercy. Verona are rampant but unable to break the deadlock.

In the 75th minute, a Fanna effort from outside the box is deflected into the path of Elkjær, who lunges to force the ball over the line from close range. Roma claim handball or maybe offside – anything to annul the goal. But their protests are in vain. Verona 1 Roma 0! Roma are incandescent but it's not entirely clear what their grievance is.

Hellas have found their rhythm and, just two minutes later, almost double their lead. Elkjær steals the ball from Bonetti and finds Galderisi, who shoots from inside the box but somehow fails to beat Tancredi. Three minutes later, Roma captain Bruno Conti spits in the direction of the linesman following a marginal offside decision and is sent off, extinguishing any vague possibility of a Roma comeback.

With less than five minutes remaining, Mauro Ferroni enters to a rapturous reception from the home fans. A Roman by birth, the *curva* has embraced him as one of their own. As the final whistle sounds, relief gives way to joy as the significance of another impressive result sinks in. Six points from a run of games that has included Udinese, Inter, Juventus and Roma. For Roma, it's the third consecutive defeat in the championship, four days after their surprise exit from the Coppa Italia following a 1-1 draw with Parma, who progressed on the away goals rule.[66]

Bagnoli again demonstrated his tactical agility today, switching from a *zona mista* in the first half to a pressing and man-marking system in the second. It is this kind of astute in-game management that has so often secured results when tight matches have hung in the balance. Elkjær has scored his fifth goal in the championship to add to Briegel's seven from midfield. In fact, Verona's pair of international signings represent one of the most potent attacking combos in the league, behind Platini and Boniek (17 between them) of Juventus and the Neapolitan pair of Maradona and Bertoni (also with 17).

Trevor Francis, meanwhile, has been transported to Genoa's San Martino hospital, where he will undergo X-rays

---

66 Ultimately, the 1984/85 campaign would prove to be a transitional one for Roma, who finished in a disappointing seventh place, and reached the quarter-final of the European Cup Winners' Cup. The following season, Eriksson led Roma to a much-improved second-place finish and a Coppa Italia triumph in 1986, but parted company with Roma in 1987. After spells at Fiorentina, Benfica and Sampdoria, Sven would go on to lift the Serie A title with Lazio in 2000 – only the second time in their history that the Roman club has won the Italian championship.

and a CT scan before being transferred to a private clinic. Suffering a lacerated wound to the left eyebrow arch and a concussion, doctors are confident that he will make a full and speedy recovery.

Meanwhile, another international break beckons as the *Azzurri* face Greece in Athens. Though the match will end goalless, Antonio Di Gennaro will once again lead the Italian midfield. In the 72nd minute, Pierino Fanna will enter to replace Alessandro Altobelli, earning his tenth cap since joining Verona in the summer of 1982. With nine games of the Serie A campaign still to play, speculation is already mounting about Fanna's future. According to some reports, the Hellas winger has already signed a pre-contractual agreement that will take him to Inter next season. The precise details of the deal are shrouded in secrecy but a salary of around 800m lire has been reported.

Finally, with both the referee and linesman on the receiving end of a vulgar Bruno Conti outburst at the Bentegodi this weekend, spare a thought for the referee in Puglia, who lost nearly half his moustache after he was assaulted by a player. The culprit, Alunni Ricci, is swiftly handed a four-year ban. The Roma captain can expect a lesser sentence for his transgression that left his team playing with ten men, as Verona march on towards the championship.[67]

---

67 Roma captain Bruno Conti was subsequently handed a five-match ban for twice 'confronting' the linesman.

21A GIORNATA

Atalanta 0-0 Ascoli
Avellino 0-0 Fiorentina
Como 0-0 Inter
Juventus 5-1 Cremonese
Lazio 0-0 Torino
Milan 2-1 Napoli
Sampdoria 1-0 Udinese
Verona 1-0 Roma

CLASSIFICA

Verona	**31**
Inter	29
Milan	27
Sampdoria	27
Torino	27
Juventus	25
Roma	23
Fiorentina	21
Atalanta	20
Napoli	20
Avellino	19
Como	18
Udinese	16
Ascoli	14
Lazio	11
Cremonese	8

22a Giornata

17 March 1985

SEVENTEEN-YEAR-OLD STUDENT Alessandro Fiorio is a regular at the Bentegodi. He takes the bus to the stadium with a group of friends from Veronetta, the vibrant neighbourhood where he lives with his parents. 'The gates would always open early,' Alessandro recalls, 'even as early as 10.30 or 11, so we tended to arrive as early as possible.' For Alessandro, the Sunday ritual was always the same: Mass in the morning, football in the afternoon. With little money to spare, he'd bring a panino from home; he certainly couldn't afford to frequent the bars around the stadium or buy drinks once inside.

For away games, Alessandro and his friends joined a supporters' club, '*La vecia piassa dell'Isolo*' (The Old Square of the Island), which met in a bar in Piazza Isolo in Veronetta.[68] 'There was', he remembers, 'a sheet of paper hanging in the bar and during the week before the away match, you just had to go to the bar and sign your name on that sheet. This covered you for both the bus and the stadium ticket.' With no online registration or fan cards, it now sounds like the Middle Ages but, for Alessandro, it was 'the simple beauty of an era that no longer exists'. The bus would leave between six and seven in the morning but, for once, Alessandro and his friends were happy to get up early. Since Florence was considered a 'safe' trip because of the *gemellaggio* between the fans, the trip to Tuscany was traditionally a family affair. Once on the motorway, the songs began as they waited for the obligatory stop at the

---

68 Isolo, once called Isolo di San Tommaso, is an area of the Veronetta district of Verona that was once a river island.

Autogrill, where a folding table would emerge from the belly of the coach and a picnic of salami or *bondola* sandwiches, *nervetti* with onions and chips would appear. There was also, of course, the obligatory demijohn of wine!

In the week leading up to the Fiorentina match, Verona sporting director Emiliano Mascetti is asked about the future of the club beyond the current campaign. In response, he tells the *Corriere della Sera*: '[W]e will improve the stadium, we will try to retain the squad, we will make adjustments for the better if possible [...]. The municipality wants the 1990 World Cup, so it must adapt.' An ambitious future but, as matchday approaches, there are more pressing matters to attend to.

Verona are without the disqualified Fanna, Bruni and Marangon, while Volpati and Tricella are also in doubt, adding to the sense of crisis surrounding the club. With Bagnoli, it can sometimes be difficult to tell if he is being ironic but there is no doubting his sincerity when he speaks to the press on the eve of this game: '[W]hoever aims for the *Scudetto* must also be able to overcome these [difficult] moments. They must find the motivation to react. This is where you see how much a team is worth.'

With a flu bug threatening the camp, Bagnoli's contingency plan is well rehearsed. Ferroni returns in defence, allowing the ever-versatile Volpati to move to the left, occupying Marangon's place. Sacchetti will play in midfield, with Turchetta deputising for Fanna. Whilst these are enforced changes, rotation is good for maintaining harmony in the dressing room, with a 3.5m lire player bonus (about €1,750 in today's money) at stake for each point earned. Meanwhile, Fanna, one of the stars of the season so far, reaffirms to the *Corriere della Sera* the importance of the collective: 'In Verona, individuals count for nothing. The results obtained so far have been achieved by the team.'

Elsewhere, Trevor Francis has made a good recovery from the horrific head knock he suffered against Udinese two weeks earlier. The English striker is in good spirits and has made a swift recovery from the blow that rendered him unconscious and in need of emergency resuscitation. Even so, there is no place for him in the Sampdoria squad that travels to Torino, where fourth meet fifth.

As 50,000 pack into Fiorentina's Stadio Comunale,[69] Antonio Di Gennaro concedes that, once again, Verona's objective for the day is not to lose. Things don't start well for the visitors when, with barely ten minutes on the clock, the home side take the lead with a Paolo Monelli glancing header. With slightly more composure, Fiorentina could double their lead in the first half, with Sócrates demonstrating flashes of brilliance and Claudio Gentile coming close with the goal at his mercy.

At half-time, it is left to captain Roberto Tricella to lift his team: '[T]hey're not superstars, these Fiorentina players, we can beat them!' His message, delivered with sufficient gusto to be heard by journalists outside the changing room, seems to do the trick and a much-improved Verona emerge in the second half.

Twelve minutes into the second half, Silvano Fontolan pounces on a loose ball inside the six-yard box from a trademark Fanna set piece. It's a rare goal for the Hellas defender (his first and only goal of the campaign) and seems to settle nerves, on and off the pitch. Then, with 20 minutes remaining, a mazy Briegel foray into the box concludes with a foul on the German and a penalty, which Galderisi dispatches with aplomb.

At the other end, Fiorentina are awarded a penalty of their own but the Argentine World Cup winner Daniel Passarella blasts high and wide.[70] In the space of just six minutes, with one penalty converted and one missed, the fate of the match, and possibly the championship, is sealed. Verona's third goal comes from yet another set piece. As the ball is whipped in from the right-hand corner, Di Gennaro fires in a shot which is blocked by Fiorentina keeper Giovanni Galli. Galderisi is the first to

---

69 In 1991, the Comunale was renamed Artemio Franchi after the former Italian Football Federation president.

70 Considered one of the greatest defenders of all time, Daniel Passarella captained Argentina to victory at the 1978 World Cup and was also part of the winning squad in 1986.

react, heading in from point-blank range, leaving the *Viola* keeper flailing. Just 22 years old and barely 5ft 6in (1.68m) tall, it's Nanu's tenth goal in the championship, including three penalties and four headers – not bad for a little 'un!

In his post-match summary, commentator Gian Piero Galeazzi concludes that 'Verona had its most difficult day, the most challenging, but perhaps it found the two points for the championship', before observing that 'a Veronese cyclone' changed the course of the game. In the tunnel afterwards, Fiorentina coach Ferruccio Valcareggi claims that a draw would have been a fairer result, before conceding that Verona now have a great chance of winning the *Scudetto*. Pinning down a grinning Garella, Galeazzi asks if he feels like the goalkeeper of the champions of Italy. 'Not yet,' comes the cheerful reply, before the big keeper deflects once again, insisting on the importance of the team. Galeazzi's final teasing question: 'Are Verona lucky or good?' To which Garella replies, with a glint in his eye, that they are good rather than lucky, bringing the good-natured exchange to a close.

Galderisi dedicates his second goal to his team-mate, Spuri, the reserve goalkeeper whose mother died during the week. Before the match, the grieving keeper had asked Galderisi to score a goal for him. Nanu was only too happy to oblige.

Notwithstanding the final score and the friendly relationship between the opposing fans, 17-year-old Alessandro Fiorio remembers a hard-fought contest. He recalled how Fiorentina took the lead and were 'superior to us at times' during the first half. He remembers it as a wild spring day, cold one moment, then rain and even some sleet. It was 'going badly', admitted Alessandro. '[B]ut fate was on our side that day and Passarella kicked that penalty really high.' Victory was in the bag once Galderisi struck at the double and Alessandro concluded: 'A ray of sunshine even appeared from behind the big black clouds. It seemed like a message from God.'

Elsewhere that day, results are favourable for Verona, with 90,000 turning out to witness a thrilling Milan derby that ends in a 2-2 draw, with Rummenigge on the scoresheet for the first time in three months. Torino share the points with Sampdoria and Juve and Roma also draw, leaving Hellas the only team in the top seven to take full points. The net result is that Hellas extend their lead to three points.

Meanwhile, speculation about Bagnoli's future has taken centre stage in the print media, leaving club president Celestino Guidotti to reassure fans that 'the club is willing to do anything to keep him' but that Bagnoli is 'a guy capable of anything'. Guidotti continues: '[U]nfortunately, I cannot conceive of Verona without Bagnoli. So, if Bagnoli doesn't sign the contract renewal, the *Scudetto* celebrations would be ruined by his departure.' Majority shareholder Ferdinando Chiampan adds to the sense of impending loss, telling the *Corriere della Sera:* '[A]t this point it's easier to win the championship than to keep Bagnoli.'

Match-winner Galderisi is asked if Verona have a secret. 'The secret,' the diminutive striker explains, 'is togetherness, friendship, team spirit. I don't even think about the possibility of being the top Italian scorer. I would be selfish if I thought about such objectives. I am completely focussed, like the others, on the wonderful reality that is about to materialise.' While such platitudes are now part of every striker's post-match repertoire, with Bagnoli's Verona they are more than just well-worn cliches meaninglessly trotted out for the press. For Bagnoli and his players, the team is everything. There are no superstars. No single player is bigger than the club. Everyone has their part to play.

Bagnoli's men return from Florence with their sixth away win from 12 games on the road. With Inter drawing, Hellas surge to a three-point lead with just eight games to go. No wonder the headline of Monday morning's *Corriere Sportivo* declares: 'Verona in Paradiso'.

22A GIORNATA

Ascoli 1-0 Como
Cremonese 1-1 Lazio
Fiorentina 1-3 Verona
Napoli 1-0 Atalanta
Roma 1-1 Juventus
Torino 1-1 Sampdoria
Inter 2-2 Milan
Udinese 2-0 Avellino

CLASSIFICA

Verona	**33**
Inter	30
Sampdoria	28
Torino	28
Milan	28
Juventus	26
Roma	24
Napoli	22
Fiorentina	21
Atalanta	20
Avellino	19
Udinese	18
Como	18
Ascoli	16
Lazio	12
Cremonese	9

23a Giornata

24 March 1985

THE CRYPTOPORTICUS of the Capitolium of Verona may not sound like an obvious place to be discussing football but when the man you're looking for is not only a renowned local archaeologist but also a long-standing follower of Hellas Verona, then perhaps you have come to the right place after all. One stiflingly hot Sunday morning in early September 2024, I descended into the cryptoporticus and found the unassuming archaeologist sitting behind a makeshift desk in a cool corner of the crypt, welcoming visitors in a fluent Italian tinged with an indelible hint of Mancunian. Simon Thompson arrived in Verona in June 1981 to work with his friend, a pioneering young archaeologist named Peter Hudson, on the Scavi Scaligeri, a major archaeological site in the city, not far from Juliet's Balcony. Simon planned to spend a few months on the dig before returning to England at the end of the summer. Nearly 45 years later, he's still here.

Simon was a big Manchester United fan and grew up in the era of Bobby Charlton, George Best and Denis Law. Despite being a regular at Old Trafford, he didn't immediately throw himself into the local football scene in Verona but by the 1984/85 season, he was a regular. He was in the stands for Maradona's debut, Elkjær's shoeless goal and that narrow victory against Roma.

Every now and then, he would encounter the team out running in the Torricelle hills. So, what was Verona like back then? 'Well,' Simon explains, 'it was completely different. For a start, there was no mass tourism. In fact, there were very few foreigners at all.'

Nor was there any trouble at the stadium but he could sense something darker was brewing: '[T]he right-wing thuggery for which Hellas has now become synonymous came later,' he remembers. On 29 May 1985, Simon invited a group of friends to his house to watch the European Cup Final between Liverpool and Juventus. Among them were fans of both teams. They watched on in horror as events at Heysel Stadium unfolded in front of their eyes. So distressed by what he saw that evening, Simon never stepped foot inside a football stadium again.

On 20 December 1989, while working on the construction of an underpass as part of the infrastructure improvements for the 1990 World Cup, bulldozers uncovered what appeared to be some kind of burial site. Building work was suspended and a team of international archaeologists, led by Peter Hudson and his friend, Simon Thompson, were brought in to excavate the site. They made a series of startling discoveries, uncovering multiple burial sites in what turned out to be a major Roman era necropolis. Across two plots, 1,343 burial sites were eventually uncovered, providing fresh insight into Roman burial rituals and the life and times of the ancient Venetians.

On a pleasant early spring afternoon in late March 1985, 41,000 are packed into the Bentegodi, including Simon. The atmosphere is expectant as Hellas face a team who haven't picked up a single point on the road all season.[71] Back in November, Verona beat Cremonese 2-0, thanks to second-half goals from Galderisi (a penalty) and Briegel. Elsewhere, AC Milan host Torino and Inter face Juventus at the Stadio Comunale in another crucial round of games that will bring us one step closer to determining the fate of the *Scudetto.* The build-up to this round of fixtures is overshadowed after a midweek European Cup Winners' Cup tie between Roma and Bayern Munich was marred by violence, with seven fans injured, two of them seriously, when clashes between

71 In fact, Cremonese's only point on the road this season will not come until 21 April, when they draw 1-1 with Fiorentina.

opposing fans broke out in the streets around the Stadio Olimpico.

Verona start well and Cremonese do themselves no favours when Walter Viganò is sent off after 22 minutes for a late challenge on Fanna. The visitors are already without several key players and the loss of Viganò for a challenge that was clumsy rather than malicious effectively ends their hopes of causing an unlikely upset. Despite the odds being against Cremonese, it is still goalless at half-time.

At the interval, Bagnoli replaces Bruni with the more impactful Sacchetti. Within a few minutes, it's the substitute who launches Briegel, who makes one of his rampant surges down the left wing before releasing an unmarked Di Gennaro. His lob is deflected into his own net by Fausto Borin, the Cremonese keeper. Forty-nine minutes played. Verona 1 Cremonese 0.

The visitors respond immediately but Garella is as alert as ever and, when he is, for once, beaten, the post comes to his rescue. The brief storm abates and Verona retake control. In the 61st minute, Fanna drills a fierce long-range shot, which Borin parries. Di Gennaro is the first to react and his cross finds Elkjær, who dives headfirst to make it 2-0.

Emanating from the *Curva Sud*, one cry above all the others reverberates around the stadium: '*Bagnoli resta con noi!*' (Bagnoli stay with us!). With offers reportedly coming in from Fiorentina and Napoli (as well as Inter), it is a desperate plea for loyalty. While discreet negotiations are taking place behind the scenes, it is surely not a question of money for Bagnoli. His primary concern is that the team he has assembled over the past four years is not broken up at the end of the season. Whatever the coach's intentions, he doesn't flinch as his name rings out from every corner of the stadium. His undivided attention remains, as ever, on the game of football being played out in front of him.

It was around this point in the season that Italian coaches gathered in Rome for a conference entitled 'Tactical Evolution of World Football'. Everyone was there, from Trapattoni to

Nedo Sonetti. Bagnoli, the leading coach in the country at that moment, took a discreet place in the second-to-back row. At a certain point, the event co-ordinator, Marino Bartoletti, called him forward to explain the Verona phenomenon. Scratching his nose, a nervous habit, Bagnoli reluctantly took the stage and said: '[N]ow I'm going to look stupid, because there's nothing to explain. I'll just say one thing – Verona play traditional football. I read in the papers that we "press". I've never noticed that on the pitch. I'm sorry but you are asking me for a recipe that I don't have.'

Back at the Bentegodi, with just minutes remaining, a Fanna free kick comes off the crossbar and Briegel bundles it over the line to score with his head. Once again, a goal by the Dane is followed by one from the German. It is almost as if they are competing against each other! The margin of victory certainly flatters Hellas, while the likeable team from Cremona once again demonstrate their capacity to play well but come away with nothing.

There are seismic results elsewhere, as Inter lose 3-1 to Juve (with Altobelli, Tardelli, Boniek and Briaschi on the scoresheet), leaving the Milan giants five points adrift of Verona. Inter president Ernesto Pellegrini admits: '[T]he gap with Verona seems unbridgeable.' Torino, meanwhile, who win against AC Milan at the San Siro thanks to a Schachner goal, join the *Nerazzurri* in second place in the standings, causing a defiant Júnior to proclaim that 'after this victory, we can even win at Verona' and 'the battle for the *Scudetto* isn't over yet'.

Edmondo Fabbri, coach of the Italian national team at the 1966 World Cup, observes Verona's victory from the Bentegodi press gallery and remarks: '[A]t five in the evening, the championship was killed by the Veronese bullfighter Di Gennaro.' So, a reporter probes, has the *Scudetto* already been won with seven Sundays to go? Fabbri responds: 'Only an idiot would doubt it.'

With his compact squad in good health, even Bagnoli has to admit the outcome of the championship is now in his team's hands. Is it time to finally pop open a bottle of champagne, the famously prudent coach is asked. Bagnoli responds with a wry smile: '[T]hat's up to you. But I'd keep it in the fridge for a bit longer.' Briegel and Elkjær are less discreet. In fact, the two foreigners can barely conceal their joy. Veering wildly off script, the towering German gushes: '[N]ow there's no point in telling lies, this championship is ours!' Elkjær is equally forthright, telling the *Corriere della Sera*: 'I have to say thank you to the *Bianconeri* [Juventus]. They handed us the *Scudetto*. In my career, I have never won anything. And now I can only say thank you to Verona, who have allowed me to win the most beautiful championship in the world.' The Italians in the team are still sticking to the script and refuse to be drawn on the *Scudetto*: 'The most I can say', mutters Galderisi, 'is that if we don't win it, we'll have to shoot ourselves!'

With a run of fixtures that involves Sampdoria, Torino and AC Milan, perhaps Bagnoli's reticence is understandable. Besides, such hubris would be completely out of character. Bigger sides than Verona have crumbled at this point and, while Torino are now the most obvious title challengers, keep an eye on an in-form Juventus. Could they mount a serious challenge at this late stage in the season? Even Verona's mayor, Gabriele Sboarina, tells the *Corriere della Sera*: 'You don't sell the grapes before the harvest.' Behind the scenes, however, his administration is quietly making contingency plans for the biggest party the city has ever seen.

With Verona nudging ever closer to a glorious footballing fairy tale, the international football community, from Toronto to Tel Aviv, is beginning to sit up and take notice. The club's switchboard is inundated with invitations to participate in friendly matches, exhibition games and pre-season tours. Meanwhile, Volpati, Tricella and Fontolan, the 'trade unionists' of the team, have opened negotiations with the club, seeking a 1bn lire championship bonus, in addition to the 3.5m lire per point they already take home. According to the deal made at the beginning of the season, when Bagnoli's team exceed 38 points in the standings, a 'joker' kicks in and the point bonus doubles.

Meanwhile, as the front page of Monday's *Corriere della Sera* reports an upsurge in racial violence in South Africa and news that the Italian super tanker *Volere* has been attacked by Iraqi jets in the Persian Gulf, below the fold, a headline for the ages reads: 'Inter fall and Verona soar towards the Scudetto'. The following day, the *Corriere* carries a rare personal insight from Bagnoli himself: 'I told my two daughters "I think it [the championship] is done here". And they started crying with joy. Could there be anything more beautiful? It's strange, because we never talk about football at home. But this is an adventure. We're outside the norm. Now, in Verona, even 70-year-old women are talking about football.'

23A GIORNATA

Atalanta 0-1 Udinese
Avellino 0-1 Napoli
Como 0-0 Sampdoria
Milan 0-1 Torino
Lazio 1-1 Roma
Ascoli 2-1 Fiorentina
Juventus 3-1 Inter
Verona 3-0 Cremonese

CLASSIFICA

Verona	**35**
Torino	30
Inter	30
Sampdoria	29
Juventus	28
Milan	28
Roma	25
Napoli	24
Fiorentina	21
Atalanta	20
Udinese	20
Avellino	19
Como	19
Ascoli	18
Lazio	13
Cremonese	9

24a Giornata

31 March 1985

AS BAGNOLI'S men march inexorably towards the *Scudetto*, a trip to Genoa to face an ambitious Sampdoria represents a potential banana skin. Pre-match, Sampdoria coach Eugenio Bersellini concedes that the race for the title is effectively over but says he remains focussed on a top five finish that would guarantee European football for his team next season. Two points today will go some way towards securing that objective for yet another coach nicknamed '*Il sergente di ferro*' (the Iron Sergeant) because of his robust and professional approach to fitness. Maximum points for Verona, on the other hand, will surely remove any lingering doubts about the outcome of the championship.

According to the *Corriere della Sera*, in the 17 previous championships in which Serie A has involved 16 clubs, the team leading at this point in the season have gone on to win the championship on 15 occasions. Naturally, the two exceptions both involved Juventus. In the 1972/73 season, AC Milan were top of the league and five points above Juventus with six games remaining but it was *La Signora* who went on to win the championship. And in 1980/81, Roma were leading but Juventus again caused a late upset, though the deficit was just a single point in that case.

For once, Bagnoli has his full roster of players available and reverts to his preferred starting XI. Ferroni returns at the back against his former club, as Volpati pushes up into midfield just behind Di Gennaro, unshackling Fanna on the wing, with Elkjær and Galderisi up front. For Sampdoria, Trevor Francis is keen to return after that terrible incident at Udinese but may have to settle for a place on the bench, a thin red scar that extends 3cm from his left eyebrow a lasting reminder of that violent clash of heads that knocked him out just a few weeks ago.

Francis has been in Italy for two and a half years and has followed with great interest the emergence of a constantly improving Verona. He is a big fan of Hellas and of Bagnoli (because of the *gemellaggio*, he is even able to say so publicly) and welcomes what they have achieved. The masterstroke, according to Francis, was the acquisition of Briegel and Elkjær, who found themselves surrounded by a motivated and rapidly maturing group with an exceptional leader. 'They remind me of an English team,' Francis explains to the *Corriere della Sera*. 'They always run, they always play, they never give up.'

With expectations high, by Saturday it's heading for a complete sell-out at the Stadio Luigi Ferraris, with record takings of nearly 600m lire. The *gemellaggio* agreement means that Hellas fans can expect a warm welcome, as an unruly convoy of 60 buses makes its way south from Verona to the Ligurian coast. Hundreds more travel by train and car. The mood is celebratory and there is just one unsavoury incident at a motorway Autogrill after four coachloads of Hellas fans are refused entry. A handful of disgruntled fans react violently and two are subsequently arrested and charged with theft and criminal damage.

When the 8,000 Hellas fans finally arrive at the Ferraris, they occupy every part of the stadium. In one corner of the *curva*, usually reserved for Sampdoria's most hardcore fans, a banner is unfurled which reads: 'Welcome champions of Italy.' Also in the stands today is the national team coach, Enzo Bearzot. Known affectionately as '*Il Vecio*' (The Old Man), he even smokes a pipe! With Paolo Rossi now approaching the twilight of his international career, Bearzot will be keeping a close eye on the in-form Verona striker Giuseppe Galderisi, not to mention the two emerging Sampdoria stars, Vialli and Mancini.

With both Inter and AC Milan losing last weekend and Juve and Torino both winning, the momentum among the chasing pack has shifted west. In fact, Inter's form of late has capitulated, having picked up just seven points from the last seven fixtures (compared to Verona's 13) and today they face a tricky trip to Zico's Udinese. A resurgent Juve, meanwhile, having taken full points from Inter last weekend, face Torino in a tantalising '*Derby della Mole*', Italy's oldest city derby. AC Milan, meanwhile, face Avellino at the San Siro.

Verona, in all yellow, start well. After just six minutes, Elkjær releases Galderisi, who surges into the penalty area, past Vierchowod and Alessandro Renica with a couple of deft feints, and beats Bordon with a precise diagonal shot. The Marassi explodes![72] Sampdoria 0 Verona 1.

Barely five minutes later, the *Blucerchiati* win a free kick in a promising area. From long range, Renica, a towering defender with an eye for goal, unleashes a missile that Garella parries into his own net. Though Verona's defence had seemed impenetrable, it has taken Sampdoria just five minutes to snatch an equaliser from a set piece. With just 11 minutes played and goals at either end, the game is certainly living up to its pre-match billing.

In the 24th minute, Fontolan almost restores the *Gialloblù* lead with a rare offensive foray. Nine minutes later, Di Gennaro – who is unburdened by Volpati offering cover in midfield and Briegel providing extra muscle – forces a decent save from Ivano Bordon. With the national coach watching on, the Verona midfielder is doing his reputation no harm with a lively performance in the heart of the Hellas midfield.

Despite the best efforts of Mancini and Vialli, Verona's defence stands firm, with Ferroni, Fontolan and Tricella letting nothing through. It has been an enthralling 45 minutes of end-to-end football played out under a grey Ligurian sky. In the second half, as the sun drops and shadows lengthen, the pace

72 Genoa's Stadio Luigi Ferraris is colloquially known as the Marassi after the neighbourhood where it is located. It is the oldest football facility in Italy still in operation, having been inaugurated in 1911.

inevitably eases off, with Galderisi and Elkjær on the receiving end of some assertive Sampdoria defending.

In the 78th minute, Bagnoli takes Nanu off, replacing him with Sacchetti, while Fanna drops deeper before being replaced by Bruni at the close, a clear statement of intent that a point at this stage is sufficient.

With just a few minutes remaining, there's a final flurry of activity but, in the end, it's honours even for two of the most exciting teams in the league. It's a mature performance from Verona, who again achieve what they set out to do. For Sampdoria, the disappointment of a point dropped at home is tempered by the sure signs that they have what it takes to become tomorrow's champions – not least in the form of the blossoming offensive partnership between Mancini and Vialli.

Meanwhile, results elsewhere mean Verona's lead has stretched to six points. Inter lose 2-1 to Udinese in another massive blow to their championship hopes, while Torino lose 0-2 to Juventus in another impressive result for *La Signora*. Once again, Verona's closest rivals have spurned the opportunity to close the gap, with only AC Milan closing ground, thanks to a 2-0 victory against Avellino. But keep a close eye on Juventus who, after a sluggish start, have now joined that chasing group on 30 points.

Di Gennaro is in celebratory mood, telling the *Corriere della Sera*: 'Damn! In 1985, I really have everything: my first daughter was born, I made it to the national team, now the championship. What more could I ask for? We deserve the title.' Roberto Mancini, disappointed to be substituted for Trevor Francis 14 minutes into the second half, strikes a similar note in his post-match comments: 'Verona deserve the *Scudetto*. They have a terrifying counter-attack.'

Meanwhile, Bearzot has called up an unprecedented four Hellas players (Di Gennaro, Fanna, Tricella and Galderisi) for the forthcoming friendly against Portugal. With Verona just a few steps away from the *Scudetto*, the national team coach offers his assessment of Verona's success: '[F]or five years, Bagnoli's team has been on the crest of a wave. They deserve this title. And I like Verona, because they play like Italy: a mixed tactical approach – zonal and man-to-man – great fluidity, a nicely manoeuvred counter-attack. The secrets? Two above all. Bagnoli's wisdom and the athletic power that Briegel and Elkjær have brought to the team.'

After the international break, Hellas will welcome Torino to the Bentegodi. Another formidable adversary who must win if they are to close the massive six-point gap at the top of the table.

While a hard-earned point is enough to send the snaking convoy of fans home from Genoa with a smile on their faces, even better news comes in the aftermath of the game, with confirmation that Bagnoli will be staying on as Hellas coach next season. Responding to questions about his decision to stay, Bagnoli emphasises the importance of retaining his team: '[L]et's say that I hope to be able to count on all the players this year, especially because I already know that next season will be much more difficult than this one.' With offers already coming in thick and fast for his key players, keeping the team together for another season will be a true test of loyalty and ambition.

24A GIORNATA

Cremonese 2-0 Como
Fiorentina 1-0 Roma
Torino 0-2 Juventus
Lazio 1-1 Atalanta
Milan 2-0 Avellino
Napoli 1-1 Ascoli
Sampdoria 1-1 Verona
Udinese 2-1 Inter

CLASSIFICA

Verona	**36**
Juventus	30
Torino	30
Sampdoria	30
Inter	30
Milan	30
Napoli	25
Roma	25
Fiorentina	23
Udinese	22
Atalanta	21
Avellino	19
Ascoli	19
Como	19
Lazio	14
Cremonese	11

25a Giornata

14 April 1985

BAGNOLI IS going nowhere. Confirmation that the taciturn coach has reached an agreement with the club to keep him in Verona next season has been met with jubilation among players and fans alike. His commitment to the club and the club's investment in him is a clear statement of intent. For those Hellas players currently considering their own futures, a gauntlet has been thrown down. The Bagnoli project is not over. No matter how the current season finishes, the miracle doesn't end here.

Speaking to the *Corriere della Sera* in the aftermath of the draw with Sampdoria, Galderisi is amongst the first to welcome the announcement: '[T]he news about Bagnoli staying is the best news of the day. Better than scoring a goal [...]. He [Bagnoli] created the group – it was formed around him, he shaped it.' The Hellas striker has already won two league titles with Juventus, but this experience with Verona just feels different: '[I]n Turin, I was an 18-year-old boy who played when I could be useful, maybe scoring seven goals, but always as a young prospect who had to fight for everything. Here it's different. I contributed to this championship with all my strength, day after day, one piece at a time. In Verona, Bagnoli and his team made me feel like a man, they gave me confidence by entrusting me with specific responsibilities.'

Bagnoli will earn 300m lire next season, with the objective of finishing in the UEFA zone and progressing beyond the first round of the European Cup. He could, as far as majority shareholder Ferdinando Chiampan is concerned, lose eight games in a row and he would never be fired. For his results this season and the loyalty he has shown, Bagnoli's position is guaranteed.

With six games to go and a six-point advantage, Verona could be excused for taking their foot of the pedal, for getting caught up in the hype that the championship has already been won. But there are two tough games to come, against Torino today and then at the San Siro against AC Milan next weekend. Even Bagnoli, who for so long has denied even the remote possibility of a *Scudetto,* is prepared to concede that his team can afford to lose one, but not both, of those games. But he is not prepared to play for a draw. He has his principles and playing for a draw is not amongst them. Although he would certainly *settle* for a draw against Torino (and again against AC Milan), it is not in his footballing mindset to actually *play* for a draw. Doing so carries too much risk. Meanwhile, Torino coach Gigi Radice is acutely aware of the risk Hellas pose: 'Verona is a team that is always dangerous. We'd settle for a draw and even that might be asking for too much.'

Just three days after that thrilling encounter with Sampdoria, four players from the champions elect (by now, most pundits and commentators have already declared the outcome of the championship in Verona's favour) were called up to bring freshness and vigour to the Italian national team that faced Portugal in a friendly in Ascoli. The international friendly against Greece little more than a month ago ended in what was regarded as an embarrassing goalless draw and Bearzot is keen to breathe new life into his sluggish team with the clock ticking down to the World Cup in Mexico in little over a year's time. In addition to Di Gennaro, Fanna, Tricella and Galderisi were also included in the squad. Bearzot has even hinted that the in-form Hellas centre-forward could be the natural successor to Paolo Rossi and repeatedly extolled the virtues of the player. Meanwhile, emerging talent like Gianluca Vialli, Roberto Mancini and Roberto Donadoni are waiting in the wings, gaining experience with the Under-21s, but it can only be a matter of time before such generational talent explodes on the international scene.

In the event, a disappointed Galderisi didn't make his international debut against Portugal.[73] Antonio Di Gennaro, meanwhile, took his place in the heart of Italy's midfield, while Pierino Fanna made an appearance 15 minutes into the second half to earn his 11th cap, as Italy emerged comfortable 2-0 winners with goals from Bruno Conti and Paolo Rossi. Perhaps Conti and Rossi were spurred on by the mere presence of Fanna and Galderisi on the bench. Perhaps Bearzot never intended to play them but merely wanted to apply pressure to the notoriously fickle Rossi, reminding him that other options were available. Whatever mind games were at play, Nanu was magnanimous despite his exclusion. Rossi was, after all, a footballing legend who had mentored the young striker when they were at Juventus together.

Despite losing 2-0 to Juventus in the derby last weekend, Torino remain one of five teams in the chasing pack currently trailing Hellas by six points. Never at this point in the season have the league leaders had a six-point advantage over a group of five competitors all on the same number of points. After 24 games, it's an unprecedented situation. While anything is possible, those in the chasing pack (Juventus, Torino, Sampdoria, Inter and AC Milan) are now primarily concerned with the battle for a European place, while Inter and Juve have the added distraction of the latter stages of the European and UEFA cups to contend with.[74]

As matchday approaches, expectations are high. On Saturday, after the last training session ahead of the game, a noisy group of Hellas fans gathers at the pitches behind

---

73 Giuseppe Galderisi made his international debut on 2 June 1985, as a half-time substitute in a friendly against Mexico, at the end of a season in which he emerged as one of the most prolific Italian scorers in Serie A. Only Platini (18), Altobelli (17) and Maradona (14) scored more than Galderisi (11) in the 1984/85 season. He would go on to earn ten caps, including four appearances at the 1986 World Cup.

74 Juventus have reached the semi-final of the European Cup, beating Bordeaux 3-0 in the first leg on 11 April with the return leg to be played on 24 April. Inter, meanwhile, have reached the semi-final of the UEFA Cup, beating Real Madrid 2-0 in the first leg with the return leg to be played in Madrid on 24 April.

the Bentegodi to make their views known to Fanna and Marangon. The message is clear and impassioned: 'Don't leave. We need you.' Behind the scenes, negotiations about their future continue.

As matchday dawns, football has taken over the city. The stadium is the only place to be. Every seat is occupied, a joyous wave of yellow and blue. There is a shimmering pageant of scarves, flags and banners, a haze of yellow and blue smoke engulfing the stadium in a mood of jubilant expectation. Is it possible to simply enjoy the moment? Or is it necessary to dwell on its implications for a club who have never known success? Every fan is swept up in the euphoria of the occasion, each subconsciously aware that they might be on the brink of something that will live forever. This is uncharted territory. Can it even be happening? In their wildest fantasies, not even the most hardcore fan expected to be living this dream.

Garella, forever associated with that distinctive red jersey, is today wearing grey. Some of his best performances – against Juventus, Sampdoria and Lazio – have come while he was wearing that lucky red top. The alternative is green (did he wear it against Roma at the Olimpico?); less striking but just as effective. 'It's a colour that I just don't like,' he complains ahead of kick-off. Hopefully not a bad omen.

Bagnoli demands a strong start and Elkjær, with just four minutes on the clock, surges through the Torino defence, leaving keeper Silvano Martina badly exposed and with little option but to bring down the flying Dane. Galderisi's penalty is woeful, lacking both power and precision – a wasted opportunity to take an early lead and settle any lingering nerves.

Just a few minutes later, Fanna finds Briegel from a trademark set piece but somehow Martina saves the German's header from point-blank range. Three minutes later, Fanna's cross finds Marangon arriving at the back post but his sliding effort narrowly misses the target.

It's a frenetic first 15 minutes for Verona but somehow it remains goalless as Torino gradually ease themselves into the game, with Danilo Pileggi, Paolo Beruatto, Giuseppe Dossena,

Júnior and Renato Zaccarelli beginning to exert their quality and experience. Up front, Aldo Serena keeps Fontolan and Tricella busy, while the devastatingly fast Austrian Walter Schachner is giving Ferroni a run for his money. A tense and finely balanced first half eventually ends goalless.

It will take something spectacular to finally break the deadlock and it is Aldo Serena's bicycle kick that leaves even Garella applauding once he processes what has just happened. Torino double their lead on 65 minutes with a cool Schachner finish, before Briegel grabs a 77th-minute consolation with a looping header at the back post. Verona come close to snatching a late equaliser but Torino defend with courage and discipline to deny the hosts another famous comeback.

With Verona struggling, the sight of Briegel being carried off after a heavy challenge by Giancarlo Corradini in the 85th minute is a painful one. A murmur of concern sweeps around the stadium. Then, as the final whistle sounds, that unfamiliar sense of defeat. It's the first time Hellas have lost at the Bentegodi in almost a year. Since 6 May 1984, to be precise, when they were beaten 2-1 by Inter.

Post-match, Elkjær concedes that Hellas played badly: 'Torino deserved the victory [...]. We lacked determination, the desire to win and suffer.' It is a gracious and honest assessment after a deeply disappointing result. Garella is even more scathing: '[I]t would be better if the fans took the *scudetti* off their flags. They can sew them back on at the end, when we have actually won something. We were unlucky but when we miss chances like that, I don't know who to blame.'

It is only Verona's second defeat of the season. The first came away to Avellino in January but on that occasion, Ferroni, Galderisi and Elkjær were all missing. For the first time, perhaps, signs of fatigue and frailty are showing in a squad that has played an entire season with barely 15 players. The media attention and pressure is also beginning to mount. But how will Bagnoli's men react? And what about those in the chasing pack? Can they cast aside the inconsistencies of the past and mount a serious challenge with just five games remaining?

Verona's defeat coincides with the simultaneous victores of four of the five title challengers (all except AC Milan). Inter edge out Fiorentina (1-0) and Juventus beat Udinese (3-2), while Sampdoria see off AC Milan (2-1). Apart from Torino, no one else seems to be in the best form but Verona's surprise defeat offers a glimmer of hope for the others. Inter have won again in the championship for the first time in more than two months and are now 'only' four points behind Hellas. For Walter Zenga, it's already too late: 'Verona lost? It doesn't matter. Now we're aiming for second place but, above all, to win the UEFA Cup against Real Madrid.'[75] Only Rummenigge refuses to admit defeat. 'If Verona lose next Sunday against Milan', he tells the *Corriere della Sera,* 'anything could happen.'

Next weekend, Hellas face that tricky journey to play AC Milan at the San Siro. They will make the short trip to Milan without the suspended Fontolan and the injured Briegel. Another defeat will seriously undermine morale and give the chasing pack a massive opportunity to close the gap even further with four games remaining.

Of Briegel, the news isn't good. The immediate diagnosis was just a sprain but then, because of the swelling and pain, the German was taken to hospital. An X-ray confirmed just a sprain but a cast was applied to his swollen ankle as a precaution and he is expected to be out of action for at least two weeks. Later in the week, Sacchetti, the German's natural replacement, will also withdraw with an injury.

Despite the defeat, the yellow and blue brigades are defiant as they file out of the stadium shortly before six o'clock on Sunday evening. As they sing '*Vinceremo, vinceremo, vinceremo il tricolori*' (We will win, we will win, we will the tricolour)[76], a sudden gust of unseasonably cold wind sweeps around the stadium, sending an involuntary shiver down a thousand yellow and blue spines.

---

75 On 10 April 1985, Inter secured a 2-0 victory in a European Cup semi-final first leg tie against Real Madrid with the second leg to be played on 24 April.

76 The *tricolore* is the flag of Italy which in this case represents the championship.

25A GIORNATA

Avellino 1-1 Atalanta
Como 1-0 Lazio
Cremonese 1-1 Napoli
Inter 1-0 Fiorentina
Juventus 3-2 Udinese
Roma 3-1 Ascoli
Sampdoria 2-1 Milan
Verona 1-2 Torino

CLASSIFICA

Verona	**36**
Juventus	32
Torino	32
Sampdoria	32
Inter	32
Milan	30
Roma	27
Napoli	26
Fiorentina	23
Udinese	22
Atalanta	22
Como	21
Avellino	20
Ascoli	19
Lazio	14
Cremonese	12

26a Giornata

21 April 1985

BACK AT the beginning of December, at an icy cold Bentegodi, it ended goalless. Today's trip to the San Siro is yet another massive test for Hellas as they edge ever closer to footballing immortality. Bagnoli would certainly settle for a point as Verona seek to steady the nerves after last week's disappointing defeat to Torino. Back-to-back losses would be a major blow – a sign that Verona had lost their nerve at this most critical point in the season.

All week, the pressure has been mounting, as pundits and commentators speculate about a spectacular capitulation as the season reaches its finale. The prevailing narrative is that the provincial upstarts have had their fun but now it's time for the big boys to take their ball back. As the tension builds, Fanna, Tricella and Volpati have dinner together at a secluded restaurant near Bardolino on Lake Garda. For the three senior players, it's an opportunity to take stock, to look each other in the eye and understand if they have what it takes to finish the job. Over *lasagnette* and a glass or two of local red wine, they reassure each other that it will be okay, that they have what it takes.

On Wednesday, the 19th edition of Vinitaly, the international wine fair, opens in Verona during a particularly delicate period for the sector. Over-production across the EEC has led to the compulsory distillation of 12 million hectolitres of wine, a costly own goal for the sector. Closer to home, Ferdinando Chiampan, the Canon entrepreneur, is preparing to take a majority stake in the club. After more than three hours of discussion at the shareholders' meeting, club president

Guidotti agrees to step down on 27 May, at which point Chiampan will become the new president. The move comes with a capital investment of 5bn lire but whether that will be enough to secure the futures of Pierino Fanna and Luciano Marangon remains to be seen. Chiampan and Guidotti have been prominent and influential figures, providing the acumen, investment and stability that has underpinned Bagnoli's success on the pitch. Speaking ahead of the trip to Milan, Chiampan insists that six points from the remaining five matches will be enough for Hellas to secure the championship: 'It would be difficult for the chasing teams to take ten points from five games.'

The success of the football club has shone a spotlight on the city and its politics, not least with local elections scheduled for 12 May. Verona is the most prosperous city in the Veneto region, with the highest per capita income, the highest standard of living, best access to education and green spaces and a level of healthcare rated amongst the best in Italy. As for Verona's reputation as 'the Bangkok of Italy', the city's mayor, Gabriele Sboarina, believes that the situation has been exaggerated. '[I]t's true', he tells the *Corriere della Sera*, 'there was a hard, violent impact with the city at the beginning [of the heroin epidemic]. The phenomenon developed very quickly, surprising everyone, but the reaction was prompt and responsible, both in terms of prevention and action taken against dealers.' The real issue, the mayor insists, is youth unemployment, with 10,000 out of work in the city.

At least 8,000 yellow and blue fans are expected to make the trip to Milan on a specially chartered fleet of buses led by a precautionary police escort. In addition to busloads of locals, hundreds of Germans and Danes will travel to Milan from the resorts of Lake Garda, hoping to catch a glimpse of Briegel and Elkjær.

As the battle for European places intensifies, Liedholm's AC Milan narrowly lost to Sampdoria last weekend. They've had a challenging run of games since beating Napoli back at the beginning of March, with a draw against Inter, narrow losses to Torino and Sampdoria and a solitary victory, against Avellino. Despite such mixed form, AC Milan are amongst the cluster of contenders currently vying for second place. Without any European entanglements, they have a Coppa Italia quarter-final against Juve to look forward to once league business has concluded.

With Fontolan suspended and Briegel and Sacchetti struggling with injury, Bagnoli is left with just 13 senior players to choose from, plus reserve goalkeeper Sergio Spuri and Antonio Terracciano and Francesco Residori from the youth team. The ever-versatile Volpati will once again revert to defence, with the unenviable task of marking the towering English striker Mark Hateley, while Dario Donà, who hasn't played for two months, is called upon to shore up Verona's left flank and counter the incursions of Sergio Battistini and Andrea Icardi.

Considering Verona's diminished squad, Milan's veteran Swedish coach drops defensive midfielder, Alberigo Evani, in favour of the more offensive-minded Roberto Scarnecchia, a winger capable of supplying precision crosses for Hateley and strike partner Pietro Paolo Virdis. Antonio Di Gennaro, Verona's in-form young playmaker, has taken Giuseppe Dossena's place in the national team and the two will come face to face in front of 62,000 at the San Siro. In his pre-match comments, Di Gennaro, dismissing talk of a rivalry between the two players, insists that this is a game Hellas will play to win with their customary offensive zeal.

AC Milan are patient and experienced. In Nils Liedholm, they have one of the most successful coaches in the history of the Italian game. They can congest the midfield, absorb Verona's pace and tenacity and, with the aerial power and physicality of Hateley and the explosive pace of Virdis, cause Verona real problems up front. To return from the San Siro unscathed today will require something special.

The league leaders, in all yellow, get a 'warm' welcome at the San Siro, with kick-off delayed by five minutes as groundstaff rush to repair damage caused to Garella's net by a firecracker launched from the stands. It's the home side who start the brighter, with a Virdis free kick after just three minutes finding Hateley inside the box. As the Englishman soars above the Hellas defenders, Garella seems nailed to the spot. But, with remarkable agility, he somehow deflects the header on to the post. An early warning for Verona.

In an effort to neutralise the aerial power of the English striker, and in the absence of both Briegel and Fontolan (Verona's tallest outfield players), Bagnoli instructs Garella to come off his line to 'mark' the towering Englishman himself, with Mauro Ferroni (at just 5ft 6in told to cover the goal in case the keeper is beaten in the air. But Hateley is no one-trick pony. In the tenth minute, he beats Ferroni for pace and, instead of shooting past an advancing Garella, lays it off for Sergio Battistini, who stumbles spectacularly with the goal at his mercy.

The Hateley–Garella duel is repeated when Icardi crosses from the right. Garella is equal to it but, with barely 20 minutes played, it's another warning for Verona. Finally, Verona respond with an offensive surge of their own when Fanna escapes on the right, takes on a couple of *Rossoneri* players and crosses perfectly towards Galderisi. Filippo Galli intervenes at the front post to head clear and deny Nanu a gilt-edged chance to give Verona the lead.

In the 35th minute, Roberto Scarnecchia crosses for Hateley, who anticipates Garella's intervention but grazes the post. Four minutes later, a blast from outside the box by Ray Wilkins whizzes just over the bar. Somehow, Hellas survive the onslaught until half-time and a scintillating first half ends goalless.

Four minutes into the second half, Garella pulls off another miraculous save from a Virdis shot. Five minutes later, he does it again. As the second half wears on, Ferroni and Tricella manage to suppress the supply to Hateley, while Garella continues to snuff out any high balls that penetrate the penalty box.

Then Elkjær launches a trademark counter-attack of his own, surging towards the keeper and beating him with a familiar lob. But the referee has already blown the whistle for an earlier infringement. As whistles ring around the stadium, Elkjær shares a smile with his team-mates. The mischievous Dane knew exactly what he was doing.

There is a clamorous moment in the Hellas box after 68 minutes when Hateley releases Battistini but his effort from point-blank range is blocked again by Verona's unbeatable superhero, 'Garellik'. As Milan begin to relent, Liedholm replaces Icardi with Alberigo Evani to bolster his left wing, while Bagnoli withdraws Fanna for Fabio Marangon and, in the closing minutes, Bruni for Turchetta. As the final whistle eventually sounds, it is met with exhaustion, relief and satisfaction. Yet another man of the match performance for Garella, who once again keeps a clean sheet against the odds.

Liedholm, in his post-match remarks, suggests that, based on today's result, Verona deserve to win the championship. From Bagnoli, a wry acknowledgement that once again Verona have failed to win at the San Siro – one of the few achievements that still eludes him. Inevitably, the Verona coach insists that it is still not the right moment to speak of the *Scudetto*. He then rushes off to Bovisa, where his mother is expecting him.

While it was another momentous team effort, Garella was once again the star of the show. Post-match, he emerges from the changing room looking polished and sharp, with the confident and self-satisfied air of a player who has just won rather than drawn. He explains to the bustling cluster of journalists the plan he and Bagnoli devised to deal with Hateley. Though Volpati was to mark the Englishman, inside the box it was Garella who would challenge him in the air. When asked if he wants to dedicate his performance to anyone, Garella's response surprises the assembled hacks. '[W]ell, I really speak on behalf of the whole team,' he says, 'in dedicating this performance to the son of our masseur, who is in hospital with meningitis.' A flamboyant showman on the pitch, Garella is a quiet family man off it, as Chiampan confirms to the incredulous journalists: '[T]he Veronese often see him taking his children for a walk or at the supermarket doing the weekly shopping.'

Elsewhere, Inter suffer a massive setback, losing 3-1 in Napoli, while Juventus can only manage a 1-1 draw against Ascoli. Once again, the big beasts of the game have failed to capitalise on Verona's dropped point. Meanwhile, Sampdoria make light work of Lazio at the Olimpico, winning 3-0, while Torino, Verona's most tenacious pursuer, reinvigorated by their success at the Bentegodi the previous weekend, ease past Avellino (2-0). With these results, Sampdoria and Torino close the gap to just three points with four games remaining. Juventus, meanwhile, continue their impressive fightback, moving to fourth place ahead of Inter and AC Milan.

As evening falls in Milan, several violent skirmishes break out between opposing sets of fans. In the most serious incident, a 24-year-old Hellas fan is hit on the head with a stone and will spend the next seven days recovering in hospital. Meanwhile, the Hellas team bus is ambushed by a group of Milan fans and requires a police escort on to the motorway. While that historic victory at the San Siro remains elusive, it's another invaluable point on the road for Hellas. The title race isn't over yet but Verona's next two games are at home against Lazio and Como. On paper, at least, Hellas can expect maximum points as they edge closer to immortality.

26A GIORNATA

Ascoli 1-1 Juventus
Atalanta 1-0 Como
Fiorentina 1-1 Cremonese
Lazio 0-3 Sampdoria
Milan 0-0 Verona
Napoli 3-1 Inter
Torino 2-0 Avellino
Udinese 0-2 Roma

CLASSIFICA

Verona	**37**
Sampdoria	34
Torino	34
Juventus	33
Inter	32
Milan	31
Roma	29
Napoli	28
Fiorentina	24
Atalanta	24
Udinese	22
Como	21
Ascoli	20
Avellino	20
Lazio	14
Cremonese	13

27a Giornata

28 April 1985

LAZIO ARE a club in crisis. After seven consecutive defeats, the most recent of which was a Maradona-inspired 4-0 humiliation at the San Paolo, Giancarlo Oddi and Roberto Lovati took over managerial responsibilities from Juan Carlos Lorenzo at the beginning of March. Since then, there has been a run of four consecutive draws, followed by defeats against Como (1-0) and Sampdoria (0-3). Despite having players of the calibre of Michael Laudrup, Bruno Giordano and Oliviero Garlini, Lazio are deep in the relegation zone and are once again playing for their survival in the top tier (having previously been relegated in 1980). While Hellas are the surprise package of the season, Lazio are unquestionably the biggest disappointment.

With such a gulf between the two sides on their season's form, this should be little more than a formality for the home side. With just 14 points from 27 games and only 13 goals all season, defeat at the Bentegodi would mean certain relegation for Lazio, with three games still to play. Even victory today would do little to guarantee Lazio's safety, with Ascoli and Avellino having a six-point advantage at the foot of the table. Bagnoli, of course, takes a slightly different perspective. 'On Sunday, we will face an adversary with nothing to lose,' he tells the *Corriere della Sera* on the eve of the game. Perhaps he has a point.

For Verona, last weekend's draw in Milan has given the group a renewed sense of self-confidence, as, too, does the return of Briegel and Fontolan, with Bruni and Donà taking their more familiar places on the bench. While Verona's defence was decisive in Milan last weekend, it is now the turn of their more offensive-minded players to seize the initiative and return the club to winning ways. It has, after all, been over a month since Hellas last won a football match. But, once again, Bagnoli has a slightly contrary perspective, insisting that his team could also achieve their objective with four draws. While, mathematically, that is certainly true, it would be an uninspiring way to conclude an otherwise miraculous campaign.

That once unified chasing group of five has now been scattered, with Sampdoria and Torino the only two who haven't been tottered over by recent results. Both, however, have awkward away matches to contend with this weekend, with Torino making the short trip to Como and Samp travelling south to Avellino. As far as Bagnoli is concerned, Sampdoria are the team of the moment – determined, in form and focussed, with a depth of squad that gives them an advantage over their adversaries.

As spring is slowly giving way to summer, the first early bathers at the seaside port town of Cesenatico are taking advantage of the clement weather to take a dip in the warming Adriatic. The final month of the season is approaching. Hellas Verona are just 360 minutes away from the most significant achievement in the club's history. Perhaps the biggest upset in the history of the game. But Bagnoli still refuses to talk about it.

As the match kicks off at the Bentegodi, it's Lazio who start the brighter, with Lionello Manfredonia, Michael Laudrup and Bruno Giordano combining to test Garella. On 20 minutes, Oliviero Garlini breaks through the Verona rearguard but balloons his shot skyward. Bagnoli reacts with an angry outburst from the touchline and his players respond accordingly. Fanna picks up the ball, knocks down the visiting defenders as if they were skittles and, in desperation, Fernando Orsi brings him down inside the area. Penalty! Galderisi steps up to take it, having missed from the spot 15 days previously against Torino. It's another feeble effort that Orsi anticipates and parries with ease, leaving a dejected Nanu hanging his head in shame.

Lazio are inspired by the penalty miss and increasingly impose themselves on the game, repeatedly penetrating beyond Verona's last line of defence. Just a few seconds into the second half, Manfredonia surges down the left flank and launches Laudrup, who crosses perfectly into the area for Giordano. He shoots on the volley but Garella responds in the manner we have come to expect to deny Lazio a surprise lead. From the restart, the visitors continue to probe but Garella is in no real danger, while, at the other end, Fernando Orsi continues to command his penalty area.

With 20 minutes to go, Bagnoli withdraws Ferroni and introduces Bruni, bringing Volpati into a deeper role, giving Fanna more freedom to push forward. Once again, Bagnoli demonstrates his tactical dexterity but is it enough to break the deadlock? The answer comes within barely ten minutes, with a long-awaited goal by one of Verona's most influential players of the season. From a throw-in deep in the Lazio half, Fanna seizes on a loose ball inside the penalty area and his scrambled shot finds its way through a cluster of players before slipping under the sprawling form of Orsi, who can barely have seen it coming. Struck with raw venom and barely controlled desire, it's a goal that epitomises the liberation of a player who has been shackled for too long. Remarkably, given that he has been so influential this season, it's Fanna's first goal of the championship and, as he hares off across the running track towards the exultant fans, he raises his fists and closes his eyes in rapture. The stadium erupts as Fanna is pursued by his team-mates, few of whom have the pace to catch him.

Pierino Fanna left home at 14 to begin his footballing apprenticeship in Bergamo. Barely 18, he broke through with Atalanta where, despite his youth, he was a key component of the team that won promotion from Serie B in 1977. Later that summer, he signed for Juventus with the weight of the world on his young shoulders. Quiet and introverted, he struggled to live up to expectations and failed to progress at Juventus, where he averaged just 2.6 goals a season. Despite lifting the *Scudetto* in the 1981/82 season, alongside the likes of Dino Zoff, Liam Brady, Claudio Gentile, Gaetano Scirea and Paolo Rossi (who was just coming to the end of a three-year match-fixing ban), by the end of the 1982 season it was clear that Fanna was no longer part of Giovanni Trapattoni's plans. Though still capable of devastating flashes of brilliance, he lacked the consistency and temperament to make an impact on the big stage. In 21 appearances in the 1981/82 season, he scored just once. At 24 years old, a career that had promised so much was in danger of fizzling out.

With his hairline prematurely receding, a prominent monobrow and a heavy-set appearance, he seemed to have aged prematurely. It was, Fanna told me 40 years later, 'the most difficult moment in my career'. He had lost his father just a couple of years previously and at Juventus he never really felt wanted. Although he didn't fully understand it at the time, he was suffering a crisis of identity. All he wanted to do was play football – he didn't particularly care where – but at this critical juncture in his career he needed a coach who understood him.

Fanna was amongst the first to join the Bagnoli project in Verona, arriving for that renowned summer retreat in the Dolomites in the summer of 1982. His first impression of the famously taciturn coach wasn't exactly overwhelming. In fact, on his first day in Verona, he bumped into another new arrival, Domenico Volpati, whom he knew as an adversary from their days together in Turin. The two men had stopped to chat outside the players' entrance at Gate E when Bagnoli walked by. The coach didn't even stop to say hello. He simply walked straight past his new players without so much as a nod! And worse was to come. After the first training session, which consisted mainly of sprints and stretches, Bagnoli pulled Fanna and striker Domenico Penzo to one side: '[Y]ou better roll up your sleeves, we've got work to do here.' By now, Fanna was beginning to wonder if he'd made a massive mistake.

But it didn't take long for the talented winger to understand and appreciate Bagnoli, his way of doing things and his approach to the game. Bagnoli reinvented Fanna. Unleashed him, took off the handcuffs and gave him the freedom to play as he wanted. Box to box, ambidextrous, offensive, aggressive, left wing, right wing, assists, set pieces and even the occasional finish. A total footballer. A classic old-fashioned winger, a defender's worst nightmare. He would play the first ten minutes on the right before switching to the left. In an era of strict man-marking, it was a tactic that left opposition full-backs floundering. With Bagnoli, Fanna subsequently reflected: 'We felt like birds let out of the cage.'

Fanna's 78th-minute goal against Lazio has been a long time coming. All those years of promise, of pent-up frustration, of redemption and rebirth and now he is at the epicentre of something truly miraculous. With this goal, it seems he has finally fulfilled his promise.

Lazio are unable to respond and, a few minutes later, full-back Gabriele Podavini is sent off for a second yellow card offence. The image of him leaving the field, head down and cursing, is emblematic of Lazio's season.

It has been by no means a classic Hellas performance. At times, they appeared nervous against a determined Lazio team who were playing for pride if not salvation (too late for that now). Some nerves, perhaps, were inevitable, given that Hellas are 360 minutes away from one of the most miraculous sporting achievements in the history of the game.

Elsewhere, Sampdoria lose to Avellino (2-1), with an own goal by Renica, Torino fail to break the deadlock in Como and Juventus lose at home to Fiorentina (1-2). Coupled with Verona's victory at the Bentegodi, these are significant results for the destiny of the *Scudetto*. Amongst the chasing pack, only Inter claim full points, beating Cremonese 2-0 and advancing into third place in the standings alongside Sampdoria.[77]

Hellas, meanwhile, have restored a four-point advantage with just three games to go. It's almost impossible now to deny

---

77 In midweek Inter were eliminated from the European Cup, losing the semi-final second leg 3-0 to Real Madrid.

any talk of the *Scudetto*. In fact, official approval has been given for celebrations to go ahead on 19 May, coinciding with the last game of the season, and even Bagnoli appears to have accepted the logic of the situation. A victory against Como at the Bentegodi next weekend might even be enough to clinch the championship. For the others, the battle is surely just for second place.

27A GIORNATA
Ascoli 0-1 Udinese
Atalanta 1-0 Milan
Avellino 2-1 Sampdoria
Como 0-0 Torino
Inter 2-0 Cremonese
Juventus 1-2 Fiorentina
Roma 1-1 Napoli
Verona 1-0 Lazio

CLASSIFICA

Verona	**39**
Torino	35
Sampdoria	34
Inter	34
Juventus	33
Milan	31
Roma	30
Napoli	29
Fiorentina	26
Atalanta	26
Udinese	24
Avellino	22
Como	22
Ascoli	20
Lazio	14
Cremonese	13

28a Giornata

5 May 1985

TWO POINTS at the Bentegodi today will put Hellas Verona out of reach of Inter and Torino to secure an historic *Scudetto* with two games still to play. But today's adversaries are the stubbornly unpredictable Como Calcio 1907, a team led by Ottavio Bianchi, an up-and-coming young coach destined to achieve greatness at Napoli, and unwilling to hand anything to anyone on a plate. Indeed, along with Inter, Como remain the only team in the league with an unbeaten home record this season, though they arrive at the Bentegodi on the back of a characteristically unpredictable run, having lost, drawn, lost, won, lost and drawn their last six games. Como have already secured a place in next season's Serie A, thanks to some rugged home performances and an impressive defensive record, inspired by an in-form but troubled young goalkeeper named Giuliano Giuliani.

Giuliani's story is one that deserves to be better known. Unless you're extremely well versed in Italian football of the mid-1980s, you've probably never even heard of him. In his prime, he was rated among the very best goalkeepers of his generation, regarded by some as a potential rival to the legendary Walter Zenga. Giuliani would go on to make 118 appearances for Hellas Verona and was a key figure when Napoli won their second *Scudetto* in 1990. And if that wasn't enough, he was the only Italian goalkeeper to save two Maradona penalties!

Giuliani was born in Rome in 1958. Following the break-up of his parents' marriage, he went to live with his aunt and uncle in Arezzo, Tuscany, while his mother built a new life for herself in Germany. Although well cared for in Arezzo, Giuliano carried the scars of a traumatic childhood and a violent father. Separated from his brother when his parents split up, he had a third sibling who he barely knew. Those who got to know Giuliano would describe him as quiet but with a certain self-confidence. He was thoughtful, cultured and intelligent – smarter than the average footballer – though prone to a certain melancholy.

Giuliano spent four formative years playing in Serie C for his local team, Arezzo. He was then spotted by Serie A newcomers Como and made his Serie A debut against Torino in November 1980 at the relatively tender age (for a Serie A goalkeeper) of 22. Over the next five seasons, he made 135 appearances for Como as they fluctuated between Serie A and Serie B, building a reputation as a reliable, if unspectacular, goalkeeper. Then, in the spring of 1983, news arrived from Germany that his mother had been strangled to death by her partner. She thought she had escaped domestic violence but it was, as one observer poignantly put it, just an illusion.

Somehow, Giuliano managed to suppress the turmoil and pain of his private life. That ability to control his emotions, to remain focussed in the face of adversity, was one of the attributes that made him such a formidable goalkeeper. The high point of his time at Como came in the 1984/85 season. With nine points from the opening nine fixtures, it was a solid start for the newly promoted minnows. That season, he equalled the long-standing record of AC Milan legend Fabio Cudicini, conceding just two goals at home all season as Como secured their place in the top division. By now, Giuliani was attracting the attention of some of Italy's biggest clubs, with Verona emerging as the favourites to secure his signature as a replacement for the outgoing Claudio Garella, who was on his way, if rumours were to be believed, to Napoli, where they were busy building a championship-winning team around Maradona.

Over the next three seasons, Giuliano would make 86 appearances for Hellas Verona, including rare appearances for the club in both the European and UEFA cups. He was a consistent and decisive presence for Hellas during that unprecedented period when they were competing at the highest level of domestic and European football. According to Bagnoli, Giuliani was 'an outstanding goalkeeper', second only to the great Walter Zenga and Stefano Tacconi.

In 1988, Giuliano was on his way south to Napoli, following once again in the footsteps of the legendary Claudio Garella. With a beautiful wife, and a child on the way, Giuliano seemed to have put the traumas of the past behind him and was emerging as one of the most effective Italian goalkeepers of his generation. Although they'd barely arrived in Napoli, Giuliano and his wife, Raffaella, spent their honeymoon with Maradona and his entourage on the idyllic South Pacific island of Mo'orea. Remembering the honeymoon years later, Raffaella described Maradona as 'crazy', saying: '[H]e always dances, day and night. He never sleeps. He performs in Polynesian skirts. He never sits still. Whenever he can, he plays football on the beach.' Of Maradona's renowned excesses, including his cocaine habit, Raffaella claimed to know nothing.

In 1989, Napoli won the UEFA Cup. One of the abiding memories of that campaign is Giuliano running half the length of the pitch to celebrate with team-mate Alessandro Renica. The defender had just scored Napoli's third goal in a quarter-final second leg against Juventus. The Turin giants had won the first leg 2-0 and the game was deep into extra time when Renica scored the dramatic late winner for Napoli. It was a rare outward display of emotion from the usually composed goalkeeper.

Napoli would go on to beat Bayern Munich in a semi-final that would be immortalised as the backdrop for Maradona's iconic (allegedly cocaine-fuelled) 'Live is Life' warm-up (though there is some dispute about where that scene actually took place). Napoli then beat Stuttgart in the final but Renica's late goal against Juventus would be the defining moment of the campaign.

Later that year, Giuliano was a guest at Maradona's wedding in Buenos Aires. Maradona had chartered a jet for 250 friends and team-mates to travel to Argentina for the occasion. Raffaella, heavily pregnant with the couple's daughter, didn't attend. As well as football stars and athletes, the guest list included television celebrities, pop stars and an 80-piece orchestra. Even Carlos Menem, the president of Argentina, was invited! Maradona personally ensured that his team-mates were well looked after. In every possible way.

Giuliano then played a decisive role as Napoli won that historic second *Scudetto* in 1990 – playing for the last six weeks of the season with a badly dislocated finger. For Giuliano, winning the *Scudetto* with Napoli marked the high point of his career. He was about to enter the final tragic chapter of his life, just as the Maradona era in Napoli was drawing to its own dramatic climax.

Despite his almost flawless contribution to Napoli's title success, Giuliano was transferred to Udinese, newly relegated to Serie B, at the end of the 1989/90 season. It was at this point, during a routine medical inspection, that the goalkeeper received the devastating news that he was HIV positive. He broke the news to his wife, without revealing the full nature of his illness. He also confessed that he had been unfaithful to her during the trip to Maradona's wedding. She was, understandably, devastated.

By 1993, Giuliano was beginning to show signs of physical deterioration and retired from public life to the hills above Bologna. He lived a quiet life far away from the spotlight of elite football, though he continued to work as a talent scout for Padova. Emaciated, with thin and greying hair, lesions now visible on his skin, former team-mates and adversaries shunned him.

In 1996, Giuliano went to Verona's Bentegodi Stadium for the last time. It was a cold and wet November evening when Giuliano attended a Serie B match between Chievo and Salernitana. Not really anyone's idea of fun, least of all if you have a weak immune system. Here, in the murky stands of the Bentegodi, Giuliano bumped into Alessandro Renica, Napoli's vice-captain, with whom he had shared that uncharacteristic moment of raw emotion in the UEFA Cup semi-final all those years ago. It had been one of the most joyful moments of Giuliano's career. 'The illness had hit him hard,' recalled Renica. 'I only recognised him from his eyes. But you could sense his desire to fight and to live, to lead an existence as normal as possible.' After exchanging a few emotional words, the former team-mates embraced and promised to see each other again. They never did.

Four days later, Giuliano left home early to take his daughter to school. After dropping her off, he suddenly felt unwell and was taken to Sant'Orsola Hospital in Bologna. He died later that day of pulmonary complications related to AIDS. He was just 38 years old.

For Giuliano, this whole tragic episode is in the future. Today, his objective is to keep a clean sheet against the club with whom he has already reached a pre-contractual agreement to play for next season. If he can deny Verona a goal, he'll also deny them an early championship party.

With the season now reaching its climax, an air of nervous expectation has enveloped the city. If results go the right way, Hellas could be declared champions this weekend. But Italians are notoriously superstitious. Nobody wants to tempt fate and the club have publicly refused to countenance any premature talk of winning the championship. That line has become increasingly difficult to maintain in recent weeks as the media has repeatedly sought to pin down a precise date for the championship party. No contingency plans have even been put in place should results be favourable this weekend. As Carla Riolfi, a local nursery teacher and Hellas fan, tells the *Corriere della Sera*: 'We will certainly fill the stadium but we haven't prepared anything in the event that this should be *the* Sunday. In any case, we will celebrate the great achievement of our football team on 19 May.'

In fact, the board won't meet until next week to discuss proposals to celebrate the *Scudetto*. One idea is to hold 'a small party' at the Teatro Filarmonico but, with a capacity of barely 1,200, this idea completely fails to grasp the magnitude of what is about to happen. The council, meanwhile, has more ambitious plans. It wants to host a grand gala at the Arena, with players, singers, local celebrities and city politicians. For Bagnoli, it all sounds a bit too triumphalist. In any case, there are still three games to go, not least today's match against a stubborn Como team with nothing to lose. But, with no injury problems to contend with, Bagnoli confirms he will retain the starting XI who overcame Lazio seven days ago. The encounter has an added significance for Silvano Fontolan, who spent eight years at Como. Volpati also spent a couple of seasons at the lakeside club, as well as, of course, Bagnoli, whose coaching career began with the *Lariani* almost exactly a decade ago. For those looking for good omens, Hellas play in that familiar blue and yellow jersey, while Garella is back in his preferred red.

In the opening exchanges, Verona lack urgency, while Como are understandably cautious. With Hellas players showing signs of fatigue at the end of a momentous season and Como content to sit back, the game is inevitably played out in midfield, with neither side taking the initiative. Finally, in the 24th minute, Enrico Todesco forces a save from Garella – a shot across the bows that does little to settle the fraying nerves on the home terraces. It's not until the half-hour mark that Hellas finally seem to come to life and probe their opponents' penalty area with anything approaching their customary zeal. In the 32nd minute, Briegel's header grazes the post. Then, four minutes later, Marangon squanders a decent chance by shooting directly at Giuliani. And, so, the first half ends goalless.

In the second half, little changes. Bagnoli makes his usual adjustments but, for once, to little effect. The best chance of the game falls to Como in the 69th minute when Hans Müller crosses for Enrico Todesco, left alone inside the box. The unmarked midfielder dives for the ball but squanders the simplest of chances, his header soaring harmlessly over the bar.

Bagnoli is furious and immediately removes Marangon, inserting Bruni in his place. This seems to give Verona the impetus they need. As Sacchetti drops deep, Volpati occupies the left-hand side, while Briegel advances in attack. The final exchanges are all yellow and blue. In the 78th minute Galderisi crosses from the right for Elkjær, who is unable to make contact and the ball passes harmlessly across the face of goal. Notwithstanding the slow start, there is now no shortage of effort as Hellas finally seem to sense an opening. In the 83rd minute, Di Gennaro plays a one-two and unleashes a surefire conclusion. Giuliani is beaten but Luca Fusi, Como's young midfielder, blocks a certain goal on the line and the game ends goalless. A point gained or one dropped? Either way, the championship race will extend at least into the penultimate weekend.

Hellas were caught off guard today, expecting Como to sit back and defend. Instead, Bianchi showed his class by taking a slightly more positive approach. As Bagnoli strides down the tunnel after the game, the RAI TV reporter fires a playful question in his direction: '*Meglio un uovo oggi che una gallina domani*?' ('Is it better an egg today than a hen tomorrow?') Is it better to have a sure thing now than a possibility of more later? After pausing to ponder the question for a moment, Bagnoli responds in the negative. The philosophical coach knows that the title will be concluded either in Bergamo next weekend or at the Bentegodi the following week. As for when the celebrations take place, that doesn't concern him. Meanwhile, it's the Como players who gather in the middle of the field to celebrate. Today's point has guaranteed them Serie A football next season. It's not the party anyone expected but nor is it a disaster for Hellas, who are yet another point closer to achieving the impossible.

Elsewhere, Inter triumph against Sampdoria with goals from Brady and Altobelli (Alessandro Scanziani scoring a consolation). It is a result that draws them one point closer to Verona. Meanwhile, Torino can only manage a draw at home with Atalanta, taking them to 36 points and second place in the standings alongside Inter. Maradona halts Juventus at the San Paolo and Juve now share fourth place with Sampdoria. *La Signora*, who just a couple of weeks ago looked like they might put together a late challenge, have now slumped six points behind the league leaders. With just two games to play, their championship hopes are now over. Sampdoria are also out of contention, with only Inter and Torino remaining in the title race. To cause a late upset, they would have to take maximum points from their remaining two fixtures and hope that Verona lose against both Atalanta and Avellino. In Florence, Sócrates watches his team from the stands, surrounded by young fans: 'Here, I've encountered nothing but kindness and sympathy from the young people, the friends who support me. It was right that I showed up to thank them.' Next weekend's encounter with Torino could be the Brazilian legend's last game in Italy. Meanwhile, in Liverpool, Everton are crowned champions of England for the eighth time, with a Cup Winners' Cup Final to come before the season is over.[78]

With the end of the season rapidly approaching, speculation is rife about the future of five 'jewels of the *Scudetto*'. Fanna is reported to have already signed a contract that will tie him to Inter for the next three years; Marangon has a similar agreement in place with Inter and negotiations have already begun to secure the defender's replacement; 'stopper' Fontolan has asked for a significant salary increase and an extended two-year contract, which the Verona hierarchy is currently considering; the 'goalkeeper of the championship' is still under contract but Garella is another who would like to maximise his earnings elsewhere (there are also rumours of a rift with Bagnoli), with Napoli leading the chase (Giuliano Giuliani has already been lined up as his replacement); and, finally, Sacchetti seems certain to follow Garella to Napoli with no counter offer on the table. So, while the championship is within touching distance, the team that has very nearly won it is facing decimation. The only question is how many more will be tempted away?

---

78 A 2-0 victory over Queens Park Rangers on 6 May secured the league title for Everton with five games still to play. On 15 May, they would beat Rapid Vienna 3-1 in the final of the Cup Winners' Cup, with goals from Andy Gray, Trevor Steven and Kevin Sheedy.

28A GIORNATA

Cremonese 0-5 Roma
Fiorentina 3-1 Udinese
Lazio 0-1 Avellino
Milan 2-1 Ascoli
Napoli 0-0 Juventus
Torino 0-0 Atalanta
Sampdoria 1-2 Inter
Verona 0-0 Como

CLASSIFICA

Verona	**40**
Torino	36
Inter	36
Juventus	34
Sampdoria	34
Milan	33
Roma	32
Napoli	30
Fiorentina	28
Atalanta	27
Udinese	24
Avellino	24
Como	23
Ascoli	20
Lazio	14
Cremonese	13

29a Giornata

12 May 1985

ON 11 May 1985, at the Valley Parade stadium in Bradford, the home fans are in celebratory mood as they face Lincoln City in the final game of the season. Just the week before, Bradford City clinched the English Third Division championship, so today's match is little more than a formality. Just before half-time, a carelessly discarded cigarette slips through the wooden floorboards of the terraces and on to a mound of accumulated debris below. Within minutes, the entire stand is engulfed in flames. The following morning, the front page of the *Corriere della Sera* reports more than 40 fatalities. The final tragic death toll would eventually reach 56, with at least 250 more suffering horrendous injuries.

Back in Verona, the city is also reeling from an incident that occurred closer to home on Thursday afternoon; a shoot-out in broad daylight between a gang of armed robbers and the police in the Borgo Milano neighbourhood, just a couple of kilometres from the stadium. A 45-year-old communist activist, who had been distributing leaflets in the neighbourhood, was caught in the crossfire and killed and one of the gangsters subsequently died in hospital of injuries sustained in the gun battle. Although it is an isolated incident, it's also a stark reminder that, beneath its genteel facade, Verona isn't always that quiet and peaceful place it seems on the surface.

Speaking on the eve of the biggest match of his life, Bagnoli is his usual calm, composed and philosophical self (some reports describe his demeanour as bordering on the indifferent), telling the *Corriere della Sera*: '[I]f we haven't wavered during the whole championship, I don't see why we should worry now. The story of a spanner in the works remains just a nice journalistic invention. The team is the same as always. I have no doubt about it.' When a journalist informs him that if they win the title, Fanna intends to run and hug his coach to see him smile with joy for the first time, Bagnoli's response conveys his wry sense of humour and unshakeable belief in the collective: '[T]hese are platitudes. The joys of life don't come just from football. It would, though, be a great satisfaction for everyone, the culmination of a collective effort that has yielded results beyond expectations. For my part, after Fanna's hug, if this has reason to happen, I will go and hug the other players, including those on the bench, because they have won, too.'

While the true extent of the previous day's tragedy in Bradford is still unfolding, 12 May 1985 dawns in Verona with a sense of jubilant anticipation, quite unlike anything the city has ever known before. The penultimate match of the season coincides with the regional elections, which take place over two days (12 and 13 May) but few in Verona are concerned with the trivialities of local democracy. Today, there are far more pressing matters at stake. Nothing can dampen the carnival atmosphere that is engulfing the city nor deter the tens of thousands of fans who will join the mass cavalcade heading west for Verona's penultimate game of the season in Bergamo.

Bergamo is, according to our 1984 travel companion, 'one of Lombardy's lesser-known treasures and Italy's most beautiful towns'. The city is divided into two distinct parts, Bergamo Alta and Bergamo Bassa, and they form a city that is 'lively, clean and easy to like'. The stadium itself is in the north-east corner of the city, barely a 90-minute drive from Verona. None of the so-called 'big' teams have won in Bergamo this season (draws with Inter, Roma, Torino, Sampdoria, Juventus and Fiorentina and victories against Napoli and AC Milan) and, pre-match, Nedo Sonetti, the *Nerazzurri* coach, repeats his mantra that his team give gifts to no one.

Thirteen-year-old Nicolas Legnazzi can't quite muster Bagnoli's sense of calm. In fact, last night he couldn't sleep.

Finally, as dawn breaks warm and bright on Sunday morning, he can contain himself no longer. Of modest means, his family aren't travelling to Atalanta but that doesn't mean they won't be following the match. They have an early lunch and rush to Piazza Brà, where the entire city seems to have gathered to listen to the game under the balcony of the studios of Radio Adige, where the commentary is being broadcasted via massive loudspeakers. The piazza, one of the biggest and most striking public spaces in Europe, dominated in one corner by the ancient Roman arena, is overflowing. The adjoining streets – Via Mazzini, Via Roma and Corso Porta Nuova – are rapidly filling up, too. As kick-off approaches, the noise reaches a crescendo. For the first time in his life, Nicolas is aware of the pounding of his own heart, beating in time, he imagines, with those of his heroes in Bergamo.

'I remember the departure of the buses from the piazza in front of the Bentegodi,' remembers 14-year-old Alessandro Fiorio. 'There must have been 100 or 150 coaches, practically on every pavement around the stadium where they were waiting to depart. You had to know your bus number and finding it wasn't easy, even though there were some general indications on the side of the square.' In fact, an estimated 10,000 fans are on the road from Verona to Bergamo. The club has organised 140 buses and others have been laid on for employees of various public and private organisations in the city and across the province, while many more fans have taken the train or are travelling by car.

Thirteen-year-old Barbara Salazer is joined by her whole family, who pile into her dad's car on the joyful convoy to Bergamo. 'Even my granny wanted to be part of the miracle!' she remembers. 'It was raining in Bergamo. There were a lot of us [10,000 or 15,000]. There was a lot of police and it's not like now that the away fans' area is strictly separated, both inside and outside the stadium. So, there were moments of tension and conflict. Fortunately, I personally didn't have any problems. I remember that, at the end of the match, there was a rumour that a fan had died in the clashes but it turned out to be a hoax.' In an unprovoked police charge, Barbara's dad was struck with a baton but even that couldn't detract from the celebratory mood of the day.

With two hours still to go until kick-off, the south stand of Bergamo's Stadio Comunale is already overflowing with yellow and blue. Hellas fans have infiltrated every sector of the stadium. Only a corner of the north stand remains a bastion of black and blue, from where Atalanta ultras defiantly attempt to drown out the roar of the clamorous travelling contingent. Just an hour before kick-off, two Hellas fans end up in hospital after being hit by a car, whose driver, surrounded by a group of troublemakers, had suddenly accelerated. As tensions mount in and around the stadium, it is not an isolated incident.

Meanwhile, Bagnoli has his full squad at his disposal and there are few surprises in his starting line-up, selecting those he deems to have the temperament and qualities to handle the pressure and deliver the crucial point that will secure the championship. At the back, the ever-reliable and versatile Volpati is preferred to Ferroni, with Sacchetti occupying Volpati's place in midfield. Otherwise, it's a very familiar-looking formation that takes the field: Garella, Volpati, Marangon, Tricella, Fontolan, Briegel, Fanna, Sacchetti, Galderisi, Di Gennaro and Elkjær. The objective is clear and simple – bring home a point from Bergamo.

Once again, Hellas can expect few favours from today's opponents, a team that has been safe for some time, a proud and tenacious rival but surely not one capable of causing an upset today. After all, a point is all that is required. Five minutes before kick-off, the cacophony of noise and colour diminishes for a moment as the teams make their way on to the pitch. Then, from every corner of the stadium, dozens of smoke bombs engulf the pitch in an impenetrable blanket of red, yellow and blue fog.

As the smoke subsides, Atalanta kick off. After just a few seconds, Marino Magrin fires a volley just over the crossbar. Verona respond immediately with a Fanna free kick that requires a smart save from Ottorino Piotti. With barely 15 minutes played, Roberto Donadoni evades Sacchetti and his cross finds the unmarked Eugenio Perico, whose simple header flies past the despairing Garella. Though there are nearly 40,000 fans packed into the Stadio Comunale, the entire stadium seems to fall silent. Atalanta 1 Hellas Verona 0. This was not in the script.

As the shock subsides, the game settles down and Hellas begin to exert their dominance in midfield. On the half-hour mark, Elkjær seizes the initiative, winning the ball deep in the Atalanta half, and launches a trademark assault on the *Nerazzurri* penalty area. Surrounded by Atalanta defenders, the attack eventually fizzles out. Less than a minute later, there is a goalmouth skirmish involving Tricella, Fontolan and Marangon, eager to make up for their earlier defensive lapse, but somehow the ball refuses to cross the line.

In the dressing room at half-time, Bagnoli pleads for patient and calm heads to prevail. In the stands, tempers are rising, as fans contemplate the prospect of the championship going down to the final game of the season. A mass brawl breaks out between opposing sets of fans. As a violent police charge ploughs a deep furrow in the crowd, the players re-emerge for the second half and a tense calm prevails as attention shifts back to events on the pitch.

It takes just six minutes. Fantastic one-touch interplay between Fanna, Galderisi and Elkjær. The great Dane shoots and scores. It had to be him! Once again this season, the Danish Dynamite is decisive. Atalanta 1 Hellas Verona 1.

It's raining but Barbara Salazer doesn't even notice. All she feels is a shuddering thrill pass down her spine as Elkjær celebrates. For 15-year-old Andrea 'Gotta', the rainfall hides the tears of joy that are streaming down his face. He's not the only one in tears.

In Piazza Brà, pandemonium breaks out as the massive crowd surges forward. Strangers embrace, limbs entangle and more than a few grown men end up on the floor. Thirteen-year-old Nicolas Legnazzi is smothered by his mother: 'I'm lucky to be alive! If it wasn't for my mum hugging me, I'd probably have fallen and been trampled!'

With ten minutes remaining, the party in Bergamo is in full swing, a spectacular display of yellow and blue flags, as 10,000 fans join in one voice to herald a city, a football club and a miracle. One by one, the names of the Hellas squad resound around Atalanta's Stadio Comunale. Names that will echo in Verona for eternity. Elkjær. Briegel. Bagnoli ...

In the closing minutes, one intrepid fan, subsequently identified as Moreno 'Il Matte' Metteoni, climbs up the fence separating the fans from the pitch and lets out a wild cry: 'VEEER-OOOOOO-NAAAAAA.' Another legendary fan, Doriano Recchia, known to everyone as 'Italia' because he has travelled every corner of the peninsula following Hellas, is in tears. He's been a season ticket holder since 1967 but has never experienced anything like this before. Meanwhile, Bagnoli introduces Ferroni in place of Volpati. Thoughtful, shy and serious, Ferroni is a reluctant hero but, in a season ravaged by injury, he deserves his place among the stars. For Sergio Spuri, Verona's reserve goalkeeper, a moment to savour as he makes his first appearance of the season in place of the superhuman Garella. It is a magnanimous gesture by Bagnoli and one that ensures that Garella's understudy will be entitled to join his team-mates when they claim their championship medals. With ten seconds remaining, Galderisi approaches the bench and asks Bagnoli: 'Have we won?' Bagnoli doesn't respond. He's waiting for the final whistle.

When the final whistle eventually sounds, pandemonium breaks out. The Verona players rush towards the south stand and throw their shirts into the sea of travelling fans. The crowd surges forward in a euphoric anarchy of movement. Eighteen-year-old 'Massimo' gashes his hands as he tries to climb the fence to celebrate with the players, as an unstoppable wave of yellow and blue surges on to the pitch. Bagnoli, midway through a live interview on RAI TV, is raised in triumph above the delirious heads of his players. It is a dramatic scene that encapsulates the miracle of the championship.

Hellas Verona are champions of Italy! They have led the league from the first to the last day of the season.[79] The party can finally begin!

In Udine, meanwhile, a fascinating sideshow is in progress. After two eventful seasons, 32-year-old Zico is playing in his last game in Serie A, while for the 24-year-old Maradona, his debut season at Napoli is also drawing to a close. In an epic game, the South American maestros don't disappoint. Maradona opens the scoring with a long-range free kick. Zico, not to be outdone on his swansong, responds almost immediately with a trademark free kick of his own to set up Galparoli. Zico then lays on another assist to put Udinese in front but it is Maradona who has the final say with a dubious 90th-minute goal that is an ominous foreshadowing of the infamous 'Hand of God' goal he will score against England in Mexico less than a year later. Zico is furious but the goal stands and the game finishes 2-2.

Elsewhere, both Torino and Inter fail to take maximum points. Torino draw 0-0 in Florence, while Inter lose 4-3 to Roma. Not that it matters. Even if they had won, Verona's point against Atalanta means they are four points clear with just one game to play. There is also a draw in Turin between Juventus and Sampdoria (where Platini consolidates his position as the season's top scorer), while AC Milan draw level on points with Juve and Samp thanks to a 2-0 victory against Lazio.

Back in Bergamo, Hellas captain Roberto Tricella emerges from the away dressing room with a magnum of champagne in his arms. 'I'm taking it to the Atalanta players,' he explains. 'They gave it to us but we can celebrate together.' Fanna, meanwhile, can finally admit what everyone has known for weeks: 'Now that we have won the *Scudetto* I can also say that I am leaving Verona. This success, which for me is the fourth [three with Juve], remains the best. In Turin, I wasn't a protagonist. I dedicate it to Bagnoli.' For a topless Garella, who

---

79 A feat only achieved by three other teams: Juventus (four times), Milan and Inter.

has gone looking for his wife in the stands, it is a magnificent moment; 'like a golden dream. I feel like I'm a child again.' He, too, dedicates the triumph to Bagnoli, who 'led this wonderful group'. For Briegel, rarely noted for his diplomatic skills, a moment of personal triumph: '[F]or me, it is a huge satisfaction to have arrived in front of the great Rummenigge. When it was known in Germany that I would be moving to Verona, many people turned up their noses. Someone asked "But what kind of team is this Verona?" This is what kind of team it is – a team of champions!'

As sporadic skirmishes involving opposing sets of fans are eventually broken up by the police, a triumphant yellow and blue convoy slowly returns along the *autostrada* from Bergamo to Verona. Thirteen-year-old Barbara Salazer waves back at the crowds flying their flags from every overpass along the route. For student Alessandro Fiorio, 'it goes without saying that the best party was the one in the evening when we returned from Bergamo'. The bus drops them off at the end of Corso Porta Nuova, from where they make their way to nearby Piazza Brà. Alessandro has always dreamt of taking a dip in the piazza's famous fountain and now, like so many others, he does! Verona are champions of Italy and that is something to celebrate!

29A GIORNATA

Ascoli 3-2 Cremonese
Atalanta 1-1 Verona
Avellino 1-1 Como
Fiorentina 0-0 Torino
Juventus 1-1 Sampdoria
Milan 2-0 Lazio
Roma 4-3 Inter
Udinese 2-2 Napoli

CLASSIFICA

Verona*	**41**
Torino	37
Inter	36
Juventus	35
Sampdoria	35
Milan	35
Roma	34
Napoli	31
Fiorentina	29
Atalanta	28
Udinese	25
Avellino	25
Como	24
Ascoli	22
Lazio	14
Cremonese	13

*Champions

30a Giornata

19 May 1985

AGAINST A cerulean blue sky, a cluster of giant puffy clouds drifts lazily across the horizon. It is, as 13-year-old Barbara Salazer remembers it, a stiflingly hot day. Barbara, like everyone else, arrives early, desperate to find a place to experience the once-in-a-lifetime party that is about to kick off at the Bentegodi. Student Alessandro Fiorio remembers that week vividly: '[L]et's say that the whole week between Bergamo and the final home match against Avellino was a long series of parties. The teachers at school suspended the exams and in the classroom we were allowed to hang scarves and posters of our champions. The air was lighter, we felt like we were flying!'

As the final whistle blew in Bergamo, thousands of fans poured into the city centre towards Piazza Brà. After dining at a Milanese restaurant, the players have a two-hour bus trip back to Verona during which Galderisi and Elkjær sing '*Siamo la coppia più bella del mondo*' ('We are the most beautiful couple in the world') and tease Garella by singing Neapolitan classics. Despite the rain, an estimated 10,000 jubilant fans have gathered in Piazza Brà to welcome the triumphant team back to Verona that evening, with just as many on their way, marching along Via Mazzini from Piazza delle Erbe. As fireworks light up the night sky and smoke bombs turn the air an acrid yellow and blue, the grass around the fountain in the centre of the piazza becomes a treacherous swamp of mud, beer and discarded bottles. Only as dawn breaks on Monday morning do the fans, players and backroom staff finally bring the celebrations to an end.

By nine o'clock on Monday morning, Bagnoli is up, preparing to perform his civic duty and vote in the local elections. Stepping out of his front door, he is met by a giant banner of thanks, erected by his many admirers in the neighbourhood. Arriving at the nearby polling station, he is greeted by hundreds of cheering fans. If he was standing for election, he would win by a landslide! When the notoriously grumpy coach eventually makes it to the club's offices in Piazzale Olimpia, he barely has time to greet the staff before a throng of journalists demand to know what is next for the newly crowned champions of Italy. Not even 24 hours to enjoy the moment!

On the desk of the newly installed club president, Canon boss Ferdinando Chiampan, among the many messages of congratulation is a telegram from a group of Juventus fans. It reads simply: 'Can we have our *Scudetto* back?' The mayor of Verona has also received a telegram, though his, from Sandro Pertini, the president of the Italian Republic, is suitably magnanimous: 'I rejoice with you for the well-deserved victory. Long live Verona and its superb victorious football team.'

Elsewhere, other prominent figures have been sharing their thoughts on Verona's triumph. For Juve's legendary coach, Giovanni Trapattoni, Verona's victory is hardly unexpected: 'I wouldn't call it a surprise at all, as Verona had been in the top rankings for a couple of seasons. Let's say, instead, that they made a leap in quality thanks to the addition of Briegel and Elkjær. The two foreigners didn't suffer from an adaptation crisis and this, also, is credit to the excellence of coach Bagnoli.' For Inter boss Ilario Castagner, the Hellas team have displayed two decisive attributes: 'The consistency in their performance and their ability to keep their nerves in delicate moments.' Luigi Radice, Torino's veteran coach, offers the following assessment: 'Verona is not a team that emerged from nowhere but is the fruit of careful planning [...]. Bagnoli's team had a very good start and, from there, had the drive for a well-deserved success.' For AC Milan's Nils Liedholm, Verona 'chose players from big clubs, even if they had only played a few games there. Bagnoli was able to count on the mentality acquired at the big clubs and on their understandable desire for revenge. The combination worked.' Roma's Sven-Göran Eriksson says: 'Verona played the best football. They were the team that was able to counter-attack with the greatest speed. A group of versatile players, capable of pressing and scoring with ease.'

On Tuesday, 500 fans, including 100 schoolchildren dressed entirely in yellow and blue, celebrate with the players as they return to training after a day off. In a dressing-room prank, Garella, Marangon and Fanna are given a small homemade tricolour by their team-mates, a gentle reminder that they will miss out on the honour of wearing the real thing the following season. Of the three players who are leaving, Fanna will be the hardest to replace. In Bergamo, he delivered yet another masterful display, covering every area of the pitch and running with a lucidity and tactical intelligence that make him the natural heir to Italian legend Bruno Conti. Already, speculation is mounting as to who might replace him and Verona's debonair sporting director, Emiliano 'Ciccio' Mascetti, has been busy behind the scenes weighing up the options.

Meanwhile, new club president Chiampan doesn't exactly endear himself to the Hellas faithful with his plans to slap a 1,000 lire supplement on the price of a match ticket to cover the costs of the musical extravaganza planned immediately before kick-off. But the surcharge has done little to stifle demand and, by Monday, the Bentegodi is completely sold out. Hopeful fans who show up at the stadium's ticket booths later in the week are met with a crudely written sign that simply says *esaurito* (sold out).

On matchday itself, the party kicks off at 10am, when a column of cars, vans and mopeds, laden with fans and draped with flags, banners and scarves passes through Piazza Brà on its circuitous way to the stadium, a deafening convoy of honking horns and revving engines. Yellow and blue flags, banners and scarves hang from every window, balcony and doorway along the route.

Though he lives just a stone's throw from the stadium, football-daft 13-year-old Nicolas Legnazzi has never been inside the Bentegodi. Until now! He's been queueing (if the surging mass of yellow and blue humanity edging slowly towards the turnstiles can be described as such) since nine o'clock in the morning. Already hot, tired and hungry, such concerns don't matter. The only thing that matters is football. Hellas Verona. Champions! 'My mum got us tickets in the *parterre* (the lower terraces),' Nicolas remembers, 'My dad and brother took their usual places in the *curva*. It's the worst place in the stadium to see the game but it didn't matter. Nothing mattered. Thank God, we were there!'

By midday, the stadium is overflowing – a euphoric frenzy of flags and banners, a riotous cavalcade of yellow and blue. Forty-five thousand fans have occupied every nook and cranny of the stadium. Thousands more are stranded outside, unable to bribe, talk or break their way into the stadium. For those who have paid between 3,000 and 5,000 lire for a ticket – plus the surcharge – a carnival show of dancers, acrobats, flag-wavers, parachutists, stunt planes and a band, *Viva la gente*, await them. Amongst the parachutes, hundreds of yellow and blue balloons and a giant *tricolore* descend from the sky, as red, white and green smoke engulfs the stadium. As the smog eventually clears, the formalities can finally begin.

At 2.50pm, still in their tracksuits, the Hellas Verona players emerge from the tunnel and are called one by one to take the applause of the *curva* and receive their championship medals. The biggest cheer of the day is reserved for Bagnoli. For many minutes, the entire stadium salutes him, chanting his name: 'BA-GNO-LI! BA-GNO-LI!' For Fanna, already the subject of feverish transfer speculation, 45,000 fans sing in unison '*Pierino Fanna, resta con noi*' (Pierino Fanna, stay with us). His two-year-old daughter, Cristina, is watching from the stands in a Hellas Verona jersey with her dad's No.7 on the back. On the pitch, Fanna is close to tears.

Though the match could quite easily have been overshadowed by the occasion, it kicks off briskly, with Verona seemingly determined to put on a show that lives up to their status as newly crowned champions of Italy. With barely nine minutes on the clock, Fanna cuts in from the left wing and finishes with aplomb from a tight angle for his second goal of the season; 1-0 to the champions!

Hellas create multiple chances but have to wait until the 40th minute to double their lead. Sacchetti unleashes a speculative effort from long range which, with the help of a massive deflection, finds its way into the back of the net. The goal will officially be recorded as an own goal, denying Sacchetti, who has played a crucial role all season, his second of the campaign. Two-nil and Verona are coasting at this point. Just minutes later, however, Avellino pull one back through Paolo Alberto Faccini, as Garella seems to dive in slow motion. Perhaps a week of celebrations is catching up with him! At half-time, it's Hellas 2 Avellino 1.

Almost immediately from the restart, Avellino grab a well-taken equaliser but not even that can dampen the party mood inside the stadium. Entering the final half an hour of the season, Elkjær puts on a show inside the box and eventually goes down rather spectacularly for a penalty. Despite the context, the Avellino players are, with some justification, outraged at the decision. Galderisi, for the 11th time this season, scores and the stadium, once again, erupts in a sea of noise and colour. In the final minute, Di Gennaro beats the onrushing Paradisi to a loose ball and flicks it high over the sprawling keeper towards the goal. Elkjær wins the physical battle to bundle the ball over the line for Verona's 42nd goal of the campaign. It's 4-2 and the party is now in full swing.

As the final whistle sounds, ignoring a pre-match promise to remain in their seats, many hundreds of fans can't resist the overwhelming impulse to surge on to the pitch from the lower terraces. In a radio commentary that will reverberate for generations, Roberto Puliero exclaims:

> *'È finitaaaaaaaa!! Alè alè alè alè alè alè! Bum! Bum! Bum! Bum! Bum! Campioni! Campioni! Campioni!*

Campioni! Campioni! Il Verona è Campione d'Italia 1984/85!'

As chaos and pandemonium erupts all around them, the Avellino players race towards the tunnel. The Verona players, and Bagnoli himself, are soon swept up in a rousing sea of yellow and blue euphoria. In the confusion and elation that follows, Bagnoli is raised aloft, while players are unceremoniously stripped to their underwear. Although ten young fans are detained by the police for excessive displays of exuberance, the celebrations are, for the most part, good-natured.

Of the game itself, 13-year-old Barbara Salazer remembers little, just the sheer joy as fans exploded on to the pitch at full time. As those around her surged forward, she remained in her place, frozen in time, enjoying a moment that she knew, despite her youth, she would never experience again.

Elsewhere, Inter finish with a flourish, beating Ascoli 5-1 at the San Siro, while Torino beat Roma 1-0 at the Stadio Comunale, Sampdoria win comfortably against Atalanta at the Ferraris and Juve draw 3-3 with Lazio at the Olimpico. Of course, the results barely matter. Hellas are champions and nothing can change that.

In the home changing room, captain Roberto Tricella sits alone in a corner. He's crying. His team-mates break away from the celebrations to console him. Tears of joy or tears of sorrow? It's hard to tell. Three years ago, as Verona celebrated promotion to Serie A, the Verona captain lost his mother. Today, his tears are for her.

When the celebrations inside the stadium finally die down, Barbara Salazer, tired and sweating but elated, joins the long line of fans on the triumphant march to Piazza Brà. The municipal authorities had planned to throw a big party at the Arena but the club vetoed the plan, afraid that the event would get hijacked for political purposes. Instead, the celebrations take place in Piazza Brà, where 15 giant screens, each 3m by 4m, are installed in strategic positions across the piazza to display images of the victorious campaign. Fifteen-year-old Andrea

'Gotta' makes the journey from the stadium to the piazza on the roof of a friend's car! The loudspeakers continue to broadcast the famous words of Puliero: *'Alè! Alè! Alè! Bum! Bum! Bum!'* 'People were dancing in the fountain and destroying the flowerbeds,' Barbara remembers. 'By the time I got there, the square was packed with people from the entire province and beyond, the water had been turned off and the whole place was muddy, the people as well. I said to myself "why not?" and jumped in!' Alessandro was 14 years old. His dad had bought him a flag that day, which he still keeps in his closet 40 years later: 'It's a piece of my heart [...]. I remember driving home [after the Avellino match] with my flag flying from the car window. I still get emotional remembering that perfect moment.' 'The whole day was just one big party', remembers Alessandro Fiorio, 'that continued into the evening in Piazza Brà with the arrival of the players on a festival-type stage [no open-top buses in those days] and the fireworks from the Arena.'

Bagnoli is characteristically restrained as the team arrive in Piazza Brà to join in the celebrations. At the end of the official presentation, as the players celebrate, Roberto Puliero asks the coach for a smile, at which point Bagnoli grabs the microphone and exclaims: '*Siamo campioni!*' (We are the champions!) and the entire piazza explodes with joy. At some point – no one can quite remember precisely when – Roberto Tricella performs his famous Jerry Lee Lewis impersonation in front of a cheering crowd.

That same evening, the Hellas Verona players appear on *Domenica Sportiva*, a popular light entertainment programme on RAI TV, hosted by Marino Bartoletti and Italo Allodi. Giampiero Boniperti, the president of Juventus, calls to congratulate the new champions. The Hellas players, unaccustomed to the limelight, seem somewhat disoriented. Only Galderisi and Garella seem to enjoy the show!

By midnight, more than 100,000 people (35 per cent of the city's population) have been partying hard for 14 hours! One exhausted young fan, his face painted yellow and blue, just wants to go home – he's got work the next morning!

For Bagnoli, of all the parties he attends that week, the one that makes him the happiest is with his old Hellas team-mates from the 1950s. Eros Fossetta (173 appearances), Dario Baruffi (73 appearances), Mario Marini (104 appearances), Auro Enzo Basiliani (180 appearances), Santino Ciceri (158 appearances), Gianluigi Stefanini (114 appearances) and others. From all over Italy, they have travelled to Verona with their wives to be with Bagnoli at the moment of his greatest triumph. For Bagnoli it is 'one of the most beautiful things in my life'.

30A GIORNATA

Como 0-0 Milan
Napoli 1-0 Fiorentina
Torino 1-0 Roma
Cremonese 2-0 Udinese
Lazio 3-3 Juventus
Sampdoria 3-0 Atalanta
Verona 4-2 Avellino
Inter 5-1 Ascoli

CLASSIFICA

Verona	**43**
Torino	39
Inter	38
Sampdoria	37
Milan	36
Juventus	36
Roma	34
Napoli	33
Fiorentina	29
Atalanta	28
Udinese	25
Como	25
Avellino	25
Ascoli	22
Lazio	15
Cremonese	15

Aftermath

The weight of the Scudetto

PRIDE COMES before a fall and, so, it was with a certain sense of inevitability that Hellas Verona slumped to a disappointing tenth-place finish the following season. It wasn't a disastrous campaign by any stretch of the imagination but Bagnoli's men just couldn't replicate the consistency that had been the hallmark of their championship season. The sudden attention, the disruption of national team call-ups and spiralling wage demands made it an increasingly challenging group to manage. Inevitably, some players looked for bigger stages. Others simply couldn't sustain the level of performance they'd achieved over the past three or four seasons.

Hellas suffered several humiliating defeats on the road (5-0 at Napoli, 5-1 at Udinese and 3-0 at Juventus), results that would have been unimaginable in previous seasons, and they conceded 40 goals (more than double that of the 1984/85 season). The departures of Garella and Marangon had clearly weakened Verona at the back, while the loss of influential attacking midfielder Pierino Fanna was another major blow, depriving Verona of one of their most effective offensive outlets, as the team struggled to rediscover their balance, identity and drive.

A promising European foray provided some consolation for poor results in the league but that, too, ended in disappointment. Indeed, the post-championship season is remembered above all for that European Cup run, as Verona, after a promising start (a convincing victory in the first round against PAOK Salonika) capitulated to Juventus in a notorious match, remembered locally as the '*Partita della Vergogna*' (match of shame). The game itself is primarily remembered for two notorious post-match incidents; Elkjær's famous 'signed check' gesture to the French referee, Robert Wurtz, and Bagnoli's unusually unguarded response to a policeman who came to investigate a disturbance in the Hellas locker room: '[I]f you're looking for the thieves, they're in the other changing room.'

Elsewhere, a charismatic entrepreneur took over at AC Milan. In 1988, he appointed an unknown young coach named Arrigo Sacchi, who believed in a high-pressing, attacking brand of football that would once and for all consign *catenaccio* to the dustbin. That entrepreneur was named Silvio Berlusconi and he would change the face of Italian football, and Italian politics, forever.

Change of a less dramatic variety was under way in Verona. At the end of the championship-winning season, a 5.2bn lire offer was accepted for Pierino Fanna, who was joined at Inter by team-mate Luciano Marangon, but it would ultimately prove to be a disappointing move for Fanna. On the margins of the Inter squad and having failed to replicate his form of the 1984/85 season, in the summer of 1989 he returned to Verona, the scene of his greatest achievement. It wasn't to be a triumphant return, however, as the season ended in relegation for a club that just five years previously had won the championship. Hellas bounced straight back up the following season, before returning to the second tier at the end of the 1991/92 season, a debilitating yo-yo existence that the club had strived so hard to reverse in the 1980s. In 1993, Fanna retired from the professional game, one of the great unsung players of Italian football, having won five championships with three different clubs (Juventus, Hellas and Inter). His biggest regret was leaving Verona at the end of the 1984/85 season. He's convinced Hellas could have enjoyed even more success if he had stayed. He was a truly outstanding player who found his footballing home in Verona, where he lives to this day with his family.

Garella was another hero of 85 whose departure to Napoli, who were building a team around Maradona capable of winning the championship, left a gaping hole in Verona's defence. In his first season, Napoli finished in third place. The following season, 'Garellik' kept 15 clean sheets in 29 matches as a Maradona-inspired Napoli finally won the first *Scudetto* in the club's history. Garella was also the protagonist in the Coppa Italia, as Napoli won an historic double. He would make 88 appearances for Napoli before being released in the summer of 1988 and subsequently made 63 appearances for Udinese in Serie B. He retired in 1991 at the age of 36, having made a handful of appearances for Avellino before injury forced him out of the game for good. Despite his heroics on the pitch, the unconventional goalkeeper was never selected for the national team. He died on 12 August 2022 due to cardiovascular complications following heart surgery. He was just 67 years of age.

Replacing Garella at Verona in the summer of 1985 was the in-form Como stopper Giuliano Giuliani. After a shaky start in Verona, he proved to be a worthy successor to Garella. In 1988, after 86 appearances for Hellas, he would once again follow Garella, this time to Napoli, where he would earn a championship medal as they secured their second *Scudetto* in four seasons. He died on 14 November 1996 of pulmonary complications related to AIDS. He was just 38 years old.

Along with Fanna and Garella, Luciano Marangon was the third Hellas player to leave at the end of the championship season, bound for Inter in a deal said to be worth 3bn lire. Though both he and Fanna scored on their home debuts at the San Siro, Marangon made just 19 Serie A appearances that campaign. The following season, he suffered a serious knee injury and made just three appearances in all competitions. He put in a transfer request but Inter refused to release him. In the end, he just disappeared. It was an inauspicious end for a player who just two years previously had been a key figure in Verona's historic championship. A colourful character, he worked for a while as a football agent and then opened a beach bar in Ibiza. Speaking recently to the *Corriere del Veneto*, he said: 'Three wonderful years [at Verona]. Bagnoli [was] an intelligent and prepared coach – a great man. He and Mascetti added new players every year; a perfect team emerged. Our strength was the locker room. We never wanted to stop training. Off the field, we were always together. A group of friends. And we still are today. Many years have passed but it is always the same thing. It is a friendship that goes beyond the sporting aspects. We have a group chat on WhatsApp; if one has a problem, the others are there and arrive in two and a half seconds.'

More than any other player, Elkjær has come to symbolise Verona's championship-winning season. His Hellas teammates used to tease him, saying that he was only the second-best player in Denmark. It was only when he took them on a trip to Copenhagen that they realised what an icon he was in his own country. Despite receiving several significant offers, he refused to play for any other club in Italy. In 1985, he was runner-up in the Ballon d'Or voting (behind Michel Platini), the only Hellas Verona player to ever receive such an accolade. When he drew a line under his time in Verona in the summer of 1988, he was only tempted out of retirement by the Danish club Vejle BK. His two-year spell there, however, was hampered by recurring injuries and he made just 39 appearances. Tumultuous and unpredictable to the end, he was sent off in his last competitive game, a play-off to avoid relegation in 1990. To this day, he retains a close affinity with Verona. His son, Max, was born there and he still visits the city frequently. He has said that in Verona he learned how to dress, how to eat and even how to drive!

Giuseppe Galderisi's form with Hellas earned him a place in the Italy squad for the 1986 World Cup in Mexico, where he was preferred to Paolo Rossi as Altobelli's attacking partner. At just 23 years old, Nanu started all four of Italy's matches as their title defence ended in the round of 16. After the World Cup, he didn't play another game for the national team. He left Verona in 1986 for AC Milan in a deal worth 5bn lire plus Paolo Rossi, who moved in the opposite direction. In the 1986/87 season, Galderisi made 21 appearances and scored three goals for AC Milan, winning a FIFA Club World Cup in the process. He returned to Verona the following season, scoring four goals in 28 appearances as Hellas slumped to a 14th-place finish despite the arrival of an emerging young Argentine striker named Claudio Caniggia. Galderisi rounded off his playing career in Italy with seven prolific seasons at Padova, who finally earned promotion to Serie A in 1994. After retiring, he enjoyed a long and nomadic managerial career, mainly in the Italian lower leagues but also including a short spell in the MLS.

Antonio Di Gennaro was also called up for the 1986 World Cup in Mexico. He started all three matches in the group phase but was dropped for the second-round defeat by France in favour of Giuseppe Baresi, who was given the task of marking Platini. In 1988, with Verona's financial problems mounting, Di Gennaro was sold to Bari. He had a brief foray into the world of coaching and is now a leading football commentator on RAI TV.

Roberto Tricella was also in the 1986 World Cup squad but didn't play. A remarkable achievement, nonetheless, for a player who just five years previously had been released by Inter and was playing in Serie B with Verona. He would go on to make 11 appearances for the national team, mostly in friendlies. In 1987, the Hellas captain accepted an offer from Juventus, where he made 80 appearances and was part of the team that beat Fiorentina in the first all-Italian UEFA Cup Final. He quit the game in 1992, having made 23 appearances for Bologna before a muscular injury forced him into retirement at the age of 33. He left the world of football completely, returning to his native town of Cernusco sul Naviglio, where he worked in the real estate sector. He hasn't done that Jerry Lee Lewis impression in many years!

In the stands, a darker side began to emerge almost as soon as the euphoria of the *Scudetto* subsided. Inconsistent results had an inevitably demotivating effect on the fans and the mass excursions of the championship season were seldom repeated in the following years, leaving a small hardcore of fans to sustain the team against far-flung opponents like Lecce,

Napoli, Bari and Avellino, while humiliating defeats in Naples and Udine triggered disorder and violent clashes with rival groups. By now, the *Brigate* (and its successors) were emerging as one of the most notorious ultra groups in Italy. They stole banners from opposing fans to display in the *Curva Sud* like some kind of trophy of war. Incidents in Como in January 1986 and Cavalese that August enhanced Verona's reputation as troublemakers. The 'looting' of Brescia in December 1986 (in which more than 500 cars were damaged, including that of the mayor, Gabriele Sboarina) led to the arrest of 12 people from Verona on charges of criminal association. At the Bentegodi the following Sunday, there was a protest that went down in history. The central section of the *Curva Sud* was left empty, while a massive banner written in blue and white read: '*Non 12 ma 5000 colpevoli*' (not 12 but 5,000 guilty). On 1 February 1987, the *Brigate Gialloblù* was declared a criminal organisation and the group was formally dissolved in 1991, though many former members simply joined new groups or, to avoid further trouble, dispersed themselves across the stands at home games.

On 23 February 1986, during Maradona's second trip to the Bentegodi, the home fans unfurled a banner that read '*Benvenuti in Italia*' ('Welcome to Italy') – the clear implication being that Napoli was not part of Italy. In September 1989, the notorious '*Vesuvio facci sognare*' ('Vesuvius let us dream') banner appeared. At the return fixture, the Neapolitans responded with the now legendary slogan '*Giulietta è 'na zoccola*' ('Juliet is a slag'). Harmless banter or a symptom of a deeper malaise? In the decades that followed, far-right groups, including the neo-fascist *Forza Nuova*, were quick to exploit fear and uncertainty in Italy surrounding mass migration and a more overtly politically faction began to take control of the *Curva Sud*. In one sickening incident on 28 April 1996, a black mannequin was suspended from the *curva*, where it hung for an interminable 38 minutes. The unfortunate object of the protest was a 19-year-old Dutch player named Maickel Ferrier, who was in contract negotiations with the club. Needless to say, he never signed.

In those pre-satellite TV days when corporate sponsorship was still in its infancy, clubs like Hellas were much more dependent on gate receipts. But, with dwindling attendances and spiralling wage bills, that model inevitably plunged the club into financial crisis. The 1986/87 season marked the end of the fruitful sponsorship arrangement with Canon, with another Japanese electronics giant, Ricoh, taking over. In increasingly challenging circumstances, Bagnoli hung on at Verona until the relegation of 1990 but, by then, the club were in serious financial difficulty.

In 1994, after spells at Genoa and Inter, Bagnoli brought his long and varied coaching career to an end at just 59 years of age. Ernesto Pellegrini, the Inter president who sacked him, called the decision the biggest mistake of his presidency. In his long retirement from the game, Bagnoli would occasionally return to the Bentegodi but football had moved on. He struggled to remember the names of the players. The constant churn of foreign signings and the style of football on display wasn't to his liking: '[S]even or eight passes to get to midfield and then the ball back to the goalkeeper … how boring,' he told *La Repubblica*'s Gianni Mura on the 30th anniversary of the 'Miracle of 85'.

After two seasons in Verona, Hans-Peter Briegel moved to Sampdoria, where he ended his career in 1988, but not before lifting the Coppa Italia as Sampdoria secured that first piece of silverware the club had craved for so long. Today, Briegel is a director at Kaiserslautern and runs a humanitarian project for children in Mexico. He returned to Verona as recently as October 2024, the guest of a local amateur team, where he spoke to the youngsters and shared his memories of his time in Verona.

Silvano Fontolan spent another three seasons in Verona before transferring to Serie A rivals Ascoli in 1988. In June 1989, he retired at 34 after a 14-season career in which he accumulated 277 appearances and seven goals in Serie A and 159 appearances and four goals in Serie B. He remains active in amateur and youth football and recently appeared at the

Bentegodi for a Serie A match between Verona and Juventus, where he was reduced to tears by the reception he received from the home fans.

The underwhelming form of legendary Italian striker Paolo Rossi, who signed for Hellas in the summer of 1986, was perhaps an indication of what was to come. The hero of Spain 82 managed just four goals in 20 appearances for Hellas Verona (three from the penalty spot). At the end of the season, following a recurrence of knee problems that had tormented him throughout his career, he bid a final farewell to competitive activity at just 30 years of age. Despite Rossi's problems, Hellas finished in fourth place and would enjoy another season of European football.

Forty years on from the championship season, Sergio 'Chicco' Guidotti, who played for Hellas as a schoolboy in the early 1980s, remains an active and respected figure around the club and is president of the ex-players' association and honorary president of the women's team. As the years passed, he would occasionally encounter Bagnoli at club functions. He always found the same humble, attentive and precise person he had known as a young player. Chicco's father, Celestino Guidotti, stood down as president on 10 December 1985, making way for Ferdinando Chiampan. Guidotti would stay on in an advisory capacity and would subsequently oversee Verona's successful bid to be a host city for the 1990 World Cup finals.

Within a few weeks of Verona's 1985 triumph, president Pertini, who had stood up on his seat at the Santiago Bernabéu Stadium to celebrate the Italian victory at the 1982 World Cup, stood down as president of the republic, to be replaced by Francesco Cossiga, whose term of office would subsequently become mired in controversy. In April 1987, Bettino Craxi's Socialist-led government collapsed when the Christian Democrats withdrew their support. The subsequent government, led by veteran centre-left statesman Amintore Fanfani, lasted for just 11 days before a general election was called. Craxi would subsequently go down in the notorious *Tangentopoli* scandal, the name given to the system of political corruption uncovered by the *Mani pulite* judicial investigation. His demise marked the end for the Italian Socialist Party as a political force. With the Christian Democrats already in terminal decline, the stage was set for a new force in Italian politics and the beginning of the Second Italian Republic, to be led by AC Milan's colourful president, Silvio Berlusconi.

Mayor Gabriele Sboarina is still remembered in Verona as the 'Mayor of the *Scudetto*'. A loyal Hellas fan, he was a regular at the Bentegodi during the Bagnoli era, when he would watch the game from the stands alongside 'ordinary' fans. He was also a leading figure in bringing the World Cup to Verona, responsible for delivering the public works that reshaped the city's transport infrastructure (including the renovation of the train station and the construction of a ring road to improve access to the stadium). Just two years later, the *Mani pulite* investigation swept Verona's ruling class. A teacher by profession, Sboarina led the city council throughout the 1980s but was never able to explain how his family had amassed a personal fortune which, according to some reports, amounted to 60bn lire.

His son, Federico, followed him into the family business and was elected mayor of Verona in 2017. He, too, was closely associated with the football team and its right-wing fan base. He was succeeded as mayor of Verona by Damiano Tommasi, who football fans will remember played for Verona in the 1990s before embarking on an eventful ten-year career with Roma, where he was a key figure in the team that won the *Scudetto* in 2001, playing alongside Francesco Totti and Gabriel Batistuta. His election as mayor of Verona in 2022, leading a centre-left coalition, came as a shock in a city that is more closely associated with the right.

Visitors who have come to the Bentegodi in recent years, perhaps inspired by Tim Parks's seminal *A Season with Verona*, will find a tired and dilapidated stadium, its best years behind it. Over the years, various redevelopment projects have been mooted but, to date, nothing concrete has materialised. The latest proposal emerged in December 2024, with the backing of mayor Tommasi, but was greeted locally with a healthy dose of scepticism.

The golden age of Italian football, which reached its peak at the era-defining 1990 World Cup, was coming to an end, as the game's centre of gravity shifted from Italy to England. For Verona, relegation at the end of the decade marked the point from which things really began to unravel. On 23 February 1991, Hellas Verona was declared bankrupt. The club had been paying inflated wages and using Swiss companies to launder profits from rigged transfer deals. On 24 July 1992, Ferdinando Chiampan, the Canon entrepreneur who had bankrolled Verona's success, was imprisoned for fraudulent bankruptcy, along with various others associated with the club. Chiampan spent 57 days behind bars but always protested his innocence, blaming a political, judicial and economic system that conspired against him. It was a shocking final chapter to the Bagnoli-inspired golden era.

A moment in time?

The legacy of 85

NO ONE at the start of the championship thought Verona capable of such an extraordinary achievement. They were rank outsiders. In fact, they weren't even that. It would have been ridiculous to even mention Hellas as championship contenders at the start of the season. So, how did they do it, what does it mean to the city 40 years later and could such a thing ever happen again?

Verona's more famous rivals boasted some of the most talented and celebrated football players ever to grace the Italian game. World champions, multiple Ballon d'Or winners, Brazilian legends, Argentinian superstars and West German powerhouses, all drawn to Italy to test themselves in the greatest league in the world. For all their greatness, these clubs weren't without their flaws.

Juventus, who had won the championship in three of the previous four seasons, were focussed on European glory (which they achieved in such tragic circumstances against Liverpool at Heysel Stadium). AC Milan were in the doldrums, on the brink of that seismic transition to the Berlusconi era. Inter, too, were still a work in progress, while Roma, under the leadership of the newly appointed Swede, Sven-Göran Eriksson, were recovering from the trauma of losing a penalty shoot-out to Liverpool in the 1984 European Cup Final. Sampdoria were a highly ambitious club with the raw talent, drive and experience to win silverware but not yet ready for a serious title run. Maradona was one of those generational players capable of anything. But he was still adjusting to life in Italy and didn't yet have the supporting cast around him that would propel

Napoli to greater things. The only other team that might have mounted a serious challenge to Verona in 1985 were the Torino of Júnior, Dossena, Schachner and Serena. But they lacked consistency when it mattered most.

Against such adversaries, the *Scudetto* was a surprise, a massive upset. But a miracle? A fluke? A stroke of luck? Hardly.

After Bagnoli's first season in Serie A with Hellas, even young fans sensed that something special was about to happen. Barbara Salazer, who was just 13 years old at the time, remembers feeling that something was possible from the year before: 'You could feel something was coming up. The team was amazing.' For many, including Bagnoli – now sadly afflicted by dementia and rarely seen in public – Verona played better football in the 1982/83 campaign than they did in the championship-winning season. 'We played with our feet rather than our heads,' explained the precociously talented winger, Pierino Fanna. The club retained the bulk of the team from that season (in contrast to the current trend in which the most talented players are sold on at the end of each season) and added the exceptional talents of Elkjær and Briegel.

Local sports journalist and former player Gianluca Tavellin is another to emphasise that Verona's success didn't happen overnight: 'The spine of the team was constructed between 1981, when they won Serie B, and the first season back in Serie A in 1982/83.' But, still, nobody could have predicted that Verona would be champions. A top-three finish would have been miraculous.

So, how did they do it? How did Hellas Verona go from provincial nobodies struggling in Serie B to champions of Italy in the space of just a few seasons?

For the first time in the club's history, Hellas enjoyed generous financial backing in the form of sponsorship from the Japanese multinational, Canon. Hellas invested an estimated 13bn lire on their championship-winning squad. It was a fraction of what was spent by the bigger clubs in the league – and as much as Napoli paid for a single player – but the Canon investment was critical, providing the club with the economic stability and financial clout to attract players of the calibre of Fanna, Briegel and Elkjær.

Having the cash to buy players is one thing; finding the right ones is quite another. Thanks to a long and varied playing and managerial career, Bagnoli knew the Italian peninsula intimately. He knew the clubs and the players, the hidden gems in the lower leagues and the disenchanted talent in the big cities. He knew the kind of player he wanted: team players (never a big name, prima donna or superstar) with hunger, drive and determination; individuals who shared his work ethic and professionalism. Of the team that began the 1984/85 campaign, the only player that sporting director Emiliano Mascetti didn't recruit was captain Roberto Tricella, who arrived at Verona from Inter in 1979. In just four years, and on a shoestring budget, Mascetti assembled a squad capable of causing an upset. He, as much as anyone, was the architect of Verona's *Scudetto*.

Verona provided the context in which those players thrived, not least those, such as Fanna, Di Gennaro and Galderisi, who had struggled elsewhere. They were allowed, encouraged even, to express themselves, without the stifling pressure felt at 'bigger' clubs. When Altobelli, for example, missed that crucial penalty for Inter against Torino, he was crucified. Galderisi missed two in successive games for Verona during the title season and life went on. It was only really in the final stages of the championship that the pressure began to mount and then Bagnoli was robust, creating a siege mentality, while consistently downplaying talk of a title race.

Bagnoli was a truly exceptional coach, outstanding in all areas – organisation, physical preparation, group management, pre-match preparation and analysis and in-game management. At one point, Berlusconi considered bringing him to AC Milan but changed his mind on the grounds that he was a communist. Bagnoli may not have been a communist but he was able to deploy the specific skills of each player according to the needs of the team. He demonstrated acute tactical and technical knowledge and achieved all of this without ever having to resort to the barracks-style severity of other coaches.

There was no doubting Bagnoli had a very particular personality. Frequently described in the press as '*brontolo*' (grumpy), journalists also referred to him as '*Amleto della panchina*' (Hamlet of the bench) or '*l'imperatore timido*' (the shy emperor). He was also regularly referred to as a 'philosopher coach'. He certainly had his own way of doing things but that didn't mean he was closed-minded or unable to adapt. On the contrary, he was quick to give his players autonomy on the pitch and to adapt tactically depending on the personnel at his disposal, making precise and decisive adjustments when necessary.

Like most coaches at that time, Bagnoli applied a variant of the defensive tactic known as *catenaccio*. Defensive solidity was the essence of Verona's identity. But his team were also able to maintain possession and transition quickly. Bagnoli generally played with two fixed markers in defence and a *zona mista*, a fluid rotational system, in midfield. Enzo Bearzot even modelled his approach on Bagnoli's in the second half of his reign as Italy's national team coach, basing the formation of his side on Bagnoli's at Verona.

By the summer of 1985, Bagnoli had spent three seasons in Serie A with Hellas (plus one in Serie B). Each season he played with a slightly different formation. In the first, he played with a single striker (Domenico Penzo), with Pierino Fanna in a supporting role. In the second, he played with two strikers (Maurizio Iorio and Giuseppe Galderisi), with Fanna in that more familiar wide role. In the third, he played with Galderisi and Elkjær up front, with Fanna on either wing and Di Gennaro occupying an extremely offensive midfield position. As a coach, Bagnoli was never rigidly wedded to a particular system; instead, he adapted his formation according to the players at his disposal.

Before kick-off, Bagnoli wasn't one for rousing team talks or detailed instructions to his players. Instead, he would sit in a corner and read the *Gazzetta*. I have nothing to add, he seemed to be saying to his players – we have prepared during the week and that is enough. Now I trust you to go out there and perform. Elkjær concedes that there was a language barrier between them, at least at the start, recently telling the *Corriere del Veneto*: 'I didn't speak Italian, he didn't speak English. But we understood each other. What mattered was that I trained seriously and that I did what I had to do on the pitch. And then he also let me smoke!'

Bagnoli's other defining characteristic was his humility. In a column he wrote for the *Corriere della Sera* the day after that decisive result in Bergamo, Bagnoli insisted that he had done nothing special, that he had, in fact, been fortunate. '[H]ere's the reality,' he wrote. 'I didn't do anything beyond a normal job. I led the players who deserved the championship without inventing new tactics, without Machiavellian practices, without any secrets. The game of football is simple. Here's an example. One Sunday, we were losing. During the break, I told the players "Behave as you know how, express yourselves in the way you are able." They did it and they won. It's the will that counts above all else. It's the team spirit that in this Verona has generated the team in the broadest sense of the definition.'

In terms of creating that team spirit, one of the defining features of Verona's success, Bagnoli was also humble: 'The group is made by the players, with their friendships, with their character and humanity.' Finally, Bagnoli had this to say about his famous reserve: '[S]ometimes, silence is also needed. A look can assume considerable eloquence [...]. The sincerity of the relationship and seriousness are the values that count.'

Bagnoli was hardly a revolutionary. He spent the previous two seasons making minor adjustments to his squad, keeping the same core group of players throughout. Great teams don't happen suddenly by chance but are, instead, the result of incremental progress over time. Of course, the arrival of world-class players can expedite that process but not always. Hellas had seven key points of reference that remained fundamentally unchanged in the seasons leading up to the *Scudetto*: goalkeeper Garella, defenders Luciano Marangon and Roberto Tricella, the versatile Volpati, midfielders Di Gennaro and Sacchetti and the winger, Fanna. Defender Fontolan and centre-forward Galderisi could also be added to that list.

It was, in some senses, a homogenous group. They drove an Audi, BMW or Volvo, were married with one kid, liked to play tennis and watch television in their free time, listened to Spandau Ballet or Michael Jackson and loved Robert De Niro films. The additions of Briegel and Elkjær brought a touch of international quality to the team; they were the cherries on the cake.

Hellas were by far the most consistent team in the league. They topped the table for the duration of the season. Only once, on 20 January, did any of their rivals even draw level and, even then, Inter could only keep pace for a week. By the end of March, with just six games remaining, Verona's advantage extended to a virtually unassailable six points.

Of course, there was a degree of fortune. Hellas avoided serious injuries to key players (notwithstanding the notable absences of Elkjær and Ferroni for a significant chunk of the season). For the first time in Italy that season, a fairer, more transparent system of referee allocation was introduced. It is surely no coincidence that a smaller club won the championship that year. The ballot system was swiftly abolished in favour of a 'technical committee' and the allocation of referees in Italy has been tainted by more than a whiff of corruption ever since.

The Bentegodi was, in the main, a welcoming and joyful place to spend a Sunday afternoon. Week in, week out, 40,000 expectant fans crammed into the stadium that was, in its day, state-of-the-art – certainly compared to the dangerous, ramshackle monstrosities that existed elsewhere in Europe at that time. It provided the backdrop for some of that season's greatest moments.

Verona's triumph in 1985 isn't a moment frozen in time but a legacy that lives on in the city to this day. Even with the young fans I meet in the city, 1985 resonates. They can reel off the names of the great players – Elkjær and Briegel, obviously, but also Fanna, Di Gennaro, Galderisi and others. And, of course, Bagnoli. For them, that moment is part of their lore.

In the past, yes, but still an integral part of their identity and still a source of enormous pride.

The 'miracle' championship has left an indelible mark. '[F]or those who experienced it, the *Scudetto* will remain one of the most beautiful memories of our life, like the day of a wedding or the birth of a child,' said 56-year-old Alessandro Fiorio. 'I try to pass on those memories and that passion to my son, who is 17 (exactly the age I was the year we won the championship).'

Roberto Puliero died on 19 November 2019. He was 73 years old. In the first home match following his death, 22,581 fans, scattered across the cavernous Bentegodi, stood as his trademark exclamation, *'Alè alè alè alè alè alè … Bum! Bum! Bum!'* reverberated around the stadium. There were more than a few tears shed by grown men in the stands that afternoon. His passing brought back memories of long ago Sunday afternoons gathered around the radio. As much as anyone on the pitch, Puliero represented that bygone era. A time when football was simpler, less commercial, when kids played football in the street and wireless radios conveyed the captivating ebb and flow of a game.

Reflecting 40 years later on the impact of winning the *Scudetto*, 53-year-old Nicolas Legnazzi is unequivocal: '[I]t changed the fate of our lives forever.' Of course, his life has inevitably moved on since then but he's still football daft, with a childlike enthusiasm for the game that manifests itself in Subbuteo, Panini stickers and five-a-side football. For 53-year-old Barbara Salazer, 40 is just another number: 'Ten or 100, it will be the same; the years won't change our unconditional love for our club.' Most fans, commentators and ex-players I have spoken to concede that it could never happen again. In fact, that is what makes 1985 so special.

As the years have passed, Elkjær's appreciation of that season has matured. He now understands that it was the friendships he forged with his team-mates, his relationship with Bagnoli, and with the city and its fans, rather than that moment in Bergamo when the final whistle blew that is the most significant aspect of his time in Verona. Another reason Elkjær remains a cult hero here in Verona is that he declined offers from other Italian clubs out of loyalty to the team with whom he had just won the *Scudetto*.

Despite being nearly 31 years old when he signed for Hellas in the summer of 1982, Domenico Volpati notched up 241 appearances for the club before moving on to Mantova in 1988, where he finally brought his playing career to end. In a long and varied career, he played in every role except goalkeeper. For Verona, he played right-back or stopper or *libero* to plug a hole, otherwise in midfield alongside Di Gennaro or to cover the advances of Tricella, who was quick to counter-attack. He finally graduated in medicine from the University of Pavia in 1989 and began his second career as a dentist. Originally from Novara, he still lives in the Val di Fiemme, where he met his wife, Daniela, during Bagnoli's summer training camp in Cavalese. Still incredibly lean and with that trademark mane of hair thinning slightly and now a distinguished silvery-grey, his eyes still twinkle and a smile is quick to break across his face as he remembers his team-mates and their exploits of 40 years ago. He has many vivid memories from the *Scudetto* season but the defining factor behind the success of the 1984/85 team was its unity: '[W]hen you find a spirit of group, a sense of belonging, this quality is what leads you to give 110 per cent. When this happens, you become an invincible team. The unity between us continues even now, like an infinite story. We are still friends. You feel that immediately whenever we are together.'

That team, those players, that group remain forever bound by their achievements that season – immortalised by a moment in time that can never be repeated. A group devoid of superstars but not lacking in talent, drive, ambition and charisma. A team, to employ that great Aristotelian aphorism, that was greater than the sum of its parts, with a leader who enabled them to express themselves and a city that inspired them to dream.

Fanna still has the match ball from that game against Lazio when he scored the winning goal, his first of the campaign. For him, the 1984/85 season was 'the last poem, the last story of a kind of football that was slowly changing'. When he reflects on that remarkable season and the calibre of the players they were up against, he can't quite believe that Verona actually won the *Scudetto*.

But, on closer inspection, it is clear that the 'miracle' of 1985 wasn't simply a moment in time. Nor was it a miracle. It was a dream. A project. A shared endeavour. A triumph of leadership. Of humility. Of humanity. Of pride and sacrifice. Of seizing the moment and doing enough. And then finding the strength and courage and quality to give some more. Just when it mattered most. To win the game. To settle old scores and prove a point. It was luck and love and faith and desire. It was yellow and blue. It was 1985. Verona: *Campione di Italia*.

Acknowledgements

MY GRATITUDE, as ever, to my long-standing friend and occasional drinking buddy in Verona, Matteo Fontana, for his encouragement to take this project on at the last minute.

Thanks to Domenico Volpati, a true gentleman, for sharing his memories with such passion and generosity. Thanks also to Pierino Fanna, a five-time *Scudetto* winner for sharing his memories with humility and kindness. Roberto Tricella was also extremely generous. Thanks also to Antonio Di Gennaro for sharing his memories of that season.

Thank you to Sergio 'Chicco' Guidotti for sharing, with such warmth and generosity, his deep passion and profound knowledge of Hellas Verona. He offers a unique perspective, not just as a lifelong fan, but also as a young player on the fringes of the Hellas team of the early 1980s and as the son of the club's *Scudetto*-winning president, the late Celestino Guidotti.

Thanks also to Gianluca Tavellin for sharing his perspective as a journalist, fan and player.

Thanks to Tim Parks, whose seminal work, *A Season with Verona*, remains quite simply the best football book ever.

The travel tips, unless otherwise stated, are taken from the 1984 *Let's Go* travel guide, so you might want to check for updates!

Thanks to my friends, Nicolas Legnazzi and Alessandro Fiorio, for the clarity and passion with which they shared their childhood memories of supporting Hellas. Thanks to Barbara Salazer for sharing her memories and those of her friends from that era.

Thanks to Gary Thacker, author of, amongst other things, *Dutch Masters: When Ajax's Totaalvoetbal Conquered Europe*, for his advice and encouragement.

It was a privilege to meet and spend time with the remarkable Giancarlo Savoia, a sprightly 80-year-old who played nine seasons for Hellas Verona in the 1960s in a career in which he amassed 67 appearances in Serie A and 307 appearances and nine goals in Serie B. He remains among the top ten players with the highest number of appearances in the history of the club.

Thanks to Pellegrino Chiari for kindly sharing his extensive archive of Italian Panini albums from the 1980s. They were indispensable.

Thanks to Rob Smyth and Michael Gibbons, authors of *Danish Dynamite*, for sharing their passion for Danish football in the 1980s.

Thanks to Simon Thompson for a unique interview in the cryptoporticus of the Capitolium in Verona. He has the eye for detail and objectivity you would expect of an archaeologist, even 40 years after the event, which I guess is the blink of an eye if you are more accustomed to uncovering Roman remains.

Thanks to the countless others who have shared their stories and memories.

And finally, thanks to the editorial team at Pitch Publishing who have worked tirelessly behind the scenes for their patience, expertise and encouragement.

Bibliography

Articles

Chalmers, Robert, 'Remembering the Heysel stadium disaster', *GQ Magazine*, 29 May 2015. https://www.gq-magazine.co.uk/article/heysel-stadium-disaster-30-anniversary

Foot, J. (2016), 'How Italian Football Creates Italians: The 1982 World Cup, the "Pertini Myth" and Italian National Identity', *The International Journal of the History of Sport*, *33*(3), 341–358. https://doi.org/10.1080/09523367.2016.1175440

Salazer, Barbara, 'Eroina', *Heraldo*, 31 October 2018.
https://www.heraldo.it/2018/10/31/eroina/

Scragg, Steven, 'Preben Elkjær: The Last of Football's True Mavericks', *These Football Times*. https://thesefootballtimes.co/2018/04/26/preben-Elkjær-the-last-great-maverick-of-world-football/

Sports Illustrated, 'Giovanni Trapattoni: A Career of 2 Halves That Defined the Golden Era of Calcio at Juventus', 12 August 2019. https://www.si.com/soccer/2019/08/12/giovanni-trapattoni-career-2-halves-defined-golden-era-calcio-juventus

Thacker, Gary, 'Michael Laudrup and Preben Elkjær: A Fantasy Partnership Devised in the Heavens', *These Football Times*. https://thesefootballtimes.co/2018/08/30/michael-laudrup-and-preben-Elkjær-a-fantasy-partnership-devised-in-the-heavens/by

The Mirror, 'Liam Brady reflects on Italy career where he was sacked by Juventus after winning title', 16 October 2023.

https://www.mirror.co.uk/sport/football/news/liam-brady-reflects-italy-career-31194539

Books

Agnew, Paddy, *Forza Italia, The Fall and Rise of Italian Football*, Ebury Press, 2007

Fishbein, Mark (ed), *Let's Go, the budget guide to Italy, 1984*, St. Martin's Press, 1984

Fontana, Matteo, *Elkjær sindaco!*, Eclettica, 2020

Fontana, Matteo, *Il Miracoliere Osvaldo Bagnoli, L'Allenatore Operaio*, 2016

Foot, John, *Calcio, A History of Italian Football*, 2007

Hand, Jonathan (ed), *Let's Go, the budget guide to Europe, 1981-82*, Dutton, 1981

Jones, Tobias, *The Dark Heart of Italy, Travels Through Time and Space Across Italy*, Faber and Faber, 2003

Rossi, Giambattista, *Agents and intermediaries*, 2018

Trellini, Piero, *The Match*, Pitch Publishing, 2023

Sandbrook, Dominic, *Who Dares Wins: Britain, 1979-1982,* Allen Lane, 2019

Smyth, Rob, Eriksen, Lars and Gibbons, Mike, *Danish Dynamite: The Story of Football's Greatest Cult Team,* Bloomsbury, 2015

Websites and archives

www.brera.net
www.calcioefinanza.it
www.corrieredelveneto.corriere.it
www.grandhotelcalciomercato.com
www.guerinsportivo.it
www.hellas1903.it
www.hellaslive.it
www.hellastory.net
www.ilfoglio.it
www.minimaetmoralia.it
www.republica.it
www.tuttohellasverona.it